The Bailout State

The Bailout State
Why Governments Rescue Banks, Not People

MARTIJN KONINGS

polity

First published in 2024 by Polity Press

Polity Press
65 Bridge Street
Cambridge CB2 1UR, UK

Polity Press
111 River Street
Hoboken, NJ 07030, USA

ISBN-13: 978-1-5095-6431-6
ISBN-13: 978-1-5095-6432-3(pb)

A catalogue record for this book is available from the British Library.

[LoC number here]

Typeset in 11 on 13 pt Warnock Pro
by Cheshire Typesetting Ltd, Cuddington, Cheshire
Printed and bound in Great Britain by 4edge Limited

The publisher has used its best endeavours to ensure that the URLs for external websites referred to in this book are correct and active at the time of going to press. However, the publisher has no responsibility for the websites and can make no guarantee that a site will remain live or that the content is or will remain appropriate.

Every effort has been made to trace all copyright holders, but if any have been overlooked the publisher will be pleased to include any necessary credits in any subsequent reprint or edition.

For further information on Polity, visit our website:
politybooks.com

For my family

Contents

Preface

In September of 2022, *The Economist* declared that the world had entered a new era: "Bailouts for everyone!" According to this leading voice of the global business community, the colossal bank rescues in response to the financial crisis of 2007–9 had created a veritable bailout state. During the following decade, governments had failed to roll back these extensive public guarantees for private balance sheets. And during the Covid crisis, when governments had broadened the safety net to prevent the economic hit of the pandemic from turning into a severe economic downturn, the bailout state had positively gone "into overdrive." "We are all bankers now," *The Economist* lamented, as if the democratization of that profession were a self-evidently bad idea.[1]

The existence of this bailout behemoth, the magazine went on to argue, meant that those who thought they were living in a "neoliberal" era, governed by free-market principles, were mistaken. That was a remarkable conclusion. During the previous decades, *The Economist* itself had played a prominent role mainstreaming neoliberal ideas, urging governments everywhere to rescind innovation-stifling regulations and cut back public spending. However, it had no difficulty identifying the appropriate response to the realization that its work was not done, demanding that economic and political leaders everywhere redouble their efforts to rehabilitate the neutral wisdom of markets against overweening state institutions.

Progressives, by contrast, have had a much harder time figuring out how to relate to the bailout state's sprawling infrastructure of backstops, subsidies, and guarantees. The left's understanding of the past century has been deeply shaped by the assumption that the shift from Keynesian state intervention to neoliberal free-market logics has been effective and in fact transformed our society to its core. It is a picture where the growth of a bailout state just has no real place.

The resulting blind spot has done much to confuse centrist and left-wing politics. Quick to assume that public things are worth supporting, progressives have often thrown their weight behind programs that benefit primarily business and the affluent. Of course, accepting an uneven distribution of benefits to secure some gains for the less well-off can be a rational political strategy. But in practice this has been a very slippery slope, as the terms of such lopsided compromises are typically quickly assimilated into the default configuration of economic policy. Before long, enormous corporate tax breaks and financial market backstops sit below the public's field of vision, attracting nowhere near the level of attention that comparatively inexpensive social programs do.

Getting the whole bailout edifice into view requires that we retrace how it was built. Only then can we understand how it became untethered from the political objectives that once drove its expansion, and what that growing disconnect means for the present.

The bailout state has deep historical roots. While its expansion to a size that makes it impossible to ignore occurred in recent decades, much of the scaffolding was put in place during what we remember as less economically tumultuous times. From early on in the post-World War II era, public underwriting of private financial risk was a key means for governments to manage the contradictions of welfare capitalism. As it proved an effective way to stabilize the economy and protect select constituencies from the effects of downturns, practices of risk socialization came to reshape the logic of economic policymaking from the inside out. There were significant side effects, however. Chief among these was inflationary pressure – the inevitable result of spreading downside risk across society without doing the same for upside exposure.

For progressively minded people of a certain generation (my own, in any case – old enough to have some sense of historical longue durée, but too young to recall a time when inflation played havoc with our parents' household budgets), the idea of inflation has, until recently, always been abstract and hypothetical. Instead, we have tended to ridicule this peculiar obsession of economists, likening it to a professional deformation. But, while adopting a more nonchalant attitude, we have often ended up using the same technical language and narrow definitions that mainstream economists use to think about inflation, obscuring what is at stake.

Developing a better language to talk about inflation requires some work. This book considers why it has been such a challenge for progressives – specifically, why it was so easy for Keynes to miss its full significance and how it went on to bedevil the Keynesian tradition. Keynes and many of his followers never fully broke with traditional theories of money, which tend to think of it as a freely available infrastructure for private commerce, with any malfunctioning the result of external forces. Such a perspective makes it difficult to recognize inflation when it becomes a chronic affliction, as it would during the twentieth century, not generated by policy mistakes but embedded in the most basic operations of economic life.

Conservatives have typically advocated fighting inflation with monetary contraction and fiscal austerity, but such policies posed a threat to key parts of the progressive agenda. To undercut inflation in different ways, postwar Keynesians looked to supply-side measures such as tax breaks and investment subsidies, intended to incentivize business into delivering economic growth free of inflation. Such policies were expensive and made the impact of economic policy far less egalitarian, but they rarely did much to bring down inflation. Public generosity towards business was invariably followed by measures to tighten the monetary and fiscal screws elsewhere in the system.

By the 1970s inflationary pressures had become difficult to contain, and it proved fertile ground for the rise of free-market ideology. But even though the neoliberal program has reshaped the world in numerous ways, its accomplishments have never included a shrinkage of the bailout state. To the contrary, over the past half century derisking policies have been consolidated into the baseline settings of economic policymaking. And they have been allied to a semi-permanent austerity agenda that has, on the whole, been highly effective – at times *too* effective, as we will see – in managing inflation.

Just as the dance of bailout and austerity already shaped the landscape of welfare capitalism well before neoliberals ever appeared on the scene, so the expansion of the bailout state during the past decades has enjoyed significant progressive credentials. The stabilization of a growing financial system bolstered, for some time, a middle-class politics that increasingly centered not on wage growth but on asset appreciation and capital gains. It experienced its heyday in the 1990s – a decade that has recently replaced the 1950s as the object of middle-class nostalgia.

Following the 2007–9 crisis, the ties that had bound the expansion of the bailout state to the advancement of broader social and political objectives came undone. Large banks and other too-big-to-fail institutions had long benefitted disproportionately from the arrangement, but since the Global Financial Crisis the bailout state's disbursements have flowed almost exclusively to Wall Street and its clients, benefitting a steadily shrinking group of ever-wealthier property owners. Promises of inclusive economic growth have looked increasingly thin.

True to its laissez-faire roots, *The Economist* occasionally expressed worry that a financial system depending so heavily on political grace and favor could lose legitimacy and invite ill-advised left-wing experiments. The economic policy response to the Covid crisis provided a taste of what that could look like, a glimpse of what could happen if the democratic public were to get its hands on the machinery of the bailout state. In fact, *The Economist* had neatly timed the announcement of its discovery to coincide with coordinated action by central banks around the world to get a grip on resurgent inflation, seeking to legitimate renewed financial austerity by publicizing neoliberal common sense. How could an economic system providing everyone with a bespoke bailout not be inflationary?

That question, however, does not have to be asked in a purely rhetorical register. It has actual answers, and one does not have to look too far back in history to find examples of how one can expand the remit of public generosity without undermining the stability of the monetary standard. In recent years, that point has been pressed by Modern Money Theory (or Modern Monetary Theory, but either version is better known as MMT), a theoretical framework that has existed for some time but rose to prominence as during the 2010s the policy formula of "bailouts for banks, not people" became more flagrantly absurd. When inflation made a comeback in the midst of the pandemic, and mainstream economists demanded sacrificial austerity, MMT proponents like Stephanie Kelton pointed out the hypocrisy.[2]

The idea of democratizing the banking profession is not as absurd as *The Economist* would have us believe. As Hyman Minsky, an economist whose work has deeply shaped the ideas presented in this book, put it, we can all issue an IOU – the trick is to get people to accept that note in payment for other debts without demanding a massive discount. The rules that determine whose debts get to circulate at par are shaped not by timeless economic laws, but by social conventions and political forces. Those rules will continue to evolve, and the only real question is how – whether they will evolve to drive an ever-greater concentration of wealth, or if democratic publics will find ways to put in place protocols to spread wealth.

The story told in this book concentrates on the United States. As Leo Panitch and Sam Gindin have argued, the twentieth century's wave of working-class revolutions was managed by a new imperial system that had its apex in the American state.[3] Even the public welfare states that arose in Western Europe, often held up as an alternative to American capitalism, were only viable because they occupied a particular, highly privileged place in the global dollar order. Contrary to the expectations of many observers, the past decades have not eroded but intensi-fied the dependence of the global political economy on the dollar system. As Adam Tooze has shown, that trend accel-erated following the Global Financial Crisis, and during the Covid crisis the American central bank led global recession-fighting by extending support to other nations' central banks and treasuries.[4] Just as the dollar is the world's money, the US government manages the world's bailout state. In the next chapters, we will see how the bailout colossus was built.

1

How Did We Get Here?

As the end of the Covid pandemic came in view, the world was confronted with another emergency: the return of inflation. Before anyone had caught on to what was happening, the purchasing power of the average family had shrunk by several percentage points. By early 2022, inflation was a headline issue. As price rises ate away at spending power, pundits debated what was to be done.

For a while, the argument that inflation was "transitory" – a temporary effect of the supply-chain disruptions caused by the pandemic – had significant traction. But as inflation refused to die down, "hawkish" voices soon dominated the conversation. They urged the Federal Reserve, as well as other central banks around the world, to act decisively and to slow down economic growth by raising interest rates.

More "dovish" commentators objected that this would have a devastating impact on employment and income, dealing yet another blow to American families recovering from the pandemic. They pointed out that the American economy was not yet experiencing a wage–price spiral like that of the 1970s. Back then, unions had demanded wage rises to compensate for the rising cost of living and so made the inflation problem worse. Fifty years later, with unionization rates a fraction of what they were, workers were in no position to demand compensation for anything.

Such arguments were to no avail. The Federal Reserve is legally responsible for ensuring price stability, and it has only one instrument to do so. In March of 2022, it started raising interest rates, rapidly increasing the federal funds rate from its historic low of zero to over 5 percent. In essence, the Federal Reserve tried to engineer an economic recession.

As is so often the case, the consequences have fallen disproportionately on those who have least to fall back on. There is, however, something unique about the current crisis: its effects have gone right to the heart of middle-class life.[1] We are in the midst of what has been dubbed a "cost of living crisis." Amidst declining real incomes, rising energy prices, and increased mortgage payments, it is only the most affluent who escape the pocketbook squeeze altogether.

As this crisis took shape over the course of 2022 and 2023, many left-wing commentators continued to point out the growing evidence that inflation was being driven not by wage growth but by energy shocks and staggering corporate profits. And they insisted that workers should not be made to bear the brunt of a crisis they had not caused.

From the Federal Reserve's point of view, such objections were largely beside the point. Regardless of what may have triggered inflation initially, the danger was that inflationary *expectations* could take hold and set in motion a self-perpetuating spiral. That the logic of expectations could be a powerful force not only in wage demands but also in corporate price setting is not thinkable within the framework of modern, mainstream economics.

This gave rise to some strange intellectual acrobatics. On Twitter, Olivier Blanchard, former chief economist of the International Monetary Fund, worried about the practical difficulty of persuading workers that higher unemployment was necessary to control inflation in a situation where wage rises were not responsible for inflation.[2] When his comment set off a storm of ridicule, he quickly apologized for the unfortunate phrasing, stressing that he too lamented the fact that the Federal Reserve only had the one blunt instrument for managing the price level – but he stuck to his point.

In other hands, this same line of thinking took on meaner qualities. Throughout 2022, Larry Summers – another leading Keynesian economist, who had occupied key economic policy positions in both the Clinton and Obama administrations – had urged the Federal Reserve to pursue its anti-inflation program more energetically. Moderation and gradualism could only provide false comfort.

Summers was not afraid to put numbers on it, either, demanding specific percentages of unemployment for set periods of time. His interest in sorting human livelihoods on the basis of back-of-the-envelope calculations seemed to take economic expertise beyond its reputation for cheerlessness into a more sinister realm. But Summers was only spelling out, in unpleasant detail, what it meant to think about inflation in the way that had been so widely endorsed by the mainstream media.

In early 2023, Summers went on Bloomberg TV to express his satisfaction that the Federal Reserve had come to accept his view on the seriousness of the situation. Zooming in from a tropical beachside location, he intoned once again that "there's going to need to be increases in unemployment to contain inflation."[3] Soon after, in a widely publicized interview with comedian Jon Stewart, Summers likened himself to a doctor prescribing medication that would have side effects. Obviously, he wished he could spare his patient the side effects – but there was simply no alternative. In fact, if it *was* important to assign blame, it should be placed squarely on the spendthrift Biden administration – if you keep running the water, the bathtub will eventually overflow. But this was all just crying over spilled milk, a distraction from what needed doing.

If hard-nosed discipline was the cure for the economy as a whole, sometimes economic necessity pointed in another direction. When, in May of 2023, the Silicon Valley Bank was about to fail, Summers urged the government to step in and provide guarantees for the bank's financial commitments. Although he expressed some doubt that the failure of the bank would have a particularly broad impact, he nonetheless insisted that a blanket of public insurance to cover both SVB and any other exposed institutions was required to maintain the confidence of financial markets.

Summers understood all too well that a bank bailout will draw significant criticism at the best of times. And this was a bailout for a bank serving the most affluent Americans at a time when the population at large was being forced to tighten its belt. So, preemptively, he warned people not to succumb to the temptations of populism. Now was not "the time for moral hazard lectures or for lesson administering or for alarm about the political consequences of 'bailouts'."[4]

Why did the emergency of SVB justify taxpayer assistance, while the financial distress of ordinary Americans warranted nothing but further austerity and discipline? Even *Forbes Magazine*, a business publication perhaps best known for its annual ranking of billionaires, was getting a little lost. Had not the same Summers recently argued passionately against student debt forgiveness, rejecting it as a bailout that would introduce perverse incentives into young people's menu of choices?[5]

The tendency among non-economists and the general public is to assume that, even if the apparent inconsistencies of their thinking confuse us, people like Summers understand something about how money works that we do not. But what if that is not the case? What if the hard-nosed realism of America's leading economic commentator is simply an elaborate web of rationalizations and excuses hiding the fact that there are in fact no good reasons to reserve bailouts for the affluent?

Earning market confidence

The worldview of economists like Blanchard and Summers says that there exists a "natural" rate of unemployment. If unemployment falls below that rate, it will produce upward pressure on the general price level; and if it goes over, the result will be deflation. When they talk about "full employment," they don't have in mind an economy where everyone who wants a job has one. What they mean is a level of unemployment that is consistent with price stability (or, more specifically, with a low and stable level of inflation).

That there exists such a level of unemployment is one of the key tenets of contemporary economic orthodoxy, New Keynesianism. What is that magical number? Nobody knows: formal estimates have closely tracked actual unemployment rates. The "non-accelerating inflation rate of unemployment," better known as the NAIRU, is a fiction, invented by modern-day alchemists. To be sure, the basic idea itself has a long history. The notion that capitalism requires a "reserve army" of surplus workers is often considered to be one of Marx's most radical ideas. However, suitably rephrased, it would have been perfectly comprehensible to almost all political economists of the nineteenth century. Without an oversupply of labor, wages are likely to increase, workers will not be as productive, and prices will be higher.

Nineteenth-century British political economists generally held that there existed a "wage fund," a specific amount of money that could be spent on wages without upsetting the laws of economics. Such thinking started to shift only towards the end of the nineteenth century with the rise of modern, micro-level economic analysis – so-called "neoclassical" economics, which concerns itself with how supply and demand are balanced in specific markets. It fostered the notion that labor was like any other commodity, and that labor markets should clear like any other market.

The rise of organized labor gave the idea of full employment political teeth, and mass unemployment during the Great Depression propelled it to mainstream respectability. The existence of unemployment was the central concern of the most influential economics book ever written, John Maynard Keynes' *The General Theory of Employment, Interest and Money*.[6] For Keynes, there existed no more severe indictment of capitalism than its tendency to force idleness on people. He tasked governments with ensuring full employment, urging them to use their powers of taxing and borrowing to compensate for capitalism's failings.

In the wake of the Great Depression, when unemployment reached unprecedented levels, political movements in several countries tried to make full employment a binding government objective. In the United States, a powerful push emerged to make permanent the state of real full employment that had arisen during the war. Recognizing what was at stake, business and conservatives fought it tooth and nail.

Had the movement for a full employment guarantee succeeded, postwar history would have looked very different. It would have forced the US government to manage inflation not by cutting spending, restricting credit, and pushing up unemployment, but through the kinds of price controls that were in place during the war. In that alternative history, the Federal Reserve would have remained a largely obscure regulatory agency, and we would be unlikely to know the name of its chairperson. To be sure, the 1946 Employment Act was hardly a victory for the capitalist class. But it forced the labor movement to accept trade-offs, and it shifted from strategies to expand the circle of solidarity towards an insider–outsider politics that aligned with America's racial divide.

The benefits for those who enjoyed the protections of powerful unions were real. Wage labor was no longer a marker of second-class citizenship but a ticket to a middle-class lifestyle. For a broad middle class, it became possible to build up property through waged work and to map out what sociologists referred to as a "life course," a privilege previously reserved for the bourgeoisie. The result was a society that could be depicted in the image shown below, a poster used by the American Federation of Labor and Congress of Industrial Organizations (AFL-CIO) in the 1950s. It shows the living wage as the rock of American of society: family, community, and business were all built on the foundation that it provided.

For progressives, the early postwar period has always remained an important point of political orientation, a normative ideal. It showed, they claim, that a civilized capitalism is both possible and desirable. Needless to say, business leaders

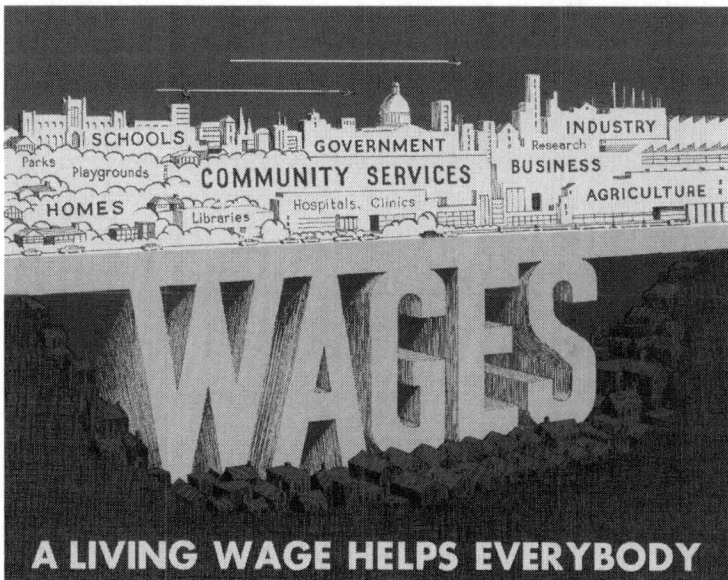

Source: Division of Political History, National Museum of American History, Smithsonian Institution.

would always have taken issue with the AFL-CIO poster, but still it captured a legitimate position in the mainstream debate. That is no longer the case. In the present, the logic depicted in the image simply no longer "makes sense." To endorse it is to advertise one's economic illiteracy. Even many labor leaders are likely to accept that wage growth can only ever be an effect, an outcome of economic growth or productivity increases – that wages are built on the strength of business, not vice versa.

Of course, it is less and less clear what the business of America and other Western countries actually consists in. The time that we worried about the ability of manufacturing companies to remain competitive is long gone, a quaint concern of the 1980s. Instead, the concern is with "market confidence": whether investors feel sufficiently optimistic about the future that they can resist the temptation to sell and cash out. Such confidence is easily damaged and not easily restored. That is how the logic of expectations works – sometimes it's more akin to gossip and rumor than rational economic judgment. The volatility of financial sentiment has replaced the security of the living wage as society's foundation.

On its face, the demand that we reorganize how our society works around the mercurial opinions of traders and investors might seem a little extravagant. But Summers' worldview was shaped during the roaring nineties, when he was part of the Clinton administration's economic policy team. Then, he had witnessed up close that when a government has the strength to stop promising handouts and free lunches, rewards will soon follow. After the hard work of financial belt-tightening was done, the second half of the 1990s saw low inflation, a rapid decline of unemployment, and booming asset markets that benefitted many working families.

So, when Summers was Treasury Secretary in the first Obama administration, the game plan was clear. The Obama administration came into office at the height of the Global Financial Crisis, and it stabilized the financial system by bailing out the banks. That was expensive, but Obama's economic team recognized the importance of paying one's bills. Indeed, being better stewards of the nation's public finances than profligate Republicans had become a major point of pride for Democrats. The bailouts were followed by drastic cuts to other parts of the public budget.

But no economic boom like that of the 1990s ever materialized. Supported by the Federal Reserve's asset-purchasing programs that went under the name of "quantitative easing," asset markets did well – very well. But capital gains were far more concentrated among the wealthy than they had been before the financial crisis, and they did not produce a broader "wealth effect" or drive general economic growth. Faithfully pandering to the whims of the marketplace no longer produced economic magic.

The absurd spectacle – lavish government assistance for the affluent, austerity for the rest of the population – sent a wave of anger through American society. The wildly different forms that such discontent took (the misgivings of Occupy Wall Street protesters often sounded remarkably similar to the concerns of Americans who joined a local Tea Party chapter) have posed a major puzzle for electoral analysts and others trying to understand the logic of Americans' political affiliations. But few any longer doubt that escalating inequality and political instability are connected.

After the financial crisis, progressives had hoped for a new beginning, and in the historic election of Barack Obama they yearned for the birth of a second New Deal. But by the end of Obama's presidency, the net worth of the average American household was lower than it had been two decades earlier. Meanwhile, the asset portfolios of the wealthy had gone from strength to strength. Thomas Piketty's unlikely bestseller *Capital in the Twenty-First Century* distilled the zeitgeist into a long series of charts, each showing the concentration of wealth in the hands of a steadily shrinking number of people.[7]

The weakness of the broader economic recovery was a source of tremendous confusion for Obama's economic policy team. What had gone wrong? How could it be that the austere management of the public finances had failed to generate strong economic performance? What was never on the table was the way of thinking depicted in the AFL-CIO image: starting with a living wage, and then building other economic institutions around it.

The election of Donald Trump became a lightning rod for progressive concerns about the state of the republic and the world at large. It appeared both to symbolize and to consolidate the conquest of democracy by moneyed interests, in the most obscene way possible. But the roots of our troubles go much deeper.

The credit boomerang

In some respects, postwar welfare capitalism is better seen as a Faustian bargain than as a limited victory or a stable compromise. The steady jobs and manicured lawns of the middle class were themselves built on foundations that make no appearance in the AFL-CIO's image of postwar society, above all severe racial inequalities.

Keynesian economists in the Kennedy and Johnson administrations worried about the concentration of disadvantage in a racially defined underclass. Their answer was to put economic growth at the center of their policy program. Wasn't that exactly what Keynes had recommended three decades earlier? In a sense, yes. But for Keynes the program had seemed straightforward: the government needed to step in and use its budget to compensate for the shortfall in aggregate demand.

The main obstacles that Keynes discerned in his own time consisted in the strength of outdated laissez-faire ideology, the aristocratic power of rentiers, and the fetishistic attachment to the gold standard. In the early postwar era, each of these obstacles seemed to have disappeared. And yet the implementation of a demand-oriented growth program was fraught with difficulties. Specifically, inflation invariably reared its head well before the economy reached a state of full employment.

Postwar Keynesians (known as "neo-Keynesians" for how they translated Keynes' insights into the formal demand-and-supply models of neoclassical economics) embarked on a long search for the missing ingredient, the key to non-inflationary growth. Increasingly preoccupied with the supply side of the economy, they developed an ever-expanding array of tax breaks and subsidies, hoping to incentivize corporations into making different investment and pricing decisions.

But there were no easy solutions. Supply-side politics has always been something of a bottomless pit: the more it has failed to be effective, the more plausible capital's insistence has been that taxes are still too high, investment incentives not sufficiently generous, and labor too expensive for what it offers.

In their search for non-inflationary growth, time and again reformers ended up looking to finance, especially mortgage credit. In our own time, finance is seen as either hero or villain, an agent of market perfection or a parasite on the body economic. But progressives of the early twentieth century did not necessarily think that way.[8] They viewed finance as a set of rules for economic life. Like all human institutions, it was both imperfect and susceptible to improvement. Finance was the nervous system of the economy, and adjusting its operating parameters could be a powerful way to change the behavior of the system for the better.

Marriner Eccles, an avid New Dealer who served as chair of the Federal Reserve from 1934 to 1948, referred to the government subsidization of lending as "the wheel within the wheel to move the whole economic engine."[9] Everyone could be happy about credit expansion: it provided new opportunities without making anyone worse off. If borrowers paid off their loans on time, there would be no reason for credit growth to be inflationary – it was just a matter of bringing opportunities forward in time.

Credit allowed workers to become owners. The reforms of the 1930s and 1940s created pathways from wage labor to property ownership – phenomena that had, until that point in history, rarely mixed. Our tendency to picture mid-twentieth-century capitalism with images of smokestacks and assembly lines notwithstanding, the postwar order did more to democratize the role of the rentiers than to euthanize them.

However, capitalism's financial nervous system turned out to have its own logic after all. It was entirely capable of fueling inflation. But maintaining the constellation of credit programs and fiscal subsidies supporting the aspirations of a broad middle class was imperative. Instead, inflation was managed by shifting economic pressures away from the white middle class onto minorities. The Federal Reserve could tighten credit to slow down economic growth, and the resulting unemployment largely bypassed workers organized in powerful unions, always hitting minorities in insecure employment hardest.

As long as each new backstop was matched by the application of austerity elsewhere in the system, inflation could be held at bay. Keynesian economists rationalized the situation by redefining full employment as a specific level of unemployment, setting in train the process that over time resulted in the NAIRU.

For several decades, credit growth allowed Keynesians to foster generalized economic growth when their other policy instruments were failing. The unwanted side effects were real but, when seen from society's center, appeared delayed and diffuse. By the 1970s, however, it worked like a boomerang, instantly creating as many new problems as it solved.

When the Federal Reserve came to the general public's attention in the 1970s, it appeared as a paradoxical combination of independence and helplessness. It enjoyed significant autonomy from other government bodies, and it was in no way accountable to the elected representatives of the American people. But, despite this tremendous freedom of action, it was unable to do the one job it had – control inflation.

In that context, *real* full employment re-emerged as a political objective, propelled by an alliance that challenged the divide-and-rule tactics of the post-New Deal state. An enforceable right to employment would have disabled the Federal Reserve's ability to inflict austerity in compensation for backstops and bailouts.

But the social and political landscape of the 1970s was different from that of the 1930s and 1940s. A middle class had grown up that owned houses and pensions, and Keynesians had lost the ability to see how an economy of actual full employment might be run. Especially after Nixon's experiment with price controls, such policies had become inconceivable – emergency measures acceptable only in wartime. Democratic politicians found themselves highly receptive to the arguments that the business community lobbed into the political arena. Those centered on the effects of outdated financial regulations, which were held responsible for weak investment and high unemployment.

The drive for a full employment guarantee was defeated, and Democrats and Keynesians did much of the heavy lifting. The watered-down legislation that was eventually passed – known as the Humphrey–Hawkins Act of 1978 – restated the Federal Reserve's responsibility for both employment and price stability. But it did nothing to make the conflict between these two objectives more manageable. And it did much to legitimate the idea that the Federal Reserve had no choice but to focus on controlling inflation first and foremost.

That same Act required the Federal Reserve to become less secretive. It instituted biannual Congressional hearings, where lawmakers would interrogate monetary policymakers about why and how they were letting down the American people. The new Act did not do anything to resolve the Federal Reserve's dilemmas, but it did expose the institution to the glare of public opinion, putting more pressure on it to exercise agency where it could.

From welfare to bailout state

Paul Volcker was appointed Federal Reserve chairperson after he assured Jimmy Carter that he would do what it took to conquer inflation. The significant pain that his policy would inflict was regrettable but unavoidable – his predecessors had allowed the problem to get out of hand. They had let the Federal Reserve get roped into maintaining an ever-expanding safety net, with generalized inflation as the unsurprising outcome. Volcker kept his word, and skyrocketing interest rates soon plunged America's economy into a ferocious recession.

He did not imagine that he could solve the problem on his own. He could help to reset expectations, but unless it was followed up by a broader process of adjustment, a program to truly break the back of inflation, it would only provide temporary respite. Volcker was not naïve about what it would mean: "The standard of living of the average American has to decline."[10]

Whereas mainstream economists think of Volcker's policy turn as the inauguration of a golden age of inflation targeting and neutral money, left-wing critics have described the same event as a frontal attack by capital on workers, democracy, and the welfare state. Such arguments have the virtue of highlighting the political stakes. But they greatly overestimate the precision of the Federal Reserve's policy tools. The Federal Reserve sets some of the main parameters for the operation of the American (and global) credit system. But it is not able to directly set employment levels or other macroeconomic indicators, and it is also not able to ensure that wide swathes of the business community will not get caught in the gears of a financial contraction.

If Volcker's program was class war, it was so in a very indirect way. During the 1980s, a seemingly unstoppable wave of failures rippled through the American economy. As the number of failures increased, it became clear that some banks were "too big to fail": their failure would have dragged down wider parts of the economic system. Volcker had always understood that the key nodes of America's financial system could not be allowed to collapse. The point of his policy shift was to stabilize the American currency, not to undermine it.

Volcker had put an abrupt end to the expansive, open-ended socialization of risk. But something, a more selective regime, needed to be put in its place. After-the-fact bailouts could only bring so much order to the system. They did not provide much "forward guidance," as we would now call it. The bailout of the mortgage sector during the late 1980s provided some clarity. An extraordinary amount of financial mischief had been pursued in what most Americans thought of as a wholesome, community-oriented sector. To let these institutions go to the wall would have been to punish the American middle class for the exploits of financiers. And so, the American government rescued not a specific firm but an entire financial sector.

Somehow, inflation did not return. During the previous years, a great deal of deadwood had been flushed out of the system. More importantly, the Reagan administration had worked hard to deliver on Volcker's declaration that the American standard of living needed to decline. Embattled unions were struggling to keep the deals they had and to prevent their plants from closing.

With Greenspan at the helm, the Federal Reserve became more and more comfortable with the logic of backstops and bailouts. The expectational regime became clear to the markets, if not always to social scientists and other onlookers: the public protection one will be able to claim is proportional to the threat one poses. With a government floor under asset markets, finance took the lead. A lackluster and uneven recovery morphed into the roaring nineties.

It took Clinton a little while to recognize history's gift. His initial plans had revolved around a radicalized supply-side Keynesianism, whereby the government would invest heavily in infrastructure and training. It had taken significant pressure from the financiers in his administration, led by Summers' mentor Robert Rubin, to convince Clinton to step back from those ambitions. But he was eventually convinced that the asset-driven growth of the 1990s, distributing its fruits to a broad middle class, was due to the budgetary rectitude his administration had displayed.

Critics never stopped pointing out that the tail was wagging the dog, that the dominance of finance over industry was not a sustainable basis for economic growth. They often invoked Keynes' dictum that "Speculators may do no harm as bubbles on a steady stream of enterprise. But the position is serious when enterprise becomes the bubble on a whirlwind of speculation."[11]

These same critics pointed out the hypocrisy in the austerity recipe. It never seemed to apply to items favored by conservative political sentiment, such as America's rapidly expanding prison complex or the military. More flagrantly, the very same bankers who insisted aggressively on public austerity were quick to demand and receive government assistance when times got tough – they were benefitting from exactly the kind of Keynesian government programs that their free-market dogmas declared anathema.

But the wave that the New Democrats were riding had longevity. Spectacular bailouts themselves became episodic. Far more significant was the growth of a web of subsidies and backstops, all uncertainly situated at the intersection of the public and private spheres. A drip-feed of liquidity support stabilized expectations and sustained asset prices. Again and again, the critics of "speculative bubbles" were left looking like desperate doomsayers.

Economic success made for ideological thickening. New Keynesianism, which emphasized the importance of "anchoring" inflationary expectations, migrated from academic theory to the public sphere. The financial safety net did not appear in its models. But it fully accepted the existence of a natural rate of unemployment. Left-wing critics have often been tempted to set this way of thinking aside as little more than Keynesian retreat in the face of the conservative Reagan revolution. But that is to downplay the energy that it brought to the reformulation of Keynesianism, and the political purchase that its promises of synergistic, inclusive, and non-inflationary growth found.

Bailouts in the age of free markets

If the bailout state is such a sprawling behemoth, why has it been so hard to see? Of course, specific groups often have reason to divert attention from the policies that benefit them. Furthermore, the bailout state works through expectations, mental maps of the future that often remain invisible. But those considerations apply to many institutions. Even experts often struggle to understand the complex details of their everyday operation, but it is rarely reason to doubt their existence.

The real reason why we often have difficulty acknowledging the very existence of a bailout state is that, by most accounts, we are meant to live in an age not of expanding government but of free markets and retreating states. In the general public's understanding, our contemporary political economy has been shaped by the historic shift from a broad-based trust in the benevolent power of the state to belief in the unobstructed play of market forces. Social scientists have used essentially the same story, seeing a shift from Keynesianism to neoliberalism as the hegemonic way of thinking about economic life and policymaking.[12]

A bailout state just has no real place in that picture. It is easy to acknowledge individual bailouts, as exceptions to or betrayals of the free-market norm. We can even recognize that this happens more often than it should, and we may well suspect that politicians and bankers are not always sincere when they sing the praises of free-market capitalism. But the two stories are inherently at odds: to the extent that the one makes sense, the other does not.

The neoliberalism debate as it has been conducted by academics has evolved to add a great deal of nuance to the basic idea of a shift from government to markets. Some authors argued that the neoliberal project included a strong role for the state from the very start, while others stressed that the instability caused by deregulation required new forms of government intervention.

Predictably, however, it also gave rise to the question of whether the neoliberalism concept still captures something distinctive. A growing number of commentators feel that it doesn't. According to them, free-market ideology has been only one among numerous factors influencing a complex and gradual process of institutional change. An institutional snapshot of today's political economy shows essentially the same as one taken fifty years ago: a mixed economy, recognizably capitalist but with an unmistakably prominent role for the state.

The differences between these perspectives on neoliberalism are not as significant as their advocates imagine them to be. For each, the post-New Deal state represents a normative ideal, a judicious balance of public institutions and private incentives. And they understand neoliberalism as an attempt to undo that marriage of social protection and capital. Where they differ is on the assessment of how effective the neoliberal assault has been.

That way of thinking suffers from two related blind spots. First, it overlooks the many oppressions and exclusions on which the Keynesian post-New Deal order was built. That order was always a *Herrenvolk* democracy, shielding the interests of a geographically and racially delineated middle class from the downside of capitalism and giving it access to a living wage, high levels of consumption, a pension, and homeownership. Second, obversely, such a perspective does not recognize the very real alliance with social and democratic citizenship that the growth of finance has enjoyed, at least in Western countries. Neoliberalism – if that is the right word – has taken shape as a middle-class politics aiming to shore up the foundations of a *Herrenvolk* democracy under pressure.

Nowhere is the continuity more evident than in the persistent centrality of stabilization as the core objective of economic policy. A Keynesian, macro-level way of viewing the economic system has specific intellectual lineages, but it did not rise to prominence as the result of a sudden cognitive shift among state officials. During the 1930s, intense popular pressure meant that the post-crash reconstruction of America's financial infrastructure needed to position it as a vehicle for middle-class aspirations. The stabilization imperative became deeply embedded in the muscle memory of economic policymaking, and it has remained there ever since.[13]

The red thread of stabilization policy has never meant stasis, however. As Hyman Minsky, a Keynesian economist whose work informs the story told in this book, understood so well, stability produces its own contradictions, and those require institutional responses. The long decade of the 1970s saw a series of policy shifts that often were pragmatic and gradual but nonetheless tremendously consequential. As the Keynesian program adapted itself to changing circumstances, in part by responding to and assimilating critiques from a neoliberal direction, it transformed both itself and the institutions of American capitalism.

In the "Keynesianism to neoliberalism" story, the tensions of the 1970s were resolved by a right-wing flank movement. The story told in this book has a different emphasis. The critical shifts of that time were driven by committed Keynesians and Democrats who, operating squarely from within the political center, sought to preserve and revitalize a middle-class politics.[14] In doing so, they built the contemporary bailout state.

All Keynesians

These arguments echo the idea that "we are all Keynesians now," a phrase (attributed to Richard Nixon) that critics of neoliberalism often use to underscore that, when crisis strikes and push comes to shove, we all believe in the benefits of government intervention. During the climax of the Global Financial Crisis of 2007–9, as the American government moved to support a financial system teetering on the brink, it was in this vein that many commentators declared the return of Keynes. What they often failed to recognize was that Keynes' presence had lingered all along – that we had never *stopped* being Keynesians.

The Obama administration came into office at the height of that financial crisis, and many progressives looked to it for a return to the original spirit of the New Deal. For them, the 2010s would be a decade of intense political disappointment, capstoned by the election of an aspiring fascist to the American presidency. Some of the world's brightest critical minds tried to make sense of it all by recommitting to the neoliberalism concept. But the focus on the radicalization of free-market thinking made it difficult to engage critically with the institutionalization of the bailout state that was taking place at the very same time.

At the end of 2008, as the Federal Reserve realized how far the uncertainty had spread and that a more predictable approach to market assistance was called for, it started buying up large amounts of financial assets to ensure their value. Quantitative easing amounted to a dramatic expansion and proactive implementation of bailouts – the bailout state became a backstop state, and forward guidance became hand-holding. As the threat that there might yet be a Second Great Depression refused to lift, the government expanded the reach of these programs time and again, creating an unprecedented safety net for the financial sector.

All this caused severe cracks in the technocratic façade of financial policy. Many wondered how we had ended up in a world where massive Keynesian state intervention was used to keep banks turning profits while the public was exposed to unrelenting austerity in the name of market discipline.

Such widespread disquiet fed the unlikely rise to prominence of Modern Money Theory (MMT).[15] It took the question that was on many people's minds – did there really exist any sound economic reasons, of a scientific and objective nature, for why the government should support the balance sheets of banks but not the pocketbooks of ordinary people? – and answered it with a simple and emphatic "no." A sovereign government can finance anything it considers valuable.

An important source of inspiration for MMT is the work of Abba Lerner on "functional finance." Not too long after the initial publication of the *General Theory*, Lerner argued that Keynes' "new fiscal theory" assumed a broader theory of how a nation's monetary structure worked.[16] If Keynes' basic analysis was correct, Lerner argued, it logically meant that government spending should be guided only by "functional" considerations, i.e., that it "should be undertaken with an eye only to the results of these actions on the economy and not to any established traditional doctrine about what is sound or unsound."[17]

That echoed Keynes' own comment, made in a 1942 radio address, that "Anything we can actually *do* we can afford."[18]

The *General Theory*, by contrast, took a more narrow approach, respecting the distinction between monetary and fiscal policy that had emerged since the start of the twentieth century and limiting its prescriptions to how the government might use its budget to stabilize capitalism. Lerner, starting to see that this had given conservative political forces room for maneuver and a set of arguments that they eagerly exploited, insisted on spelling out what he considered the logical implication: real Keynesianism implied a rejection of the fiscal/monetary distinction. The government's budget and the nation's money were one and the same.

Modern-day MMTers grew up in a time when the markets' demands for sound monetary management had become an intolerable constraint on the use of government finances for any progressive purpose. Adding insult to injury, it was people like Summers, who claimed the legacy of Keynes, who did the work here. Whatever strategic benefits Keynes' circumspection might once have had, had long worn off.

Echoing demands of earlier political movements for the radicalization of Keynesianism, some MMT authors espoused the objective of actual full employment, insisting on a job guarantee. The purpose here is the same as in the past: to deactivate the state's ability to control inflation by imposing austerity.

But it is a sign of changing times that many MMT authors view full employment as just one option on the menu of possibilities. Others demand public spending programs that would allow Americans to work *less*. Especially in a time of accelerating ecological degradation, it is no longer clear that economic growth is always desirable. But the fundamental point is that the government can finance whatever we democratically agree is worth having. The first task, then, is to democratize the bailout state.

According to MMT, Americans live in a perverse reality, where a Keynesian state is fully operative but functions to advance the interests not of people but of banks and corporations. What prevents us from discerning this is the erroneous myth of free markets.

That assessment, I believe, is essentially correct. But it is also incomplete. The idea that it is only ideological distortion and manipulation shackling us to a reality of bailouts for some and austerity for others is too simple. If we are to have any hope re-seeing the present, we need to understand what happened in the first place. How did Keynesian interventionism become an instrument of the ruling class? When and how did the Keynesian program morph from a policy manual for generalized growth into a program to keep alive the very rentier interests that Keynes had sought to euthanize? And why weren't people watching at the time? Or were they?

Roadmap

Chapter 2 expands on the ideas presented in this introduction, setting out the core idea in a more systematic way. The protagonist here is Hyman Minsky, a Keynesian economist who was critical of neo-Keynesianism and New Keynesianism, but who also kept some distance from MMT-style arguments.[19] Like Lerner, Minsky recognized the artificiality of the fiscal/monetary distinction. But he also understood that it had become an entirely real, institutional aspect of how the economic system worked and that it could not simply be bypassed or unthought.

What most varieties of Keynesianism shared, Lerner's included, was the hope for a technical fix, a simple, uncontroversial solution to capitalism's ills. Although Minsky was a strong advocate of the use of the public budget to bring about full employment, he fully recognized that this would tear at the institutional fabric of capitalism and give rise to political conflict. That was the point, at least in part – to re-politicize institutions that the public had come to treat as technical, economic, or otherwise beyond its grasp or ken.

This wider lens allowed Minsky to see the logic of Keynesianism as a practical program more clearly. The New Deal was so successful because it undertook, under tremendous democratic pressure, an inside-out reconstruction of American society's financial structure. To the extent that the Keynesian program subsequently lost sight of that basic fact, it was bound to become receptive to false promises and entangled in unreliable alliances. The focus on achievable quick wins and convenient compromises would undermine its longer-term ability to be an agent of progressive transformation.

Chapter 3 revisits the era of welfare capitalism. Formulaic characterizations of the era – as the heyday of the mixed economy, when government successfully pushed back against the reach of the market – can in fact be major obstacles to understanding it. The ability of Democratic administrations to make aggressive use of fiscal policy to bring the economy to full employment, supposedly the hallmark of such a mixed economic order, was always limited.

Instead, full employment was redefined as an acceptable level of unemployment, and sharp boundaries were drawn around the constituency of white, unionized workers who could leverage steady annual wage rises to build up property. The Federal Reserve stood at the intersection of these forces. On the one hand, it was responsible for ensuring the Treasury's ability to fund the American government and backstopping markets to facilitate the growth of credit flows to the expanded middle class. On the other hand, it was responsible for containing inflation – a job that it took just as seriously, as we have already seen.

Chapter 4 discusses the rise of "growth Keynesianism," propagated by economists in the Kennedy and Johnson administrations who discerned the bind the Keynesian program was in and were eager to undo it. They considered that earlier Keynesians had relied too much on demand stimulus alone and not done enough to undercut the inflationary pressure that it produced. Instead, they centered the supply side, seeking to reshape the economy's investment and pricing calculus with tax cuts and other incentives.

Time and again, growth Keynesians looked to credit growth as a means to reconcile economic and social objectives. To that end, they actively assisted banks in their attempts to break out of the regulatory framework of the New Deal. When inflationary pressures threatened to get out of hand, the Federal Reserve would intervene and try to shut down the banks' innovations. But by the end of the decade, such regulatory pushback only drove banks to come up with new and more effective ways to create credit.

Chapter 5 takes a fresh look at the decade of the 1970s, when the government appeared to be losing control over inflation. According to the "Keynesian to neoliberalism" story, growing economic chaos accelerated the right-wing backlash, and the Carter administration was the last gasp of tax-and-spend liberalism. In reality, the New Deal state had come under attack from the left as much as the right. It was the sustained management of social pressure by mainstream Democrats that demobilized the challenge.

A new political movement for full employment legislation sought to repurpose the machinery of the New Deal state towards the achievement of full employment. But Democratic leaders were less concerned with the maldistribution of past growth than securing high levels of future growth. They had become amenable to arguments that the barrier to non-inflationary growth consisted in supply-side obstacles, in particular financial regulations. Although that program won the day, it failed to stem the inflationary tide.

Chapter 6 shows how Volcker's policies created the conditions for the contemporary bailout state to emerge. Critical scaffolding for that structure had been put in place during the previous fifty years, but Volcker recognized that indiscriminately expanding the financial safety net was bound to be inflationary. Diametrically reversing the priorities of the Humphrey–Hawkins drive for full employment, he decided to prioritize stable consumer prices above all else.

The policy turn had a devastating impact on the American economy and its financial infrastructure. Volcker's objective, however, was not to let the economic system go into freefall, but to stabilize it by enforcing a more selective approach to risk socialization. Financial authorities began to bail out positions that they considered too systemically important to fail, and by the end of the decade an informal bailout regime had been consolidated whereby the American state guaranteed the balance sheets of too-big-to-fail banks.

Chapter 7 looks at what resulted: the roaring nineties, an economic expansion that was heavily driven by the growth of asset prices. New Democrats built a new progressive philosophy of economic policy on this fact. Their worldview could still acknowledge the importance of public expenditure as part of a supply-side growth strategy, but it fully accepted that governments incurring budget deficits to increase consumption or to fund social programs would do little except fuel inflation. Wage growth was only considered acceptable when it was an outcome of market processes.

This did not, however, mean an end to progressive ambitions. To the contrary, the 1990s was the decade when a new middle-class politics took hold, one that substituted the logic of capital gains for wage growth. In the philosophy of the New Democrats, the way ordinary people could benefit from economic growth was through the appreciation of their assets – their human capital, real estate, and pension savings. Progressives of the Clinton era, it seemed, had finally found the holy grail of Keynesianism: non-inflationary, generalized growth.

Chapter 8 examines the contradictions of the bailout state. When the financial crisis of 2007–9 crisis started, financial authorities knew what to do: bail out the banks. The cost of those interventions came on top of large budget deficits caused by a decade of wild tax cuts and expensive military ventures, and once the immediate threat had gone, the Obama administration undertook to bring order to the public finances, tightening the public financial belt by pruning social programs and public investment.

The recovery was painfully slow, and the possibility of a wholesale deflation never entirely receded from view. With interest rates near zero, the Federal Reserve turned to large-scale asset purchases to stabilize asset prices, ensure liquidity of bank portfolios, and get credit flowing again. It prevented a Second Great Depression, but nothing more – growth remained sluggish, and unemployment high.

Chapter 9 discusses how the most powerful institution in the world economy got locked in place. Cognizant that it had become trapped in an unhealthy relationship, the Federal Reserve began trying to extricate itself from the arrangement. But every time it tried to do so, the financial markets threw a massive tantrum that forced the American central bank to sound the retreat. Held hostage by too-big-to-fail interests, American financial authorities were stuck in a financial position that they were unable to exit without doing severe damage to America's financial system.

The asset price boom of the 2010s was never able to recapture the 1990s' spirit of financial democratization: it was too skewed towards the comfortably propertied to offer plausible promises of universal access and generalized growth. Its benefits flowed overwhelmingly to white households in the upper deciles of the wealth distribution, while the effects of public austerity were felt most intensely by African Americans and other minorities. The trickle-down effect of asset inflation had stopped working.

Chapter 10 reflects on the present and future of the bailout state. The public health emergency of the Covid crisis created an unusual task for economic policy: to facilitate a dramatic

reduction of economic activity without damaging the underlying economic infrastructure. That required an extension
of the financial safety net, but there existed no playbook for
this unprecedented situation and the way it mixed economic
and social considerations. When Federal Reserve chairperson
Jerome Powell stated that there existed no technical – only
political – limits to the possibility of getting money in the
hands of people who needed it, he conceded the essential truth
of MMT. But if this came dangerously close to letting the cat
out of the bag, he would soon make amends by leading the
fight against the aspirations the Federal Reserve's pandemic
policies had inadvertently engendered.

Progressive critics have not been silent, arguing that inflation is driven not by wages but primarily by profits. On this
fact, they have built a case for a renewed progressive supply-
side politics: if we can get a grip on the causes of inflation at
its presumed point of origin and target them with bespoke
policies, we will have removed the reason for austerity policy.
However, as this book shows, such a supply-side orientation
has long been a fraught part of the Keynesian program. It
has never provided a technical fix and has always pushed the
Keynesian program right to the very edge of its conceptual
frame: the monetary constitution of contemporary society,
where questions of economics become inextricably entangled
with issues of political power and control.

2

What Keynes Missed

For Keynes, capitalism's most serious flaw consisted in its tendency to let productive resources go unused amidst widespread scarcity. The existence of involuntary unemployment stood as capitalism's strongest possible indictment. This, he argued, needed to be remedied by governments making more active use of their powers of taxing, borrowing, and spending.

During the first decades of the twentieth century, governments had failed spectacularly on this account. Hostage to antiquated orthodox ideas about how the economy should be managed, they had prioritized balancing government budgets and maintaining the gold convertibility of their currencies. If such orthodox ideas had served certain purposes during the nineteenth century, by the early twentieth century they had come to serve as a straitjacket, driving governments to sacrifice growth and employment at the altar of money and property. It took an economic depression and tremendous democratic pressure for governments to recognize the profound problems with orthodox economic thinking.

The political economists of the eighteenth and nineteenth centuries had been aware of the instrumental, conventional nature of money – that was their major advance on mercantilists' fixation on the accumulation of precious metals. But, almost in the same breath, authors such as David Hume and Adam Smith had imagined that money was entirely neutral – that its only role was to facilitate transactions that would have happened anyway, albeit later rather than sooner. Abundant evidence for the non-neutrality of money did not lead them to question the idea, but rather to insist that governments devote their powers to *making* money neutral. Classical political economy had come to fetishize gold in its own way, not just urging states to accumulate it but insisting that entire societies remake themselves from the inside out to maintain the convertibility of their debts into gold.

In the age of democratic ferment through which Keynes lived, this paradoxical logic looked more and more like reactionary ideology, serving no one but a small stratum of property owners. If money was a convention, a device that society has created to solve its problems, it made no sense to think that it demanded only submission and sacrifice. Instead, it was meant – and could be made – to work for the political community that had created it. For thousands of years, Keynes argued, money had been a creature of the state. And in a time when growing democratic demands meant a rapid widening of the political community, the true spirit of modern money was not austerity and scarcity, but growth and abundance, the progressive *elimination* of scarcity.

Keynes identified two characters who prevented such progress: the speculator and the rentier. The speculator was the investor who eschewed enterprise, and instead hoped for capital gains through effortless appreciation in the value of an asset. Although Keynes considered this unproductive behavior, he also saw it as inevitable to some extent, as enterprise would inevitably throw up new opportunities for exploiting market movements. The real danger was that this situation would reverse and that the tail would end up wagging the dog.

But Keynes reserved most of his opprobrium for the rentier. Like the speculator, the rentier was unproductive; but, unlike the speculator, he did not even incur risk. Instead, he simply cashed in on the return on property. The scandal that the rentier expressed was that there existed a return on mere ownership, nothing but formal legal title. This was an absurdity produced by the growth of a fully monetized society.

Rentiers were derisked speculators, enjoying the upside of uncertainty about the future without being exposed to the downside. They had survived into the twentieth century because orthodox financial policies kept interest rates artificially high and capital artificially scarce.[1] A Keynesian program of generalized growth would overcome such artificial scarcity and starve the rentier class of its lifeblood. The *General Theory* was Keynes' policy manual for progressive elites, to use when they were next in charge. It showed how they could use the government's budget (the public "fisc," hence "fiscal policy") to ensure that the economic system operates at full capacity, hastening the rentier's demise.

Keynesianism and the money question

After the appearance of the *General Theory*, economists such as Alvin Hansen and John Hicks translated the book's insight into the models of neoclassical economics, the formal mathematical language that economists had developed to understand how markets operate and clear. Neo-Keynesian models showed how, by using the fiscal powers of the state to correct for market imperfections, societies could attain the fullest possible employment of their economic resources. This neo-Keynesian paradigm remains the lingua franca of modern economics to this day. Its core concepts are still taught to millions of students every year in high schools and universities around the world.

Neo-Keynesian models assumed the possibility of separating fiscal and monetary questions. Keynes himself had never made such a strong claim. In Keynes' time, the institutional divide between fiscal and monetary policy was not nearly as settled as it would later become. As we will see, the emergence and consolidation of that divide is of tremendous political significance. It meant that decisions about how money is organized – how society organizes its rules for determining who gets what – are shifted into a separate sphere that we no longer think of as having political significance.[2]

As the neo-Keynesian paradigm established its hegemony in the academy and beyond, it sidelined monetary questions, working with the kind of orthodox understanding of money that Keynes had been generally critical of. It relied on what Minsky called a "village fair" model of the economy, where people may struggle to find suitable partners to exchange their commodities with.[3] They can solve that problem by agreeing on a monetary standard that allows everyone to put a price on their goods – here, money is a neutral facilitator, allowing trading to take place but adding nothing new into the mix.

Minsky challenged this way of thinking about money. When considering a village fair, it is possible to model the creation of money as a simple solution to a coordination problem. But that procedure loses plausibility when we are dealing with economic interactions taking place on a society-wide scale. Economic transactions often occur for the purpose not of consumption but for investment, often involving long timelines and requiring debt finance. The resulting degree of complexity and interdependency is such that it rules out tidy, one-off solutions. Instead, it requires the ongoing management of an intricate, evolving web of financial promises and obligations. Money is an infrastructure that requires constant upkeep, and neo-Keynesian models made it invisible.[4]

Certainly, Keynes himself had opened the door for the kinds of assumptions about money that neo-Keynesians were now using to develop his ideas. Monetary questions did not receive much explicit consideration in the *General Theory*. Keynes had engaged those in earlier publications such as the *Treatise on Money*. However, reflecting the urgency of the moment, the *General Theory* squarely focused on the problem of unemployment, and it zeroed in on the problem of insufficient demand as its most proximate cause. That, he said in the preface, justified "technical monetary detail fall[ing] into the background."[5] It was no doubt also on Keynes' mind that a narrow theory focused on how use of the government's budget could solve society's main problem was more likely to find traction than a wholesale reassessment of the existing financial system.

One of Keynes' early interpreters, Abba Lerner, felt that this silence on broader monetary issues had been unwise – it left ajar a door that should have been properly shut. Already in 1943, he noted that neo-Keynesian popularizations of Keynes' work were heavily driven by the wish to make the theory acceptable to establishment viewpoints.[6] They ceded too much ground to orthodox sound money arguments by conceding that there may exist objective economic limits to fiscal expansion, levels of employment, and public budget deficits. In other words, Keynes' bracketing of the monetary question had an immediate backlash effect on the fiscal argument. The very reason why fiscal arguments were less contentious was that they were more easily contained. According to Lerner, Keynes had stepped into a trap.

Rejecting Keynes' notion that monetary questions pertained only to technical detail, Lerner brought them from the background into the foreground. And he insisted on not fudging the issue: Keynes' "new fiscal theory," properly understood, implied a full rejection of the fiscal/monetary distinction.[7] If Keynes' analysis in the *General Theory* was correct, Lerner argued, it logically meant that government spending "should be undertaken with an eye only to the results of these actions on the economy and not to any established traditional doctrine about what is sound or unsound."[8]

Lerner specified the economic role of the government as follows:

> to keep the total rate of spending in the country on goods and services neither greater nor less than that rate which at the current prices would buy all the goods that it is possible to produce. If total spending is allowed to go above this there will be inflation, and if it is allowed to go below this there will be unemployment.[9]

He recognized that this could at times require deficit spending, a particular source of anxiety for establishment opinion. But as long as such borrowing did not result in spending that exceeded economic output, this too could not logically present a problem because the government was only compensating for the leaks and squeaks elsewhere in the economic system.[10]

In a later contribution, Lerner put it plainly: the ideas of the *General Theory* only fully made sense if we accept Keynes' earlier idea, from the *Treatise of Money*, that money is "a creature of the state."[11] According to this theory of "chartal money," it is the state that designates a particular token as legal tender, and only then can it serve as the standard for private commerce and as the means of payment for settling debts.

The monetary/fiscal divide

In practice, the monetary/fiscal distinction, while entirely a human invention, has been all too real. At various points in history, events such as the Employment Act of 1946 made the conceptual distinction into an institutional divide. And the constraints that this imposed on the Keynesian program were by no means imaginary. Instead of neatly compensating for a deflationary leak elsewhere in the system, fiscal stimulus often quickly produced inflation. Such pressures emerged when the economy was still operating well below capacity and unemployment was still unacceptably high.

Keynesian policymakers and thinkers spent tremendous time and effort trying to build flanking policy models to undercut inflation and so prepare the ground for expansionary fiscal policy. From early on, the Keynesian program included an active concern with the supply side of the economy, where decisions about investment and pricing are made. Keynes himself had already suggested as much, writing in the concluding notes of the *General Theory* that the implementation of his program might in fact require a "somewhat comprehensive socialization of investment," although he quickly retreated from the more radical connotations of that idea by specifying that it "need not exclude all manner of compromises and of devices by which public authority will co-operate with private initiative."[12]

The wartime economy showed what an indisputably effective supply-side policy looked like: with a combination of planning and wage and price controls, it is possible to employ a nation's productive resources to the fullest possible extent while controlling inflation. That way, you can afford anything you can actually do, to use Keynes' words. But that option has only ever been available to national governments in situations of extreme external pressure. Outside of wartime circumstances, attempts to bring such ideas onto the political agenda have predictably provoked an aggressive capitalist counteroffensive. In such circumstances, the appeal of Keynesianism has always consisted in the promise that similar outcomes can be achieved *without* having to wage class struggle.

Although the receptiveness of business to government's attempts to harness private interests to the public interest has fluctuated over time, on the whole supply-side interventions have rarely been able to deliver the non-inflationary growth that Keynesians were looking for. The public–private cooperation that Keynes envisaged has always been far more effective in socializing the *cost* of business investment than delivering public control over investment *decisions*.

How was it possible that in modern capitalism inflation had become "chronic," as Minsky put it? Neither neo-Keynesianism nor Lerner's chartalism was capable of accounting for this deep-seated inflationary force. For all their differences, each is premised on the possibility of designating a standard in which private transactions can be conducted without that standard itself becoming subject to the maelstrom of economic life.[13] In a sense, chartalism assumes that, with the help of the state, the village fair model *can* in fact be scaled up. In a world where it is possible to create a monetary standard through legislative fiat or simple designation, inflation has no real place.

Financial Keynesianism

Minsky rejected the idea that a functional monetary standard could be created through mere designation. Like Lerner, he insisted that Keynes' fiscal theory was at its core a financial theory. "Keynes was almost exclusively a monetary economist," as he put it.[14] But he was more alert to the shared limitations of both the orthodox and chartal positions. The economy's financial structure emerges "endogenously," from the interaction of economic units' balance sheets; and yet it requires ongoing public support and maintenance.

For Minsky, the village fair model wasn't just unrealistic. More critically, it failed to grasp what was at stake in economic life: ownership and investment, not consumption. Economic interaction is shaped not primarily by the wish to exchange our surplus commodities, but by the drive of economic units to secure their future by making the right investments. Financing such investments requires economic units to borrow from others, and in this way a complex web of debt relations is spun. Minsky referred to this way of looking at the economic system as the "Wall Street" paradigm, his alternative to the village fair paradigm.[15]

We are inclined to mentally model this process as occurring in a modern economic system with a uniform national currency. But that is already to assume that – rather than explain how – economic units solve their coordination problems and create an infrastructure for their interaction. According to Minsky, we can only understand how the problem is solved if we center the role of banks.[16] By replacing heterogeneous debts owed by a variety of parties with a debt owed by the bank, banks produce currency, a debt that circulates at par and in which other debts are denominated and settled. Whereas other debts need to be discounted, bank debts do not. A bank can issue IOUs (which we all can) and have it accepted at par (which few of us can).[17]

That is certainly not, logically or historically, the only possible way in which money can be produced. But banks swapping other people's debts for their own has become the dominant mode of money creation in modern capitalism. Banks do not create credit on the basis of an existing monetary standard: they *create* that standard in the first place by "making a market" for their own debt. And they *re-create* that standard every single day. If banks were to stop operating, the monetary system would collapse in short order.

Neo-Keynesianism was never able to understand this role of banks. It viewed a bank as a credit intermediary: an institution that gathers many short-term savings, bundles them up, and passes them on in the form of longer-term credit. According to Minsky, this is a superficially plausible description of bank activity that abstracts from their core activity. A bank's defining operation is not that it accepts short-term savings and transforms them into longer-term loans; it is that it gathers up short-term debts and replaces those with its own short-term debts.

In one sense, this is a simple shift of perspective. But the intellectual challenge here is significant. It requires more than acknowledging fractional reserve banking (as in neo-Keynesian models), which maintains the channeling model and primarily views banks as creditors or lenders.[18] Heterodox, "post-Keynesian" scholars have rejected the neo-Keynesian understanding of banks as credit intermediators, arguing that banks do not have to passively wait for people to hand over deposits on the basis of which they can then make loans. Instead, banks actively create deposits as they make loans.[19] Although that is certainly a better description of the dynamics of a bank balance sheet, it still assumes symmetry between its two sides. But when a bank makes a market for its own debt, it creates a new financial standard and so *breaks* that symmetry. The failure to recognize that is why the post-Keynesian literature is predisposed to see balance sheet leverage solely as a source of instability, rarely recognizing its prior role as a source of financial stability.[20]

A different way of expressing this is that banks produce money by turning balance sheet leverage into a business model.[21] Leveraging is typically understood as borrowing funds to increase the exposure of one's investment to market fluctuations. For banks, however, it is a more fundamental operation. A grocery store without balance sheet leverage is still a grocery store; a bank without balance sheet leverage is no longer a bank. The need for banks to leverage their balance sheet exists prior to the identification of any suitable investment opportunities.

The more stable a bank, the more money-like its convertible-on-demand IOUs will be. It can assume that any counterparty will accept its debt confessions at par, allowing it to issue money unilaterally. Exploiting the stability they provide, banks can generate profits by taking risks that other economic actors cannot afford to take. They do not use this power mindlessly to buy consumer goods. Instead, they use it to lend on property, or more precisely to buy promises of future property. Bank money – our currency – is collateralized by the promise of a return on property.

When banks extend credit, they push up the price of assets. Higher asset values can in turn justify additional bank lending, which further pushes up prices. This self-reinforcing feedback loop can also work in the opposite direction, with falling asset prices and credit contractions mutually reinforcing each other. As the constellation of credit connections begins to deleverage, depositors will start withdrawing funds (a "run on the bank"), putting yet further pressure on the bank to divest itself of its assets. That dynamic, in a nutshell, is what caused the Crash of 1929 and the Great Depression of the 1930s.

Minsky viewed instability as the defining aspect of modern capitalism, and as the driving force behind the tendency of the financial system to become centralized. When banks' ability to borrow directly from the public is evaporating, banks naturally look for their own banker, an institution that is still capable of issuing IOUs whose value is not in doubt. Financial elites have never failed to advocate for such a bankers' bank, a "lender of last resort" to stabilize the financial nervous system of the economy during times of uncertainty.

As governments became more accountable to broader segments of the population for how they managed the economy, they have typically considered it to be in their own interest to support such emergency arrangements. Thus, a hierarchy of money emerged: when lower-level money (the debts of a small, local bank) fails, higher-level money (the debts of a central bank or the national treasury) can take over.[22] All stable modern currencies have emerged through such mixing of private and public forces, that is, from the use of public resources to protect private balance sheets. The problem with understanding money as either purely private or purely public is that it cannot see this "essential hybridity" of money.[23] Money is a "public–private deal."[24]

Chronic inflation

In response to the Crash and the Great Depression, the Roosevelt administration undertook a major reconstruction of America's monetary infrastructure. By insuring bank deposits with federal funds, it undercut the logic behind bank runs. It barred banks from trading stock, but it provided them with a range of subsidies and incentives to encourage lending on mortgages and Treasury debt. A large share of mortgages was guaranteed by the government, while the Federal Reserve's support for the Treasury debt market meant that federal debt was a highly liquid asset. In other words, the American state guaranteed key items on banks' balance sheets.

Minsky's understanding of what happened here represents a major clarification of the foundations of Keynesian theory. The *General Theory* relies on the assumption that a pure, laissez-faire version of capitalism would be characterized by a deflationary bias. It underpins the idea that the capitalist circuit suffers from a "leak" and that government spending would neatly plug the leak. Minsky never reproduces that line of thought. In his world, a stable financial structure can only emerge by derisking the positions of key debt issuers. Such protections have inflationary effects: they exempt a specific group of investors or class of assets from market downturns.

According to Minsky, then, deflationism is not a congenital defect of a basic version of capitalism. Instead, it is a policy to compensate for the inflationary pressures produced by other policies. It's a way to manage the pressures produced by an institutional framework guaranteeing a financial return on property.[25]

The reconstruction of American finance during the 1930s created new, more powerful sources of inflationary pressure. The lessons about the danger of a deflationary spiral had been thoroughly absorbed, and the safety net was much broader than it had been during the nineteenth century – it maintained a middle class, not a bourgeoisie. The New Deal did not abolish the rentier function but distributed it over broad swathes of American society. By putting a floor under specific asset classes, the New Deal state produced a standing source of inflation. As Minsky put it:

> the economic relations that make a debt deflation and a long-lasting deep depression like that of the 1930s unlikely in a Big Government economy can lead to chronic and, at times, accelerating inflation. In effect, inflation may be the price we pay for depression-proofing our economy.[26]

As a consequence, postwar fiscal stimulus never simply corrected for a deflationary bias, as Keynes and early Keynesians had hoped. Instead, it exacerbated an inflationary bias that was baked into the post-New Deal financial framework. This inconvenient fact made itself felt at the same time as something else became clear – that the state's budget was in fact an indisputably effective tool to produce full employment and improve social conditions. This conflict shaped much of the postwar period.

Keynesianism in government

During the 1960s, a roster of leading neo-Keynesian economists occupied key positions in government and were ready to implement the Keynesian recipe for growth and full employment. But time and again, the economy showed signs of inflation well before a situation of full employment had been reached. For conservatives, the diagnosis was simple: inflation indicated that demand was excessive and that the economy was overheating, and the solution would have to consist in monetary tightening and fiscal restraint.

Trying to upend the orthodox way of thinking, neo-Keynesians like Paul Samuelson and Robert Solow looked to locate the cause of inflation on the supply side. If you could learn the *specific* causes of inflation, you can target them without having to hold the economy as a whole hostage. It was in this context that they formulated the famous Phillips curve, which depicted a trade-off between unemployment and inflation.[27]

From a Minskyan perspective, this neo-Keynesian response to conservative perspectives on inflation misses something important. Deconstructing the general price level into its supply-side components can provide important information, but such a factorial approach can have difficulty putting its finger on the *systemic* character of inflation. Even though Minsky undertook such factorial analysis himself,[28] he did not mistake it for an explanation of the phenomenon of inflation itself – that is, the constant build-up of pressure that the system is not able to clear and consequently shows up as the devaluation of the monetary standard itself.

Minsky's understanding of inflation in fact bore some similarity to orthodox theory. The latter understands inflation in terms of an excess of liquidity in relation to the amount of commodities in circulation (that is, "too much money chasing too few goods"). That is in keeping with the village fair model, where all trade is in consumables. Minsky exploded that model by introducing debt-financed property. But he never seemed to see the point of disputing the commonsensical idea that there was likely to exist a certain proportionality between the amount of liquidity in the system and the price level. It was obviously not the case that inflation is always and everywhere a purely monetary phenomenon (as in Milton Friedman's monetarism), but there is some truth to the idea that without sustained money creation it is not possible to have sustained inflation.

An analogy may be useful here. To attempt to understand inflationary pressure through a lens focused on its supply-side causes is a little like trying to understand the operation of a hot air balloon by focusing on the behavior of the molecules in the gases that compose air. It can be a very useful re-description that can demystify the experience of seeing a balloon go up. But if you take that approach too literally, you end up missing the essential elements: the presence of a heat source that produces constant pressure, in combination with a limit against which that pressure strains.

If you're in a hot air balloon and want to descend, you need to reduce the influx of energy. If your analysis of molecule velocity has somehow led you to the idea that you need to decelerate a specific set of particles (say, the fastest ones), you have managed to define the problem in a very misleading way. Even if you somehow manage to accomplish that feat, the continued pressure from the heat source that you're not turning off means that you need to find ever more extreme ways to decelerate the particles you can control just to compensate.

Keynesian supply-side politics has always had this inexhaustible, never-good-enough quality. Despite large tax cuts, investment credits, publicly funded training programs, and other business incentives, supply-side politics has never given Keynesians the policy levers they needed to be able to get to the centerpiece of demand stimulus.

The Phillips curve, it turned out, was not nearly as shiftable as had been hoped or imagined. So, what had at an earlier time been a depiction of the relationship between unemployment and inflation that was meant to give Keynesian policymakers a better grip on how inflation was produced came to be seen as a static menu of available combinations. The Phillips curve thinking that Keynesians had promoted now became the basis of a wage-push theory of inflation that logically implied increasing unemployment as the main way of fighting inflation.

When faced with the limits to their demand-side and supply-side programs, Keynesian policymakers looked to credit growth. Banks were more than happy to play their part in this, but they found their lending capacity constrained by the New Deal regulations, particularly the interest rate ceiling that limited their ability to attract deposits. Banks responded with a series of complex legal constructions that allowed them to source deposits in financial markets. These new forms of banking relied on short-term funding sources that were not guaranteed by the government and were therefore far more volatile.

From the 1930s until the 1950s, the neo-Keynesian notion of banks as credit intermediaries had made some degree of sense. But banks actively going into financial markets to indebt themselves just had no place in that framework. Postwar Keynesianism developed a paradoxical relationship to the expansion of finance: it was unable to generate any meaningful analysis of a banking revolution that was happening right under its nose and that it had done so much to foster.

The inflation problem

The Federal Reserve was situated at the intersection of these conflicting forces. Especially once new financing mechanisms were in place and supplying credit for important areas of economic activity (often mortgage lending), the central bank was often reluctant to shut them down. It would adapt its programs to sustain these new financial channels, further building out an uneven infrastructure of financial support. The inflationary pressure that resulted would then become the reason for tightening credit for the economy as a whole.

This logic will only be visible when we look at the relations between banks and the Federal Reserve dynamically and holistically. If we look at any given situation by itself, and do not scratch the surface of official statements too much, it might seem reasonable to understand the Federal Reserve's role as "leaning against the winds of deflation of inflation, whichever way they are blowing," as William McChesney Martin, Federal Reserve chair during the 1950s and 1960s, put it.[29] But that model only attends to the tip of the iceberg. It ignores all the derisked financial positions that have become part of the system's baseline settings, and it is unable to see the systematic pattern whereby the Federal Reserve blocks the deleveraging dynamic of downturns much more forcefully than it dampens the upturns.

Conversely, the effects of credit tightening are never distributed evenly. It always leaves intact an extensive infrastructure of mechanisms for liquidity provision for too-big-to-fail entities, and is often combined with new such facilities. In our current post-Covid moment, we can see that clearly enough: interest rate increases have had a severe impact on the financial health of many households, but banks can count on guarantees and backstops, and, when they actually fail, bailouts. The leverage that has been built up in the system is never completely unwound, and the system is never reset to a neutral state.

It is important to appreciate this point, as it goes against much post-Keynesian work that has claimed Minsky as its standard bearer. Such approaches criticize finance for generating bubbles that are out of touch with real values, and understand financial instability as reflecting the law that "what goes up, must come down." Minsky's understanding of whether and how speculative financial claims might be "validated" was more nuanced. He made no strong claims about what constituted real value, and assigned a central role to the judgments made by the actors situated at the key nodes of the public–private nexus. For Minsky, the development of capitalism was shaped not primarily by financial instability as such, but more fundamentally by how governments respond to such instability.

The inflation problem came to a head during the 1970s, when it became anchored in the ability of unions to demand wage rises to compensate for anticipated increases in the cost of living. It is at this point in the story that the neoliberalism argument usually takes over: a right-wing revolution resolved the economic chaos of the 1970s by imposing strict limits on the reach of politics and installing the market as judge, jury, and executioner. While a useful shorthand to make a political point, the "Keynesianism to neoliberalism" story is not all that accurate. Inflation was not conquered by restoring a laissez-faire system of unregulated capitalism – far from it. It would be contained by making the logic of bailout work in more selective ways.

Naturally, the emergence of this new bailout state was hard to discern for contemporaneous observers. The rhetoric of neoliberalism was strident, and its politics uncompromising. Like many others, Minsky found it difficult to separate rhetoric from reality. But he was always entirely clear that some version of big government was here to stay. Any government unwilling to plunge the American economy into another Great Depression would have to maintain an elaborate system of public guarantees in some form or another.

3

How Welfare Capitalism Worked

Little about the past century will make sense unless we recognize how it was shaped by the experience of the Great Depression. Although the depth and duration of the economic depression of the 1930s effects were new, the crisis that precipitated it did not strike out of the blue. Since colonial times, financial instability had been a prominent feature of the American economy. Especially since the Civil War, financial crises had been severe, and the effects had been felt more widely with each.

Other countries, notably Britain, had created a system of emergency lending to help the banking system weather financial turmoil. When markets froze and depositors were wondering if they should empty their accounts, banks could turn to the Bank of England. Walter Bagehot formalized this "lender of last resort" principle: at times of financial stress, the central bank should lend freely (to banks only), but at high rates (it should be a "last resort") and against collateral of unquestioned value (banks that held too many bad assets should be allowed to go under).[1]

In this way, the Bagehot doctrine tried to separate temporary problems that banks experienced from more fundamental ones: questions of liquidity from issues of solvency. It was the former that a central bank should help with, not the latter. The Bank of England's lender-of-last-resort role was therefore considered broadly consistent with the orthodox commitment to "sound money," the commitment to a non-inflationary currency, enforced through gold convertibility. In practice, the Bank of England's interventions were rarely neutral. The operation of the lender-of-last-resort doctrine was based on the possibility of *exempting* key financial institutions from the discipline of the market, i.e., not just on "tiding over" but on "bailing out."

Throughout the nineteenth century, American financial elites sought to create a central bank on the English model. But the American public viewed such proposals as little more than attempts by elites to support their self-serving financial dealings with a bespoke safety net – one to which the rest of society would not have access. Andrew Jackson's destruction of the Second Bank of the United States in the name of the common man is only the most storied instance of a political logic that dominated American capitalism right up until the end of the nineteenth century. All the while, financial instability grew. Americans who were excluded from the benefits of the credit system were still exposed to the effects of its instability, and each crisis triggered new calls for the decimation of moneyed interests.

Growing volatility and deepening crises towards the end of the nineteenth century meant that greater control over the dynamics of American finance came to be seen as imperative. But that this would take the form of a central bank – a bank for bankers – rather than a monetary authority controlled by democratic power was by no means a foregone conclusion.

Chartal ideas enjoyed wide popularity. The paper money issued directly by the American government during the Civil War had reminded Americans of the political possibilities here, and during the post-Civil War era the "greenbacks" had become a rallying point for populists seeking the democratization of credit creation.[2] The populist program had tremendous political power. The late nineteenth century saw a proliferation of ideas for the democratization of money that, to a twenty-first-century observer, easily looks confusing.

It was not until the end of the nineteenth century that the threat of democratic control over money creation receded. William Jennings Bryan had staked his 1896 presidential campaign on a rejection of the gold standard, and his defeat was a tremendous blow to the populist movement. The crisis of 1907 shifted the conversation further. J.P. Morgan played a central, and highly publicized role in orchestrating the rescue operations, reminding people of the far-reaching and pernicious influence of the collusive network of financiers that was known as the "Money Trust." It allowed progressive reformers to push the argument that expert-led public regulation was preferable to the indefinite growth of bankers' control over government.

The Federal Reserve System that was established in 1913 was the result of political compromise.[3] The System was decentralized – there was no "Fed" in the way we now refer to that institution, and the central Board of Governors, located in Washington, D.C., would only be created later. The regional banks could only lend against commercial bills presented to them, which limited room for discretionary interventions and opportunities for collusion.

For their part, elites had ensured that the Federal Reserve System would be barred from holding government debt. That would have brought the federal budget and the democratic public dangerously close to the mechanisms of credit creation, inviting the kind of populist schemes that had just been fended off. The Federal Reserve soon broke this rule to support the Treasury's ability to fund its debts when the United States entered World War I, but it dutifully unwound these policies following the war.

During the 1920s, American banks invested heavily in the booming stock market. The Crash of 1929 had a dramatic impact on stock values, and as banks sought to unwind their positions, they set in motion a fire-sale of assets that fed on itself. When news of the banks' troubles spread, the public lined up to cash out their deposits. As the scramble for cash drove asset prices into the ground, it became apparent that there was no natural floor to this dynamic. Anything the Federal Reserve might have done to stop the deleveraging movement would have conflicted with its institutional setup and legal role. The premise of the Bagehot doctrine – that liquidity problems could be separated from asset values – had some plausibility for the British system but virtually none for the American one.

Just as the Federal Reserve System was caught in a deflationary logic that it could not see or act its way out of, so was the US Treasury. Until the start of the twentieth century, the Treasury had been the closest thing the US had had to a federal regulator, and, as in the 1907 crisis, it had often worked directly with New York financiers to contain the fall-out of financial failures.[4] Since the founding of the Federal Reserve, the Treasury had extricated itself from those politically sensitive entanglements.

But it was soon faced with another, no less daunting task: how to manage the nation's growing budget. Before the twentieth century, public expenditure had increased rapidly only during periods of war. The government would finance this with the issuance of public debt, and it would repay the debt soon after the war with revenues put together from a patchwork of different sources.[5] But during the first decades of the twentieth century, the government budget had grown significantly. In this pre-Keynesian era, the growing size of the federal budget *reinforced* the importance of balanced budgets as a core pillar of sound finance.[6] After 1929, the fall in tax revenues almost automatically produced a budget deficit, and Hoover's response was to insist that the Treasury balance its budget by bringing down its expenditures, further contributing to the spiral of debt deflation.[7]

The devastation that the Great Depression wrought on the American economy was immense. Income levels plummeted, and a quarter of the American population became unemployed. About a quarter of America's banks went out of business, and many Americans lost their savings. As people were unable to repay their mortgage debt, banks foreclosed on numerous properties, sending real estate values spiraling downward to about half of their pre-Crash values.[8]

New Deal reforms

The Crash and Depression did much to discredit the orthodox economic policy mindset that was preoccupied with sound money and balanced budgets. Discontent with Hoover's handling of the economic crisis was not confined to the people who had lost their job or home. The business community too was growing impatient with the administration's doctrinaire orthodoxy, which was not just bad for business but also fed social unrest and the radicalization of organized labor.[9]

The Roosevelt administration's first order of business was to arrest the American economy's downhill slide, and to do so in a way that would not align it too closely with the people the public held responsible for the disaster: the bankers. Suspicion of big finance was already widespread, and public investigations revealed dense networks of collusive ties. The administration's financial reform task was made easier by the fact that business did not pose a united front. Corporate America felt that it had been dragged into a crisis not of its own making, and many captains of industry questioned whether the exploits of the Money Trust really benefitted more than a handful of wealthy financiers. Even within the financial sector itself, major lines of division existed. Regional and country bankers had no more sympathy for the Morgan empire than did the average person, and they were eager to see the "Money Trust" dismantled.

Across the country, people had lost money that they had
entrusted to banks, and the Roosevelt administration understood that such trust was not easily restored with mere words.
The first wave of legislation prohibited deposit-taking institutions from investing in the stock market. It also put in place a
federal system of deposit insurance through the creation of the
Federal Deposit Insurance Corporation (FDIC). Doctrinaire
objections that such socialization of risk undermined the spirit
of free enterprise and individual responsibility rang hollow in
the aftermath of the crisis. Nor was it lost on bankers that
deposit insurance would have important advantages. Once the
American public was assured that its deposits were safe, bank
runs would be a thing of the past, and banks could manage
their balance sheet knowing their deposit base was stable.

In other areas, notably industrial relations, it was harder
for the Roosevelt administration to play off divisions running
through the business community. But the need to restore trust
in American capitalism was paramount. The centerpiece of
that effort was the National Labor Relations Act of 1935, more
commonly known as the Wagner Act. It recognized the right
of workers to organize in unions and the right of unions to
bargain collectively on behalf of their members. Although the
Wagner Act ushered in a new era of labor relations, it was
never a symbol of consensus. As soon as it was in place, it
became an object of conservative attempts to undo it or at least
reverse those aspects that business found most constraining.

These legislative reforms provided key parameters for the
recovery, but they did not answer a broader question: what
would the ongoing role of the state in managing the economy
be? Since the Progressive Era, the government's presence in the
American economy had grown steadily. Even before Hoover's
response to the financial crisis had exposed the contradictions
of orthodoxy, many had come to recognize that government
decisions affected the economic system by design or default –
and that, at least in that sense, laissez-faire was an incoherent

ideology. In the throes of the Depression, the question was not whether or not a more purposeful and ongoing approach to economic management was needed – it was what that would look like.

Libraries have been filled with volumes about the specific areas where the American state expanded its administrative and regulatory reach during the New Deal. For our purposes, three areas hold special interest: planning, public spending, and credit programs.

Of these, planning carried the most explicit threat of creeping communism. It was never difficult to get corporate support for programs that sought to limit competition by replicating the logic of cartelization and giving it a public stamp of approval. But business had little tolerance for programs that were more directive in nature or that might empower labor.[10]

The business community had offered initial support for Roosevelt's plans to spur recovery through the National Industrial Recovery Administration (NIRA).[11] But when the administration proved reluctant to follow the lead of business, cautious support quickly turned into outright hostility. After a series of legal challenges, the NIRA was declared unconstitutional only a few years after its founding.

Reformers increasingly focused on the federal budget,[12] but public spending would not always be less contentious than public planning. The administration was determined not to repeat Hoover's mistakes, which entailed a general receptiveness to the idea that government spending had a legitimate role to play. But beyond that proto-Keynesian sentiment, there existed no roadmap or handbook.

In the administration itself, a powerful strain of fiscal conservatism persisted. Treasury Secretary Henry Morgenthau, Jr, recognized that the recovery was worryingly slow, but he insisted that balanced budgets were the best hope for new business investment. Roosevelt was not entirely sure what to make of such arguments but never dismissed them out of hand. He also recognized that they aligned with popular hostility towards taxation and could not simply be set aside as reactionary.[13]

The business community, faced with the uncompromising reality of the lack of demand for its products, was at times more open to the idea of temporarily increasing public spending.[14] But such acquiescence was entirely conditional on the government's willingness to let business shape its spending priorities. It strongly opposed the growth of social programs, fearing that it would embolden organized labor and feed the idea that the public should be in charge of the nation's financial affairs.[15] By 1935, Roosevelt had lost much of the initial goodwill from the business community.[16]

Caught between contending ideological and political currents, the Roosevelt administration's approach to fiscal expansion remained hesitant until the end of the 1930s.[17] The contentious character of fiscal policy was a key driver behind the growing use of credit programs. As Sarah Quinn summarizes their appeal, "credit flourished as a policy tool because it could be reconciled with free-market rhetoric, because it could be easily taken off-budget and run through partnerships, and because it could sidestep congressional appropriations and all the veto points that process entailed."[18]

Housing credit in particular was seen not just as a way to enable people to buy or keep a home, but also as a way to stimulate economic growth.[19] Government subsidization of mortgage credit was, in Eccles' words, "the wheel within the wheel to move the whole economic engine."[20] During the first decades of the twentieth century, progressive reformers had worked hard to make mortgage credit more widely available. They had enjoyed limited success. Banks considered mortgages a cumbersome kind of credit. They were large and long-term, and so they took up a great deal of space in a bank's portfolio. Because they were highly specific loans, tied to local knowledge and regulations, they were almost impossible to sell on to other investors. In order to protect themselves from fluctuations in the property value, banks typically asked for high down payments, putting mortgage credit out of reach for most households.

The credit programs incentivized banks to extend home loans. Through the Federal Housing Administration (and later the Veterans' Administration), the government insured mortgages, relieving banks of any default risk and obviating the need for large down payments.[21] At the same time, the Federal National Mortgage Administration (better known as Fannie Mae) created an infrastructure for the standardization and securitization of mortgage loans, allowing banks to sell and buy such assets and greatly reducing liquidity risk.[22]

Of the various programs introduced during the New Deal, it was always the credit programs that could count on most support from business. The free flow of credit was not threatening and in fact offered considerable business opportunities. If lending was done properly and borrowers repaid their loans on schedule, it could not logically be inflationary. Unlike planning, it worked through inducement rather than direction. And unlike public spending, it worked without bringing democracy dangerously close to property and without emboldening organized labor. Increasingly, credit programs came to be seen as a model for how government policy could obtain collaboration from business and induce investment decisions that would advance the common good.

Stagnation and war

By the end of the first Roosevelt administration, it was clear that, while its programs had arrested the economic freefall, they had not been able to kickstart an economic recovery. The United States had slowly but surely been climbing out of the trough of the Depression, but private investment remained weak and unemployment failed to come down to acceptable levels.

In this context, Alvin Hansen, the most influential Keynesian economist of the age, formulated his theory of secular stagnation, hypothesizing that American capitalism had exhausted its growth potential.[23] The end of America's western expansion, the absence of any major new discoveries and technologies, and the slowdown of population growth had combined to reduce the economy's prospects for growth. Under such circumstances, increased demand does not automatically produce investment opportunities.[24]

Hansen did not mean this diagnosis to inspire pessimism or helplessness. To the contrary, it reinforced his belief in the need for the aggressive implementation of the Keynesian program. But that program could not *limit* itself to socializing demand and increasing public expenditure. Keynesianism needed to supplement demand-side stimulus with ways to engage the supply side of the economy – while also accepting that anything reeking of planning or central direction was off-limits.[25] The government needed to think more deeply about what it might be able to do to induce particular levels and kinds of investment.[26] But the Roosevelt administration's reluctance to pursue expensive programs limited options in that respect too.

The turning point was the so-called Roosevelt Recession of 1937–8. Faced with unexpected financing requirements, the Treasury made a series of spending cuts in order to maintain a balanced budget.[27] It triggered a major recession, which added to existing discontent about the already slow recovery. These circumstances gave advocates of increased federal spending a strong platform to make their case.[28]

The Roosevelt administration, and Federal Reserve chair Eccles in particular, had hired many proto-Keynesian economists who thought of public spending not as an emergency stopgap but as a catalyst of economic growth.[29] During the first Roosevelt administration their influence had remained limited, but the recession of 1937–8 gave them an opportunity to press their arguments. The *General Theory* had been published in the meantime and provided additional ammunition. And by this time Roosevelt sensed a clear danger that he might go into history as a second Hoover, a fate he was determined to avoid.

The administration pushed public expenditure up to unprecedented levels. The effects were soon visible: unemployment dropped, and growth accelerated. Calls for fiscal moderation could be heard soon enough, and there is no guarantee that this recovery would have escaped the gravity well of fiscal conservatism if the US had not started mobilizing for World War II soon after. The exceptional circumstances of the wartime economy blew calls for fiscal moderation out of the water. They also required business to fall in line with national priorities, although the government made it profitable for them to do so.

In the end, it was only the crude instrument of government expenditure that had been able to pull the US economy out of its slump. The wartime full employment economy would be a pivotal moment in the development of the Keynesian state. The US state had shown itself, with deceptive simplicity, to be capable of ensuring that all Americans (all men, at any rate) could have a job. This was not easily forgotten. The idea of returning millions of families to a wageless life in the name of abstract financial considerations was not on the table.[30] As Herbert Stein put it, "Full employment became a national goal in a much more imperative and operational sense than it had ever been during the Depression."[31]

The Federal Reserve refounded

The reorientation of fiscal policy during the New Deal and the war was supported by the Federal Reserve. Already during the 1920s, its economists had become aware of the contradictions of sound money doctrines as the foundation for financial governance. The Crash and the Depression had reinforced those concerns. In response, the Federal Reserve shifted its modus operandi from passively standing by, waiting for banks to present debts for discounting, towards the active buying and selling of government debt. Its ability to do so across an institution composed of many regional branches was facilitated by the creation of a centralized Board, located in Washington, D.C.[32]

To support the Treasury's ability to borrow, the Federal Reserve maintained the price of government debt at a minimum level. Government debt now became a very attractive asset for banks: it was highly liquid and extremely low-risk, but it generated a return all the same. In this way, the Federal Reserve supported the monetization of government debt – the transformation of public debt into currency.

It did not do so lightly. Part of its motivation was to stave off more radical proposals from winning political support.[33] The *indirect* monetization of public debt, which maintained banks as the central loci of money and credit creation, was considered far preferable to ideas for *direct* ways of monetization that were growing in popular support as the Great Depression wore on.[34] Of course, the Federal Reserve studiously avoided any suggestion that it was helping to convert America's debt into currency. Instead, it spoke of the need to maintain an "orderly" market, where Treasury debt could be sold at a moment's notice and without loss of value, and where the Treasury's public debt sales would be consistently and reliably successful.[35]

As banks filled their portfolios with government debt, the Treasury market came to serve as a cornerstone of the financial system that the Federal Reserve was charged with stabilizing. Only two decades earlier, the Federal Reserve had been founded on the principle that money creation and public debt should be kept strictly separated. Now, the role and mandate of the Federal Reserve had changed entirely. As Aaron Wistar puts it, "Money was increasingly backed not by the real economic activity ostensibly underlying commercial loans, but by the debt issuance of a growing fiscal state."[36]

The subordination of the Federal Reserve's operations to the Treasury's debt funding needs enjoyed broad political support. New Dealers naturally saw in it the foundation for expansionary fiscal policy and low rates. Many fiscal conservatives considered that, as undesirable as an expanding federal debt was, the Federal Reserve's policies at least kept government borrowing affordable.[37]

A consensus formed that, after the war, the Federal Reserve would have to maintain the peg. This meant that the central bank would have no instruments to control inflation. During the war itself, such pressures were contained by price and wage controls, but it was always clear that controls would be repealed as soon as possible following the end of the war. For several years, even a partial and gradual unwinding of Federal Reserve support was unacceptable to the Treasury, however. It was only with the outbreak of the Korean War, which meant further growth of the federal debt, that the Federal Reserve's concerns found a hearing. This was in part because, without any plan to manage inflation, a restoration of price controls began to seem unavoidable.[38]

Forced to reconcile their differences, in 1951 the Treasury and the Federal Reserve reached an agreement, asserting their "common purpose to assure the successful financing of the Government's requirements and at the same time, to minimize monetization of the public debt."[39] The wording of the compromise made little sense, as the two objectives were inherently in conflict. But it gave the Fed a degree of institutional autonomy to pursue restrictive policies when it judged it necessary to do so. This institutional independence would become central to what David Stein refers to as the "containment of Keynesianism."[40]

As the Federal Reserve reduced its support for the market in government debt, the Treasury was forced to pay higher rates to borrow. This was of major concern to Eisenhower, whose fiscal conservatism balked at the prospect of financing public debt at higher prices. But opportunities for reducing public spending were limited.

To ease the government's concerns, the Federal Reserve created an alternative infrastructure for the placement of federal debt.[41] If non-bank institutions held government debt, its monetization would be logically impossible – so the reasoning went.[42] To encourage dealers to trade in Treasury securities, the Federal Reserve offered them an incentive in the form of cheap financing.[43] Barred by law from lending directly to non-banks, the Federal Reserve developed a workaround – the repurchase agreement, or what would later become known as the "repo."[44]

The arrangement was highly effective in improving the tradability of Treasury securities and in increasing their uptake outside the formal banking system. But what was not clearly on policymakers' radar was the likelihood that this formally non-bank area of the financial system would develop its own banking mechanisms. For Minsky, these developments were entirely unsurprising – banks are private enterprises that emerge in response to opportunities for making profits, not public utilities that answer to formal regulatory definitions.[45]

The market for Treasury debt became the basis of a "shadow" banking system, where non-bank financial institutions created liquidity in much the same way regular banks did. Their short-term commitments were not money in the sense of official currency of course, and for some time these systems operated in parallel. But before too long, commercial banks found ways to access the shadow liquidity, using it to boost their capacity to produce real dollars.[46]

Containing Keynesianism

The ramping up of public spending, first following the Roosevelt Recession and then during the war, had made clear how powerful an instrument fiscal expansion was as a means to get economic growth going and to bring the economy near full employment. It gave the idea of full employment political power, and a movement emerged to enshrine the affirmative right to employment in law.[47]

Critical histories of the New Deal have rarely recognized the radicalism of the full employment movement. They have tended to focus on the gradual decline of the New Deal's ambitions and labor's settlement into a compromise with business. Full employment is then taken to be part of that quid pro quo: labor was given full employment in exchange for abandoning more radical claims.[48] But such claims are part of the mythology of the postwar era.

The capitalist class never viewed the full employment objective as a manageable demand that could form the basis of a compromise.[49] It was not quite as threatening as the abolition of private property, but close enough. Its radicalism was also evident in the cross-racial alliances that it opened up, weakening the racism and nativism that had historically been such a pronounced feature of American organized labor. As Michael Dennis notes, "the idea of full employment probed the very horizons of a post-capitalist society."[50]

That the demand for full employment was so radical may be hard to imagine from a present-day perspective, where that term has been so thoroughly redefined and defanged. But for contemporaneous authors like Michael Kalecki the issue was very clear: full employment was bound to be inflationary and therefore unacceptable to capital.[51] Minsky too recognized that "full employment is itself destabilizing – that is, it is a disequilibrium state."[52] It was perhaps Keynes' *own* notions about full employment that were unusual. Overexposure to the ethereal abstractions of neoclassical theory had produced in his mind the idea that the real-world operation of the capitalist labor market could be assessed against the benchmark of a properly clearing market.

Although the New Deal and the war had raised the expectations of American workers, they had also given business and conservatives an opportunity to mobilize politically. Especially when it came to fighting the full employment objective, they found plenty of allies among political moderates.[53] Even Eccles, as committed a Keynesian and New Dealer as one could hope to find, expressed his strong opposition to a legally binding full employment objective because of the "uncontrollable inflation" it would create.[54]

The eventual Employment Act of 1946 did not include an employment guarantee. It merely set "maximum employment" as a non-binding objective, and stipulated that it be balanced with other objectives, above all the containment of inflation.[55] Ongoing assessments of the economic situation would be undertaken by the newly created Council of Economic Advisers (CEA) and Congress's Joint Economic Committee. But no one indicator was to be taken as an ultimate, overriding objective.[56] The CEA would be an important vehicle for the spread of Keynesian ideas in government.[57] But the uncertain and highly conditional status of full employment as a policy objective would be a major source of contradictions for the Keynesian program.

Business scored another major victory with the Taft–Hartley Act of 1947, which gave employees the right to opt out of union membership and so provided employers with a potent weapon to divide and rule. Labor subsequently lost a great deal of influence during the Eisenhower administration, which prioritized fighting inflation and simply accepted that it would entail painful reductions in growth and employment.[58] These developments restored the logic of the reserve army.[59]

The political retreat of organized labor, in combination with the rapid growth of unemployment during the recession of the late 1940s, reinforced the insider–outsider logic of trade unionism. Throughout the postwar era, the unemployment rate for African American groups would be more than twice as high as in the rest of the population.[60] Tolerating Jim Crow in Southern states had always been a key condition for the ability of the Democratic Party to gain electoral power. But the war and the full employment objective had militated against long-standing racial divisions in the labor movement. This was now rapidly being undone.

White middle class

Welfare capitalism offered carrots as well as sticks. The flipside of the retreat from aspirations for widening the circle of solidarity was that many jobs were no longer just jobs. The New Deal revalued wage labor not simply in a quantitative sense (that is, higher wages), but also in a qualitative way. For select constituencies, it repositioned wage labor, socially and culturally. From a marker of second-class citizenship, a condition without future prospects, wage labor was transformed into a gateway to property ownership, a basis for building a future.

For a broad middle class, New Deal institutions made it possible to live a propertied life on the basis of wage labor. These constituencies could now plan for the future of their family in the areas of housing, education, and retirement. The public subsidization of mortgage credit and homeownership was central to this model. It allowed a generation of wage earners to leverage their wage, secure a mortgage, and build up property.

Taking its cue from long-standing wisdom in the real estate sector, the American government did not guarantee loans collateralized by homes in African American neighborhoods.[61] The limitation of insurance to white households was famously enshrined in the formal underwriting protocols of the Federal Housing Administration.[62] Later programs, such as those of the Veterans' Administration, were built on top of the FHA programs and reinforced the basic inequity.

Unlike the Federal Housing Administration's 1938 underwriting manual, none of those postwar programs was explicitly racist.[63] Indeed, they gradually replaced the language of racial differentiation with a more sanitized economic language that was highly effective in locking in the basic pattern of discrimination while obscuring the racial logic at work.[64] What public and private organizations were doing when they "redlined" neighborhoods appeared to be simply dictated by economic considerations.[65]

The effect was to make wealth accumulation almost impossible for African American families.[66] Without the government guarantee, a home loan was much harder to get, and even when it could be obtained it was more expensive and required a higher down payment.[67] Legal restrictions built into property deeds often prevented white families from selling their house to families of color.[68] As a consequence, even when they owned their home, minority families lived in areas where property values did not go up by much. Unlike their white counterparts, they were unable to benefit from the preferential tax treatment of capital gains.[69] More typically, they rented in areas segregated from all-white suburbs.[70] As Gary Dymski summarizes, "the Golden Age never crossed the race line: African-American and other minorities largely functioned as a labour buffer-stock, spatially segregated in lower-income neighbourhoods with low home-ownership rates."[71]

Segregated homeownership interacted with other parts of the New Deal state, such as the management of workers' pension savings and the distribution of educational opportunity. Occupational pension plans (to which employers could make tax-free contributions) grew rapidly after the war,[72] and these funds invested heavily in municipal and local bonds, ensuring that the savings of prosperous communities would not be socialized across society.[73] In addition, the funding of community resources through local property taxes meant that white suburbs created the kinds of school systems that could efficiently transmit privilege to the next generation.[74]

But the subordination of the African American population never *guaranteed* the prosperity of white workers and their families. Unemployment was not stably concentrated among minorities, but an ever-looming threat to white unionized workers. That was the point of having a reserve army: unemployment could happen to anyone, and this awareness had a disciplinary effect. Furthermore, African American and other minorities never resigned themselves to their marginalization in the name of social stability. The Civil Rights movement that gathered strength during the 1950s took aim at discrimination in work, housing, and education.

How these social tensions were managed found expression in public spending priorities. But this was never an unconstrained arena. Whenever Congress was responsive to pressure from disadvantaged constituencies, the specter of inflation soon reared its head. Especially when Congress took to funding programs that reduced the dependence of disadvantaged Americans on the labor market, the Federal Reserve stood ready to make credit more expensive, slow down demand and investment, and push up unemployment.[75]

In this way, the Federal Reserve came to occupy a central place in managing the tensions of the post-New Deal order. It was positioned at the intersection of conflicting imperatives. On the one hand, it was responsible for supporting the financial infrastructure of the New Deal state, which included safeguarding the ability of the Treasury to place its debt and maintaining the credit facilities of the welfare state. On the other hand, it was supposed to contain inflation. These objectives were in dynamic conflict and any trade-off was a temporary and unstable one.

The Federal Reserve had become an arbiter of employment and life chances. When in 1965 Federal Reserve chair Martin signaled that he planned to raise interest rates (which he eventually did), President Lyndon Johnson replied, "It would amount to squeezing blood from the American working man in the interest of Wall Street."[76] Johnson might have been channeling the comment that Wright Patman, the populist chair of the House Banking Committee, had made to him a year earlier: "the Federal Reserve can create far more poverty than can be eliminated by your entire antipoverty program."[77] The American central bank had come to play a pivotal role in the management of race relations and industrial relations.[78]

4

The Promise of Growth

Progressives worried about the concentration of disadvantage in a racial underclass. They did not fail to note that each slowdown in growth, whether engineered by the Federal Reserve or stemming from another one of Eisenhower's austerity budgets, hit minorities much harder than the white middle class. The 1957–8 recession had been particularly brutal in this regard. It provoked considerable social unrest and added extra urgency to Democratic efforts to unseat Republicans.[1]

Broadening access to the middle class was one of the Kennedy administration's main objectives. Central to this ambition was economic growth.[2] Without growth, the pursuit of social justice was entirely dependent on redistribution, taking away something from one family to give it to another.[3] That was to be avoided at all cost. For fear of alienating its Southern constituencies, the Kennedy administration dragged its feet when it came to supporting the Civil Rights movement's demands for the redistribution of economic resources. Growing the pie was essential.[4]

The image of economic growth that Kennedy held up – a tide that lifts all boats – has become the oldest politician's cliché in the book, but that's not what it was when Kennedy used it. It represented the return to public discourse of an idea that had never properly taken root. That a zero-sum game makes distributional questions harder to solve is somewhat of a truism. But the Keynesian program of the 1960s was distinctive for the idea that distributional questions should be almost entirely absorbed into, and resolved by, economic policy expertise. Neo-Keynesian economists such as Paul Samuelson occupied key positions in the Kennedy administration.

Walter Heller, another such economist who served as Kennedy's Council of Economic Advisers chair, referred to the administration's economic program as "Keynes-*cum*-growth."[5] Keynes had been concerned with growth of course, but, in his eagerness to bring the wonder drug of demand-side stimulus to governments' attention, he had paid insufficient attention to supply-side factors.[6] Keynesians of Hansen's generation had recognized this lacuna to some extent, observing that the problem was not simply a shortfall of demand but equally "the problem of inadequate private investment outlets."[7] But they had not provided any real solution. In fact, the deepening marriage of Keynesianism to neoclassical economics had produced elegant but static models that provided little insight into the dynamic sources of growth.[8]

The Kennedy administration was receptive to fiscal demand stimulus in a way that no previous administration had been – even for Roosevelt and Truman the idea of fiscal stimulus had never entirely lost its stopgap character. But unless the Keynesian program could influence investment decisions and count on cooperation from the business community, the demand-side program was bound to be inflationary.[9]

Neo-Keynesians had seen the economy start to sputter during the second half of the 1950s. Unemployment was going up, gradually but unmistakably.[10] But despite lackluster performance on growth and employment, inflationary pressures were already making themselves felt. The return of inflation revived orthodox theories of inflation, and they were accompanied by calls for tighter money and balanced budgets.

In an extraordinarily influential paper, Paul Samuelson and Robert Solow argued that such classic, "demand-pull" theories could not explain the situation.[11] The issue was not that the system was being overheated by stimulus – the problem was something else, something located on the supply side of the economy that drove "cost-push" inflation.[12] To better understand the behavior of such inflation, they drew the Phillips curve, which depicted an inverse relation between inflation and unemployment. Their point in doing so was to argue that tight monetary policy and fiscal austerity to dampen demand would be of limited use in tackling inflation. What an economy performing below full capacity yet exhibiting inflationary tendencies needed was not a reduction in demand or general deflation, but a supply-side program that could support demand stimulus.[13]

Crucially, neo-Keynesians did not see themselves as trying to strike a "balance" between conflicting objectives here. They rejected that there fundamentally *was* a conflict between growth and price stability, even if in the short term it often appeared that way. The only coherent response to a recognition of the inflation problem was to place *greater* emphasis on the need for growth.[14] Keynes-*cum*-growth was about "realizing and enlarging the economy's non-inflationary potential," in Heller's words.[15] To imagine that beneficial things would ensue if only the economy was left to its deflationary devices was to return to the naïve certainties of gold standard orthodoxy – to put the cart before the horse. The point was to get out in front of the game rather than being forced to play it on unfavorable terms.[16]

Central to the program of growth Keynesianism were tax cuts, viewed as a way to influence the operation of demand-side and supply-side factors at the same time.[17] Progressives had no difficulty thinking of tax cuts as properly Keynesian – the reason that Keynes had not considered this as a key vehicle for fiscal stimulus was simply that, in his time, taxes were much lower. As Seymour Harris, a prominent adviser to Kennedy and Johnson on economic policy, said of the 1964 tax cuts, "This is a Keynesian technique scarcely known to Keynes because when Keynes wrote, taxes were not high, and hence a tax cut was not likely to be very effective."[18]

Tax cuts explicitly relied on the argument that lowering taxes would not just promote economic growth but also would serve to increase tax revenue. That idea is typically associated with the Reagan administration's supply-side politics, and in particular with Arthur Laffer, an economist who is said to have scribbled it on a napkin while explaining it to Ronald Reagan. But it has in fact solid roots in the Keynesian era.[19] As Elizabeth Berman and Nicholas Pagnucco show, their supporters justified the 1962 and 1964 tax cuts advocates in terms of their ability to induce investment.[20] As Kennedy himself put it, "it is a paradoxical truth that tax rates are too high today and tax revenues are too low and the soundest way to raise the revenues in the long run is to cut the rates now."[21]

Financial constraints

The Keynesian program was always dependent on cooperation from the Federal Reserve. The effects of fiscal stimulus could be, and often were, undone by monetary tightening. Under chair Martin, the Federal Reserve had achieved significant institutional independence. Its declared policy was to "lean against the wind" – that is, to tighten credit during times of expansion and to make it more freely available during recessionary periods.

That was a highly idealized representation of the central bank's modus operandi. The Federal Reserve routinely condoned and backstopped new financing channels despite their obvious inflationary effects, especially when such mechanisms supported the ability of banks to extend mortgage credit. But when it came to interest rate policy, the Federal Reserve now had a mind of its own, using it to limit inflationary pressure by depressing economic activity.

The changing external position of the American economy played a major role here. The country's trade balance had deteriorated as the postwar recovery of Europe and Japan gathered pace, and the willingness of foreigners to hold dollars became more conditional. America's international economic power was also prominently on Kennedy's own mind. Often, he realized, rate increases were needed to suppress inflation and maintain the international position of the dollar. It made him reluctant to act on Heller's advice that "the Federal Reserve must be petted, pressured, or pushed into firm resistance of rising interest rates."[22]

The threat of inflation functioned as a permanent constraint on the administration's economic policy ambitions. As a consequence, Keynesians found it extremely difficult to get to the more traditional parts of their agenda: programs requiring the sustained growth of public spending. Instead, generous tax cuts were often followed by cutbacks elsewhere, introducing strong elements of fiscal austerity into the program of growth Keynesianism.[23]

Martin indicated that he would be more willing to keep interest rates down if wage growth was brought under control, an idea that slotted neatly into the new Phillips curve thinking.[24] The Kennedy administration tried to achieve such wage moderation through wage–price guideposts, but to little effect. Business was strongly supportive of the wage moderation aspect but resisted price controls; labor's attitude was the reverse. Sometimes confrontation proved unavoidable, but on the whole the balance of forces was such that neither capital nor labor was able to force the other party to shoulder the burden of ensuring price stability.

Kennedy's economic policy team turned its mind to other ways to spur growth. The administration designated industrial zones where investment was encouraged through a variety of regulatory exemptions, tax credits, and direct subsidies. When such programs came with few strings attached, they were entirely acceptable to the business community but often did little more than reinforce existing patterns of inequality and exclusion.[25] To the extent that they empowered local communities and came with strings that advanced specific policy objectives, business obstruction soon ensued.

Heller was an ardent advocate of human capital programs: that is, public investment in training and education that allowed workers to build and retool their skills.[26] Such programs were able to address mismatches and local bottlenecks, but it was never clear that they were effective in inducing business to make different investment decisions or in improving aggregate outcomes. Minsky viewed these programs as misguided attempts to improve people, often for hypothetical jobs, whereas the objective should be to create jobs for existing people.[27]

The Keynesian program of the 1960s developed a wide array of supply-side policy instruments: tax cuts, investment credits, industrial policy and subsidies, wage–price guidelines, and training and education programs.[28] Although progress was rarely entirely absent, obstacles to a sustained implementation of the fiscal Keynesian program were always clear and present.

The headwinds were reflected in the gradual redefinition of what constituted full employment. Until the early 1960s, full employment meant what a layperson would take it to mean: no involuntary unemployment. But now economists began redefining the term to mean a level of unemployment that was consistent with price stability – so that an economy where millions of people were involuntarily without a job could still be considered as having achieved the full employment objective.[29] The CEA's first attempt, in 1962, to estimate a natural rate of unemployment suggested 4 percent unemployment as "a reasonable target for full utilization of resources consistent with reasonable price stability."[30] This soon turned out to be too conservative, and the next two decades would demonstrate that there is no natural landing point for this logic of revising downward expectations.[31]

The power of credit

From day one, credit growth had been an integral part of the Keynesian program. But its prominence increased as the other part parts of the Keynesian growth program disappointed or malfunctioned. The appeal of credit growth was that it always appeared to be a readily available, non-inflationary way of achieving high levels of growth, a means to keep the tide rising. We won't be able to understand this way of thinking if we bring in too many contemporary preconceptions – for instance, if we view it as "financialization," a flight out of "real" economic activity.[32] To the contrary, it was a way of reaching into the inner mechanisms of capitalism and greasing its wheels, above all the "wheel within the wheel" of subsidized mortgage credit.

The New Deal framework had done an exceptional job channeling credit to wage earners. But during the 1960s those same regulations had begun to hamper the continued growth of credit. The creation of the National Commission on Money and Credit in 1957 was motivated by the growing sense that the financial system was characterized by a level of complexity that could not be handled by the existing regulatory framework. The Commission's conclusions indicated that more could be gained from relaxing outdated regulations than from attempts to strengthen them.[33]

While the Commission offered its recommendations in a spirit of administrative problem-solving, the Kennedy administration saw political opportunity. The appointment of James

Saxon as Comptroller of the Currency was a key move. Saxon felt that many of the New Deal regulations had outlived their original purpose, and he actively supported banks' attempts to find ways around them. He advocated for the abolition of the interest rate ceilings, provided regulatory exemptions to enable bank mergers, approved bank plans to expand the range of their activities, and even challenged the authority of the Securities and Exchange Commission to police the boundaries between commercial banking and securities trading.[34]

For all the setbacks that it had experienced, by the middle of the decade the Keynesian program had nonetheless produced results. Investment and growth were up, and unemployment had come down. Although racial inequality remained stark, there were signs that the divide in unemployment levels, income, and wealth was becoming smaller.[35] The Civil Rights Acts of 1964 and 1965 finally made both economic and political discrimination illegal, and Johnson felt that the time had come to deliver more fully on the social promises of the Keynesian program.[36] Crucially, this was not a shift from economic to social priorities, but rather an attempt to include the latter more fully in the former. Redistribution in a stagnant economy remained anathema.[37]

The CEA made a forceful case for a renewed commitment to fiscal stimulus and was able to build a broad political alliance in support of its position.[38] International organizations like the International Monetary Fund agreed that insufficient American stimulus could destabilize international financial order further.[39] But the Federal Reserve stood ready to raise rates at the first sign of new inflation, and before long, the Johnson administration was caught in familiar dilemmas and trade-offs.[40] Initially, Johnson wanted to stay the course, hoping that inflationary pressure and balance of payment pressures would ease of their own accord.[41] But soon enough even the CEA, the bastion of Keynesianism, reversed course and recommended that Johnson take some inflationary pressure out of the system by raising taxes and cutting spending.[42]

The growth of finance was always a double-edged sword. It solved problems in the short run, but it exacerbated the pressures on the Keynesian program over the longer term. This boomerang effect, with an ever-shortening turnaround time, was not comprehensible to neo-Keynesians. They intuitively recognized the power of credit, but their conception of banking as a public utility, a freely available infrastructure, did not allow them to grasp the contradictions that this process produced.

The more economic policy relied on credit growth, the greater the centrality of the financial system. The more systemically important finance, the more effective the financial markets' veto was as a constraint on what governments could so. And the less budgetary autonomy the government thought it had, the more it came to see "mobilizing" private financing through public–private partnerships as the only way to get anything done.

Financial transformations

But fresh challenges were already in the making. At this point, tightening credit was no longer a straightforward matter even for the Federal Reserve itself. Until the early 1960s, the business model of banks could somewhat plausibly be understood from a neo-Keynesian view of banks as "channelers." Banks were conservative operations, taking in a stable base of insured deposits and investing in risk-free government paper and guaranteed mortgage loans.[43] That tranquil situation also lent credence to Martin's understanding of how the Federal Reserve interfaced with the banks and markets. The Federal Reserve's role, according to him, was to keep money as neutral as possible, symmetrically smoothing out the ups and downs of the business cycle – "leaning against the wind."

That may have been what things looked like from the top of the iceberg. But it was held up by the submerged part of America's financial infrastructure, an elaborate constellation of guarantees, subsidies, and backstops. At the core of financial governance was "the role of the government as an insurer-guarantor of various private liabilities," in Minsky's words.[44] When the financial seas were calm, it was easy to turn a blind eye to that entire constellation, much like we ignore the internal machinery of a car when it works well. But when instability hit, it became all too material. "If financial distress does occur, the efficacy of the various government guarantees, insurance, devices and built-in stabilizers will be tested."[45]

As the postwar peacetime economy picked up pace and the Federal Reserve wound down its support for government debt, banks expanded their lending into new areas. By the late 1950s, they had approached the limits of their existing lending capacity (dictated, at any given point in time, by reserve requirements). Once a bank reached that point, it could only make new loans if it was able access new sources of funds. But New Deal regulations – specifically, the caps that Regulation Q imposed on the rates that banks could offer depositors – constrained banks' ability to compete for deposits. As interest rates rose above the Reg Q ceilings during the 1960s, banks and thrifts even started losing depositors as the American public shifted funds from bank deposits into financial markets to take advantage of the higher rates that mutual funds could offer.

Banks responded to these pressures by developing strategies that made no sense from the neo-Keynesian view of banking as passive channelers of the nation's savings.[46] Armed with complex legal redefinitions of what constituted a deposit, banks went into the money market to borrow funds. A watershed moment was the Citibank's introduction of the "certificate of deposit" in 1961.[47] Its original purpose was to recapture funds that corporate treasurers had shifted out of banks, but once this strategy proved successful banks were not constrained in its use. It meant that banks had "virtually unlimited borrowing power."[48] They would make loans first, and then source deposit liabilities as needed to satisfy regulatory reserve requirements.

These dynamics started to interact with the shadow market for Treasury debt. The Federal Reserve's original hope was that the placement of Treasury debt outside the formal banking system would prevent it from serving as the basis for credit creation and causing inflation. But that arrangement was premised on the institutional dividers of the New Deal framework holding firm. Banks were now bypassing those barriers, transforming shadow liquidity into real money.

What became known as "liability management" drove a major transformation of the business model of banks. New ways of funding required new ways of lending.[49] Unlike deposits insured by the FDIC, what became known as "bought" or "brokered" deposits were volatile. In addition, banks' competition for funds drove up their price, which put pressure on banks to invest in high-return assets.[50] Adjusting their lending operations, banks started looking for assets that could serve as collateral and enhance their ability to borrow.

We find here the origins of what is often referred to as "marketized banking." But we will misunderstand its significance if we think of it as a process whereby the distinctions between banks and market were eroded and banks increasingly became just another financial market actor. A far more accurate depiction of the transformation is almost contrary: banks enlisted financial markets in their distinctive core business model, that is, balance sheet leveraging.

These developments made it much harder for the Federal Reserve to control the creation of credit: when it raised rates, it often just triggered another round of financial innovation – that is, the creation of new legal constructions that allowed banks to source funds in the wholesale money markets. The

Federal Reserve could, and often did, close down particular channels that routed liquidity from the wholesale money markets to commercial lending. But banks would find new ways around such restrictions before too long. Just as important, new funding channels often developed so quickly that the Federal Reserve did not think it could shut them down without precipitating a financial crisis – which would have put it at loggerheads with the administration. In this way, it gradually extended the financial safety net to cover new market segments and instruments.

Anticipating pressure from Congress to do more to contain inflation, from the mid-1960s the Federal Reserve started tangling with the banks in a more serious way. In 1966, concerned that inflationary pressures were getting out of hand, the Federal Reserve engineered a contraction of credit while policing vigilantly banks' efforts to open up new funding channels. The resulting credit crunch had a severe impact on housing finance and the construction sector.[51] But it only stopped banks in their tracks for a brief moment. Limited in domestic opportunities to counter the Federal Reserve's tightening moves, they turned to the London-based market in dollars that had grown during the previous decade as the US had spent on commodities, war, and fuel.[52]

To make matters worse, the 1966 shock severely upset the Treasury market. Although the Federal Reserve no longer considered itself responsible for keeping the Treasury's borrowing cheap, it was most definitely responsible for ensuring an "orderly" market in Treasury debt. It had adopted an "even keel" policy, which meant that it would not pursue policies that would interfere with the successful placement of Treasury debt.[53] Indeed, as Minsky pointed out, its failure to do so would instantly open up the prospect of *direct* monetization.[54]

But attempts to stabilize credit growth and control inflation were now at odds with maintaining an even keel. The US Treasury had growing difficulty placing new debt and rolling over existing debt.[55] The Treasury's refunding effort of 1970 almost failed – from today's perspective, an almost unimaginable event.[56] Use of the repo backstop had grown throughout the 1960s, but the Federal Reserve now threw the doors wide open.[57] It underscored the Federal Reserve's structurally impossible position, forever combating inflationary pressures that its own operations engendered and that its own programs maintained.

Harnessing finance

Kennedy had been careful to avoid a fight with the Federal Reserve, much to Heller's aggravation.[58] Johnson had initially been more belligerent and, following the 1966 credit crunch, he had put significant pressure on the Federal Reserve to ease.[59] That was to little avail, and he too had eventually come to recognize that within the existing institutional settings there were inevitable trade-offs.

In these circumstances, new sensibilities germinated that recognized the achievements of the New Deal's financial framework but felt that it had now become an obstacle to continued growth. By this logic, the aim should not be to shore up old regulations, but to modernize America's financial infrastructure by putting in place new arrangements appropriate to the times.

Old-school Democrats like Patman had always viewed the high interest rates produced by the Federal Reserve as a direct threat to the American Dream. But a younger generation of Democratic politicians argued that the housing sector needed to work more like Wall Street, where things could be financed whether rates were high or low.[60] These groups looked far more favorably on the idea of firms combining under one roof business activities that the New Deal had assigned to different institutional compartments. They saw in such supermarket

firms the promise of non-inflationary growth. Financial institutions had devised complex strategies to connect commercial
banking activities to the capital and money markets, but the
need for such extensive workarounds introduced considerable
inefficiencies into banks' attempts to respond to Americans'
credit needs. Moreover, they were dependent on regulatory
forbearance and the politically fragile tutelage of people
like Saxon – not a sustainable state of affairs. Functionally
integrated financial organizations would be able to support
their lending activities with access to the money and capital
markets, efficiently sourcing funds and extending credit as
needed.

This ethos was by no means reactionary, a precursor of a
right-wing revolution. What animated it was the growing recognition that existing regulations had made the middle class
inaccessible and were maintaining America's racial divide.[61]
The New Deal institutions no longer worked to spread wealth
but benefitted primarily a white middle class ensconced in
suburban properties. Public housing programs, institutionally
segregated from the subsidization of private homeownership
through the FHA, were increasingly held responsible for the
entrenchment of an African American underclass.[62] When the
National Advisory Commission on Civil Disorders emphasized that a poorly functioning housing market was a major
cause behind civil unrest, it was giving voice to sentiments held
widely across civil society.[63]

The 1968 Housing and Urban Development Act created an
elaborate network of subsidies, guarantees, and refinancing
options to encourage the construction of affordable homes and
bring mortgage credit within reach of new strata. The political project of expanding homeownership had always relied
heavily on collaboration with private industry, but a decade of
frustrated ambitions had left on Johnson a deep impression of
the limits on government action when it tried to go against the
grain of private industry.[64] The larger those obstacles loomed,

the more imperative it was to pursue public objectives by harnessing private money.[65]

The Act positioned the public–private partnership as a central organizational vehicle, looking to coalitions of "bankers, real estate brokers, and homebuilders" to implement solutions to the "urban crisis."[66] It greatly expanded government insurance for securitized mortgages, removing the remaining default risk.[67] Through the creation of the Government National Mortgage Association, or Ginnie Mae, the Act created a nationwide market for securitized mortgage debt, which removed the remaining liquidity risk associated with mortgages.[68] The hopes and ambitions of growth Keynesianism were now fully bound up with the uninterrupted growth of credit.[69]

5

The Inflation Decade

When we think about the origins of our present era, it is common to view Jimmy Carter as the last gasp of progressive Keynesianism and Reagan as the first neoliberal president. In reality, many of the policies that we associate with neoliberalism were in motion under Johnson. It was Nixon who pressed pause, centering his economic policy on deficit spending and demand stimulus.[1] And, following the Ford hiatus, it was the Carter administration that would shift middle-class politics into a new register in a more decisive way.[2]

To be sure, Nixon had come into office determined to tackle inflation by tightening economic policy.[3] His administration's first budget generated a surplus, which slowed down growth but failed to bring down inflation.[4] It was taken as yet further evidence of the limitations of demand-pull theories, lending credibility to what had become a dominant way of thinking about inflation – the wage-push logic embedded in the Phillips curve.[5]

The right did not take the growing consensus around the existence of an unemployment–inflation trade-off as a reason for imagining sophisticated supply-side programs to underpin ambitious government spending. Instead, and admittedly more logically, they saw it as pointing to the need for combined austerity and wage repression. Nixon came under growing pressure from business and his own economic advisers to adopt a hardline anti-labor stance.

But he saw that route as leading to electoral ruin, so he resisted. The institutions of the New Deal had come under pressure, but the social constituencies that it had produced remained powerful.[6] Not constrained by political correctness, Nixon understood that life under welfare capitalism required drawing boundaries. Maintaining it meant expanding the middle class of working homeowners to include "new white" groups as full members, while explicitly excluding African Americans and other minorities.[7] With his New Economic Policy, Nixon turned to old-fashioned Keynesian stimulus.[8]

Nixon appointed his long-time ally Arthur Burns as chair of the Federal Reserve. Burns quickly found himself impressed by the severity of the inflationary situation he had inherited, but he was nonetheless unable to resist pressure from the administration to adopt an easy money policy.[9] Nixon's decision to abandon the Bretton Woods system of fixed exchange rates – on the occasion of which he declared himself a Keynesian – was motivated by his refusal to impose austerity domestically.

To manage the inflationary pressures that were bound to intensify, Nixon turned to mandatory wage and price controls – an approach that the Kennedy and Johnson administrations had considered beyond the pale.[10] Analysts of the 1972 election have tended to agree that Nixon's political calculation was correct. Fiscal stimulus, it was shown again, albeit by a Republican president, was an effective way of preventing a recession, maintaining growth and employment, and building political support.

By 1973 the wage–price controls had become difficult to maintain. Business leaders felt that labor benefitted too much from the arrangement.[11] Union leaders too were increasingly frustrated. At a time when the union movement had wider

appeal than it had in a long time and membership was climbing, they were unable to exploit their growing bargaining
power.[12] After the abandonment of the wage–price controls in
1974, inflation shot up.[13]

The Ford administration declared inflation a national emergency.[14] A much more doctrinaire character than Nixon, Ford
accepted the need for fiscal austerity, never considered bringing back price and wage controls, and gave full support when
Burns signaled his intention to tighten monetary policy.[15]

Whereas the Burns of the early decade had rationalized his
loyalty to Nixon with hopeful stories that inflation might yet
die down of its own accord, he now saw a new economic world
where the Keynesian program just added fuel to a raging fire of
inflationary expectations:

> Keynesian policies designed to counter high unemployment
> – policies such as tax reductions, larger governmental expen-
> ditures, easier credit – were . . . based on the premise of a
> declining or stable price level. . . . We have entered a different
> world, a world in which inflation is present in fact proceeding
> at an accelerated pace in recent times, a world in which trade
> union leaders, workers, and businessmen are all influenced
> heavily by expectations of inflation.[16]

The combination of fiscal austerity and monetary tightening
produced a recession that pushed up unemployment, particularly among African Americans and other minorities who did
not enjoy protection from powerful unions.[17] Social pressures
now started boiling over.

Challenging welfare capitalism

When trying to make sense of the 1970s, left-wing critics have
tended to see a right-wing backlash against the welfare state.

There was such a movement, of course. But for much of the 1970s, business was on the defensive. The Watergate scandal was not seen as the wrongdoing of one person but as a window into the webs of collusion between business and politics.[18] The commonly held idea that the 1970s protest movements were concerned not with questions of political economy, but with culture and identity, is victor's history. The Civil Rights movement in particular had a strong and explicit focus on economic issues: inequality in housing, employment, and taxation – the pillars of America's racially delineated welfare capitalism.

Indeed, the grassroots fight against racial discrimination in housing was distinctive for its focus not just on consequences, but on the inner workings of the problem. The 1968 Fair Housing Act had formally ended discrimination in housing, but mortgage lenders had calibrated their redlining methodologies accordingly. Increasingly, institutional racism worked through seemingly objective economic criteria. The community reinvestment movement sought to intercept this logic of color-blind racism at the source, demanding not ameliorative social policy but a more fundamental reconstruction of the logic governing public and private investment.[19] The Equal Credit Opportunity Act of 1974 and the Home Mortgage Disclosure Act of 1975 made redlining more difficult, and the Community Reinvestment Act of 1977 provided communities with limited but meaningful instruments to enforce equal treatment.[20]

What animated the community reinvestment movement was the perception that the expanding fiscal state had come to serve primarily the interests of business and the affluent. This critique of welfare capitalism had broader purchase, and it brought into play class and racial solidarities that seem unfamiliar to a contemporary observer. That was apparent even in the poster child of the neoliberal backlash story, the property tax revolt. That story did not start with California's

Proposition 13, and it did have not a naturally conservative inclination. In origin, it rather expressed how far discontent had spread beyond the lowest income groups.[21]

As Josh Mound has demonstrated, resistance to local property taxes was a response to the effects of supply-side Keynesianism. Successive federal tax cuts had made America's structure of taxation far less progressive, while putting pressure on state and local governments to increase their own sources of tax revenue.[22] Local authorities tended to give well-organized business communities a pass and typically found it easier to tax homeowners instead.[23] As inflation accelerated, these groups shifted into even higher tax brackets. The result was "a pocketbook squeeze on lower- and middle-income Americans."[24] Many who at an earlier point had thought of themselves as solidly part of the middle class began to see themselves as being shortchanged. The property tax became such a prominent issue because it was the only tax that was determined directly through local elections.[25]

The perception that drove the community reinvestment and tax revolt movements – that the new barriers to middle-class prosperity were created not by impersonal markets but by political decisions – also animated the resurgent movement for full employment legislation. The initial version of what would eventually become the Humphrey–Hawkins bill tried to create a legally enforceable right to employment, requiring the federal government to expand public employment as needed.[26] Such a federal commitment to full employment would have deactivated the Federal Reserve's ability to fight inflation by increasing unemployment.[27]

In the original bill, the full employment objective was embedded in a range of planning mechanisms.[28] Radicalizing the supply-side analysis of inflation, it required economic policymakers to study inflation as a multifaceted phenomenon and to develop policies to target its specific sources.[29] The case was consciously built on the awareness that the state was *already*

heavily involved in picking winners and losers, and that existing institutions could be repurposed to serve other ends.

An Initiative Committee for National Economic Planning
was formed to publicly campaign for economic planning in
support of the bill. Its members included trade union leaders
and left-wing economists, but also prominent establishment
figures such as Robert Roosa, who had been in charge of international economic policy during the Kennedy administration
and had subsequently become an investment banker. He
declared the Committee's objective to be "to develop a truly
homegrown American form of national economic planning.
Practically all the pieces of a planning process already exist.
They are just not pulled together."[30]

The full employment drive challenged the divide-and-rule
logic of welfare capitalism.[31] The 1963 March on Washington,
typically remembered as a demand for civic and political rights,
had in fact been a march for "Jobs and Freedom."[32] Soon after
the legislative victories of the mid-1960s, the Freedom Budget
sought to use the fiscal powers of government to provide not
"tax incentives for industry" but "full employment and a guaranteed income, the rebuilding of our cities, the provision of
superior schools for all of our children, and free medical care
for all our citizens," in the words of Bayard Rustin, one of its
main proponents.[33]

Although the Johnson administration took problems of
poverty and unemployment in African American communities
seriously, it viewed the proposals of the Freedom Budget as
simply unaffordable – period.[34] The War on Poverty included
no real mechanism for enlarging the number of available jobs,
and it ended up reproducing all the problems of traditional
social welfare and relief approaches that growth Keynesianism
had been so eager to avoid.[35]

The full employment idea did not die, however. When the
limits of the War on Poverty became clear, and as the austerity of the Ford administration pushed up unemployment

rates, it re-entered public debate. In the mid-1970s, groups that had traditionally been excluded by organized labor began transforming existing unions and organizing new ones. The percentage of African American union members grew rapidly in the 1970s,[36] and such activism often went hand-in-hand with activism on access to credit and discrimination in housing.[37]

Conceptualizing stagnation

As the American economy sputtered, concerns reminiscent of the secular stagnation debate of the 1930s resurfaced. This time, there was also a pronounced international dimension: anxiety about America's decline as the world's economic superpower ran high. While the recession of the mid-1970s radicalized popular demands, in Washington it drove a shift in the way economic issues were discussed.

Following Nixon's resignation, the 1974 midterm elections had delivered a decisive victory for the Democrats, bringing a new generation of politicians into office who had only heard of the Great Depression from their parents.[38] Their view of politics had been shaped by the disastrous McGovern campaign of 1972 (when Nixon had won forty-nine states), which had further undermined the authority of Democratic leaders who still thought of themselves as the heirs of Roosevelt.[39]

These Democrats did not dismiss the idea that the problems of the 1970s were at least in part a consequence of Keynesian stimulus. They were receptive to arguments from the business community that attributed the weak performance of the American economy to a "capital shortage" caused by high taxes, overregulation, expensive labor, and inflation – all of which made it unprofitable to be an investor.[40]

As Julia Ott documents, these debates took shape through Congressional debates on pension reform.[41] At an earlier point in time, the role of pension funds had been heavily shaped by the communities in which they operated and the corporations they were associated with. The funds had invested heavily in municipal bonds, so supporting the ability of local government to fund itself at low rates. That arrangement had been under pressure throughout the 1960s, as pension funds had gone on the hunt for higher returns. In the early postwar years, US pension funds held most of their assets in public debt and corporate bonds. By the 1970s, their asset holdings were heavily dominated by corporate stock, and they held virtually no public debt anymore.[42]

The changing role of the pension funds raised questions of how they should be regulated. The importance of the pension funds to the broader economy was well understood, as was the fact that their growth would accelerate as the baby boomer generation started saving for retirement. Consideration in Congress of what would become the Employee Retirement Security Act provided representatives from the high-tech sector with a platform to argue that the future of the American economy was in their hands. What these companies needed were not investment tax write-offs, in the spirit of Fordist bookkeeping, but large amounts of up-front financing for high-risk, high-reward ventures. Proper reform of the nation's pension savings, they argued, would kill several birds with one stone: in addition to securing employees' retirement income, it would reduce inflationary pressures by diverting funds from wages to savings and by freeing up capital for investment.[43]

The requirement that asset portfolios be managed in the interest of the beneficiaries was a double-edged sword. It meant that employers would be unable to cream off capital gains, as they had tried to do. But it also meant that employees were denied a say over the fund's investment decisions – as that was likely to come at the expense of individuals' interest in the long-term value of their savings.[44] These debates set the tone for the role of Democrats during the 1970s, inflecting their concerns, decisions, and strategies at every turn.[45]

Democrats managing change

Carter had more affinity with the legacy of growth Keynesianism than the Watergate babies did, and he had an all-star team of Keynesian economists to advise him.[46] But he agreed that the need for growth had been pushed out of the frame by demands for redistribution.[47] And, as a former state governor (required, by law, to balance the books), he had a strong dislike of deficit spending. Although he accepted the principle of using fiscal policy to affect the level of employment at a theoretical level, in practice the commitment to fiscal prudence dominated.[48] In his memoirs, Carter expressed his belief in a way that would become trademark Third Way conviction:

> I had inherited the largest deficit in history—more than $66 billion—and it was important to me to stop the constantly escalating federal expenditures that tended to drive up interest rates and were one of the root causes of inflation and unemployment.[49]

Carter's first budget was nonetheless a cautious attempt to spur economic growth through tax reductions, infrastructure investment, and job and training programs.[50] Old-fashioned Keynesians like Heller thought the package was too small;[51] Federal Reserve chair Arthur Burns thought it was too big.[52] The administration went out of its way to reassure Congress and the public that the size of the stimulus was carefully calibrated and would not exacerbate the inflation problem. In support of that claim, Carter's CEA chair Charles Schultze argued that the economy was suffering from a special kind of inflation: "momentum inflation," which "has not been and will not be cured by a policy of sluggish recovery, high unemployment and idle plant capacity. Equally important, it will not be accelerated by a prudent policy of economic stimulus that restores a steady and sustainable rate of economic recovery."[53]

But the package did fuel inflation, prompting a swift policy turnaround. The administration's next budget was an austerity budget – but insufficiently so, bond traders thought, and the markets reacted strongly.[54] Carter responded with a revised, this time fully balanced budget that included severe cuts in a range of social programs and a freeze on public sector hiring.[55] It pushed the economy deeper into recession.[56]

"Momentum inflation," an inflation that has been locked in through self-fulfilling expectations and continues even after it is no longer actively fueled by policy decisions, was what neoliberal thinkers of the monetarist and rational expectations schools had identified as the *worst* kind of inflation. Although it was easily triggered, it could not be managed through specific policies – all that policymakers could do was to observe monetary and fiscal austerity and wait for expectations to resettle.

The contradictions of Keynesian thinking about inflation were now making themselves felt. Two decades earlier, Samuelson and Solow had advanced the Phillips curve to demonstrate that inflation could be generated by specific causal factors that had little to do with the general overheating of the economic system. But Keynesians had not experienced much success managing inflation with their supply-side measures. Whatever reality the Phillips curve had, right-wing economists like Milton Friedman and Robert Lucas argued, was confined to the short term.[57] Beyond such ephemeral trade-offs, they said, the following law held: if unemployment was below its "natural rate," the general price level would increase in a self-reinforcing, expectation-driven way (and vice versa). Schultze's idiosyncratic idea of "momentum inflation" articulated the new wisdom even as he was trying to make the case for the continued relevance of old Keynesianism.

Inflation had become so clearly and heavily driven by expectations backed up by market power that arguments rejecting the possibility of any stable trade-off were impossible to ignore.[58] But this wasn't just a matter of turning back the clock. Almost two decades of discussing inflation in terms of employment levels and wage costs (rather than profits or markups) meant that excessive expectations had become exclusively associated with wage demands. In other words, while Phillips curve thinking had been unable to dislodge the orthodox common sense about inflation, it had very success-fully advertised that inflation could be fought by increasing unemployment. Retrofitting explanation to solution, the very existence of inflation was increasingly taken as indicating that unemployment was too low and wages too high.

These sensibilities came to dominate the Humphrey–Hawkins debate, especially because the bill's backers had taken price and wage controls off the table. They had done so in part to ward off accusations of ideological radicalism, but also to placate the AFL-CIO leaders, who viewed such controls as jeopardizing their ability to deliver higher wages for their members.[59] In this context, arguments about the inflationary impact of full employment found a great deal of traction, con-stantly putting the bill's advocates on the back foot.[60]

Federal Reserve chair Burns voiced his strong opposition – it would have been impossible for him not to, seeing as the bill proposed to abolish his job.[61] The business community too made grateful use of the inflation argument. The idea that "full employment" should not be taken literally, and always meant a specific level of unemployment set by the laws of economics, now migrated from economic theory to public opinion.[62]

During his campaign, Carter had expressed support for the Humphrey–Hawkins bill, but without conviction.[63] As inflation woes grew, lukewarm support morphed into quiet opposition and strong behind-the-scenes pushback. CEA chair Schultze commented that "the combination of the 'employer-of-last-resort' provisions . . . and the wage standards that go with it threatens to make the inflation problem worse."[64] Internal Democratic negotiations revolved around watering down targets and transforming the government's legal responsibility into non-committal goals.[65]

The final bill did not have an enforceable right to employment, and it did not create any new programs for public employment. It required that inflation be controlled in a way that would not jeopardize the achievement of the government's employment objectives, but it provided no indication as to how the principal tension here might be attenuated or tackled.[66] The bill's main practical innovation was to create a new set of processes for the formulation and implementation of economic policy objectives, which included the requirement that the Federal Reserve chair appear before Congress.[67]

Reinforcing the supply side

At its halfway point, the Carter administration had little to show for having disconnected from left-wing coalitions and agendas. Inflation was soaring and Carter's approval ratings were tanking.[68] With its back against the wall and the next election in sight, the Carter administration turned to industrial policy, aiming to reinvent growth liberalism's supply-side politics in a micro-economic frame.

In part, this turn was prompted by acute difficulties in key economic sectors, which had dragged the administration into funneling support to private business in highly visible ways. Its assistance for the steel industry had ended up looking like a no-strings-attached bailout.[69] The public consternation shaped the administration's approach to the bailout of Chrysler, where it imposed an austerity package including significant wage concessions.[70] Each course of action left the administration politically vulnerable and reinforced Carter's growing reputation for haplessness. If the government was going to be forced to intervene, it needed to be able to (be seen to) do so with purpose and conviction.

Here, what Elizabeth Berman refers to as the "economic style" of thinking – a focus on measurable, micro-level cost and benefits – rose to prominence in economic policymaking. During the 1960s, as macroeconomic instruments and goals had come under pressure, this style had taken flight as a way to justify and guide the expansion of Johnson's Great Society programs – there was efficiency, not just equity on offer.[71]

During the Carter era, this way of thinking really soared.[72] It was seen as providing a calculus to guide decisions about public support for private interests. It also provided a specific lens on the inflation question, one that centered on productivity growth.[73] As long as technological innovation ensured that productivity growth was higher than wage growth, it was logically impossible for the latter to be inflationary.

Of course, innovation is an uncertain business. And it was in exploiting this uncertainty that the economic style did its real work. When it came to committing public resources to save jobs, the style demanded hard evidence and ironclad guarantees. But it displayed a tremendous willingness to take at face value capital's promises of synergistic, inclusive growth. This combination of hard-nosed empiricism and idealistic gullibility would become a defining aspect of the ethos of Clinton's Third Way.

The Carter administration became highly receptive to business claims that government red tape was the main threat to investment.[74] The legal and institutional framework for the public–private partnership had been put in place during the previous decade, and the administration made extensive use of it. Believing that previous attempts at industrial policy often had found insufficient take-up because the terms were insufficiently appealing, Carter recognized the need to give sufficient weight to the "private" aspect of the public–private partnership.[75] Wage moderation seemed an important building block for an ambitious supply-side program, but unions were in no mood to voluntarily moderate their demands.[76]

The impact of micro-level supply-siderism was felt nowhere more keenly than in the changing tone of the tax reform debate. Carter had campaigned on the issue. He recognized that much of the tax cutting done during the previous decades had benefitted special interests, and that it had turned the tax code into a Swiss cheese – "a disgrace to the human race" he called it.[77] His vision had been to close loopholes for corporations, cut taxes for low income, and equalize the treatment of different kinds of income (in particular to get rid of preferential treatment of capital gains).[78]

Building on their success during the pension debates, an alliance of high-tech and venture capital firms argued that the taxation of capital gains amounted to a form of double taxation that held investors back from putting their money towards the high-risk, high-reward ventures that held the key to America's economic recovery.[79] By their reasoning, equal treatment of income sources should mean the *abolition* of the capital gains tax.

They also took an idea that supply-side Keynesianism had made respectable – that reducing tax rates could mean increased revenues – and argued that it applied to capital gains in particular, since it was easier for asset owners simply not to sell than it was for workers not to sell their labor.[80] Democrats had become highly sensitized to such arguments and, as the declining competitiveness of American manufacturing vis-à-vis Europe and Japan came to symbolize a more general decline of American global leadership in the world, they viewed the high-tech sector as holding the key to America's future.[81] The right's victory on Proposition 13 sealed the deal on an emerging consensus, and the Revenue Act of 1978 did not only not increase, but in fact drastically *lowered* the capital gains tax rate.[82]

Financial deregulation

None of these measures was likely to generate their effects in time to help Carter's chances of re-election. For more immediate stimulus, the administration looked to financial deregulation. Almost a decade earlier, the Hunt Commission had urged such deregulation to allow more activities to be undertaken by one firm and to enhance the capacity of financial institutions to provide mortgage credit in particular.[83] As the 1970s wore on and the problems of economic governance piled up, the idea that such large, multi-service banks would be able to deliver non-inflationary growth became very popular with Democrats.[84]

Carter felt that supermarket banks could offer the kind of efficiency gains that would counteract inflation.[85] His predecessors had entertained similar ambitions, but their efforts had run aground on the strong interest that different financial institutions had in protecting their own playing field, even as they were always eager to step onto others'.[86] Carter initially faced very similar problems,[87] but a legal challenge to the interest rate ceilings – launched by a coalition of savers who saw the value of their savings shrink as inflation surpassed the rate on deposits – gave the administration a platform to pursue its agenda. In the name of the small saver, legislation to deregulate financial services and phase out the interest rate ceilings was fast tracked.[88]

By 1979 the inflation problem was nevertheless escalating. Investors started selling Treasury debt, and the *Wall Street Journal* reported that yields on government debt were higher than "the extreme levels set during the Civil War, when a viable market for long-term Treasuries simply didn't exist."[89] Carter was desperate for a way to tackle inflation. Burns had refused to afford him the same forbearance he had shown Nixon, but even then, he had been unable to bring inflation down. When Burns' term finished in 1978, Carter seized the opportunity to put in place a new Federal Reserve chair.[90]

After a brief interlude when businessperson William Miller held the reins, Carter appointed Paul Volcker, a career economic bureaucrat who was upfront about the fact that he would work to tackle inflation and be immune to political influence. This was, at that point, what Carter was looking for: he had abandoned hopes that he could turn the economy around with a recombination of existing policies and accepted that a major reset was in order. Whether it would pay off in time to secure re-election was anyone's guess.

Writing before the attention radar of social scientists became colonized by the pros and cons of neoliberalism as an explanatory framework, in an unpublished doctoral dissertation no less, Patrick Akard accurately and pithily summarized the role of the Carter administration as follows:

> the policies of a *Democratic* administration included deregulation, reduction of domestic government expenditures (while defense expenditures increased), and cuts in tax (especially on capital income). A new Federal Reserve chairman instituted a strict monetarist program to reduce inflation, sending the country into another recession. These measures were all undertaken before the 1980 election.[91]

6

Building the Bailout State

At no point during his tenure had Arthur Burns, Federal Reserve chair from 1970 to 1978, really known what he was supposed to do. "The rules of economics are not working in quite the way they used to," he despaired in the middle of the decade, and he had left his job feeling pessimistic about the prospect of conquering inflation.[1] In 1979 he expressed his feelings in a lecture with the title "The Anguish of Central Banking." Surveying the numerous specific factors that were often cited as the causes of inflation (public spending, currency shifts, supply shocks, and unsettled expectations), he argued that such perspectives all captured aspects of the phenomenon but all failed to recognize "a more fundamental factor: the persistent inflationary bias that has emerged from the philosophic and political currents that have been transforming economic life in the United States and elsewhere since the 1930s."[2]

Acknowledging that many New Deal programs had been necessary to tackle the unprecedented circumstances of the Depression, he asserted that, over time, they had fostered unrealistic expectations among the American public. Postwar Keynesians had been overly receptive to the demands of a growing range of interests for inclusion in the benefits of postwar prosperity. The resulting "interplay of governmental action and private demands had an internal dynamic that led to their concurrent escalation."[3] America's institutions were now buckling under the weight of the public's ever-intensifying expectations.

There was, Burns thought, not much that a central bank could do, on its own, to change this dynamic. Its "practical capacity for curbing an inflation that is continually driven by political forces is very limited."[4] Burns realized that, from a purely economic perspective, the Federal Reserve could have done more to enforce financial discipline. But steering the economy into a severe recession would have angered virtually every constituency, and political pressure would no doubt force the Federal Reserve to reverse course before too long. What was the point in even trying?

Volcker had been Undersecretary at the Treasury during the first half of the 1970s, and president of the New York branch of the Federal Reserve System during the second half. In both roles he had been able to see up close the devastation wrought by accelerating inflation, and the impact this was having on the global status of the dollar. His understanding of the problem resembled Burns' diagnosis. The Federal Reserve had allowed itself to be suckered into maintaining an ever-widening financial safety net, keeping everyone liquid and backstopping new markets wherever they arose.[5] Promising to make everyone's life better had naturally fostered exaggerated expectations and unhealthy dependency. Having spread itself too thin, the Federal Reserve had lost credibility. In this way, it had endangered its ability to discharge its core responsibility of stabilizing the American economy's financial nervous system.

To be sure, Volcker did not think that financial markets could ever function *without* Federal Reserve support – that was a fantasy induced by economic abstractions that only true believers took literally. The Federal Reserve's policies were intimately involved in the everyday upkeep of financial markets, and to a large extent this state of affairs was irreversible. Any tightening policy would have to leave intact an extensive network of government subsidies and guarantees. Volcker certainly did not imagine that the Federal Reserve would be shifting to a "leaning against the wind" approach anytime soon – that was a fair-weather philosophy, of little relevance to the hard choices required by difficult economic times. Like Burns, he was incapable of enjoying Martin's innocence.

Whereas this had induced anxious despair in Burns, it filled Volcker with a clear sense of purpose and mission. He considered moralistic handwringing the enemy of decisive action, an unhelpful obstacle to actually fixing the institutional problem. He did not see monetary policy as a helpless victim, but, to the contrary, considered that central banking was the "only game in town."[6] The Federal Reserve was by no means the source of all the problems, but it was nonetheless the only institutional actor that could right the ship.

Volcker abandoned Burns' reservation and ambivalence, not out of recklessness but because the stability that Burns had thought he was preserving was increasingly exposed as imaginary. As Volcker put it during a meeting of the Federal Open Market Committee in October of 1979: "On the inflation front, we're probably losing ground. In an expectational sense, I think we certainly are, and that is being reflected in extremely volatile financial markets."[7]

Cognizant as Volcker was of the expectational aspect of inflation, he did not look to the rational expectations school of thought for practical guidance. Its core proposition was that any attempt to interfere with market mechanisms would backfire to produce inflation – such sit-on-your-hands advice had limited use for policymakers aiming to bring about specific changes. Instead, Volcker looked to monetarist theory, which overlapped with rational expectations thinking in many ways but was distinctive for its insistence that money could be clearly defined, and its circulating quantity easily controlled.

Whereas the rational expectations thought originated in the postwar academy and had a strong reactionary quality, monetarism enjoyed a longer historical lineage (going back at least to David Hume's quantity theory) that had included more complex political affiliations.

Monetarism had received a great deal of airtime in Congress under Wright Patman's chairmanship of the House Banking Committee. Patman was a Democratic populist from Texas who valued smallness of scale above all else. He thought that the New Deal had relied too much on the large corporation, fanatically fought legislation that would allow banks to develop branch networks, and harbored a deep suspicion of the Federal Reserve, viewing its affinity for tight money as a standing threat to American workers and the dream of property ownership. Patman considered monetarism an ally insofar as it insisted on the need for Federal Reserve policy to be rule-bound and transparent, its role limited to ensuring the growth of the money supply according to set rules.[8] That postwar monetarism was not a natural ally of conservative austerity was indicated by the fact that the paradigm-defining book by Milton Friedman and Anna Schwartz had pinned the blame for the Great Depression on the Federal Reserve's tightening policies.[9] The approach first rose to prominence in policy circles when the Nixon administration viewed it as offering arguments to support its demand for more accommodating Federal Reserve policies.[10]

Of course, Patman recognized of course that inflation fighting through quantitative tightening would produce higher rates. But what he correctly understood was that the higher interest rates produced by the Federal Reserve never had even effects to begin with – they had a dramatic impact on labor markets, the construction sector, and aggregate demand, but they never did much to disturb the activities of Wall Street banks.[11] Better to have simple rules in place that did not lend themselves to discretionary interventions susceptible to favoritism and collusion.

Amidst the troubles of the 1970s, Congress had taken a strong interest in making the Federal Reserve more accountable.[12] Patman's work laid the foundation for the adoption of House Concurrent Resolution 133, which required the Federal Reserve to set annual targets for the growth of the money supply, to track its performance against them, and to report on those to Congress.[13]

Burns had never been sympathetic to monetarist ideas, viewing them as irredeemably simplistic. One of the key problems facing the Federal Reserve was precisely that it was *not* possible to distinguish money from other forms of liquid assets, and money-issuing banks from other financial institutions. Furthermore, the idea that financial governance could be boiled down to a few transparent rules of thumb militated against his firmly held belief that central banking required specialized expertise, and, especially during hard times, nuanced judgments that should be insulated from democratic scrutiny.[14]

Where Burns perceived naïve simplicity, Volcker discerned helpful simplification. Monetarism offered practical ways of defining monetary aggregates, which the Federal Reserve could then work to contain. It was clear that inflation was driven by many things other than monetary conditions.[15] But without constant money creation, inflation would not be able to grow – that was the practical truth in monetarism.

That "in the long run . . . an excess supply of money contributes not to real income or wealth, but simply to inflation" was "one of the oldest propositions in the history of economic thought," according to Volcker.[16] Insofar as politicians and policymakers had "lost sight of it amid the urgent search for solutions to immediate policy problems,"[17] the monetarists provided an important public service by communicating that foundational truth in a way that was able to gain traction in the age of public scrutiny and democratic expectations. "The day is past when any instrument of Governmental policy, including monetary policy, can expect to be effective without exposing the objectives and policies to public scrutiny. Monetary targets lend themselves to such scrutiny."[18]

Resetting expectations

In October 1979, Volcker threw a massive wrench into the gears of the American – and global – financial system. He announced that the Federal Reserve would until further notice focus all its energies on controlling the growth of the money supply, letting interest rates adjust as needed.

A first round of shock therapy failed to deliver the reset that was needed, and a second, more sustained offensive pushed interest rates close to 20 percent. By way of comparison, during the 1960s Johnson had been upset with the Federal Reserve for letting interest climb past *5 percent*. Unemployment eventually soared past 10 percent, the highest level since the Great Depression, and it remained at alarmingly high levels for most of the decade.[19] America's "wheel within the wheel" came to an abrupt standstill. Contractors sent Volcker pieces of lumber in the mail to remind him of the homes that they were unable to build.

This was not a smooth process whereby business efficiently averted the cost of adjustment onto workers. The drastic increase of financing costs raised the bar across the board and caused many overleveraged balance sheets to come apart. If Volcker's policy turn was class war, as many have argued, it was certainly not precision warfare. Carpet bombing might be a more suitable metaphor. During the 1980s, more banks failed than during the 1930s.[20] Corporate profits plummeted. Public intellectuals from across the political spectrum wrung their hands at the decline of the American economy.

Volcker washed his hands. He recognized that his policies were causing pain, but he considered that he was simply correcting the unrealistic expectations that his predecessors had fostered. He didn't like it more than any other well-adjusted citizen, but there was no way around it. The Federal Reserve's lack of discipline had allowed numerous economically unviable institutions to stay in business, and inflation would not be conquered unless this problem was dealt with. Volcker's impartiality was plausible, and, by all accounts, entirely sincere: he was in nobody's pocket, business leaders and presidents included. Reagan was deeply unhappy with Volcker's policies, fully mirroring how Johnson had resented Martin's tight money policies.[21] It was only when the benefits of higher interest rates became apparent (primarily large capital inflows) that the animosity softened.

In a sense, nothing much rides on a correct assessment of Volcker's personal motivations and intentions of course. But the widespread tendency to misinterpret the Volcker shock as functional to capital or neoliberal ideology is indicative of a misunderstanding of what happened. Volcker was, by all accounts, earnestly committed to advancing the public good and impervious to corruption. Highlighting the ability of such a mindset to serve as an agent of draconian restructuring allows us to understand something important about the process: the extent to which inequity was built into the everyday operations of the financial system and the degree to which public policy had become dependent on the cooperation of the submerged state, where public authority and private leverage were often hard to tell apart.

For left-wing critics of Volcker's policies, William Greider's book *Secrets of the Temple*, which depicts the Federal Reserve as a secretive bastion protecting creditor interests at all costs, has long been an authoritative statement.[22] Minsky wrote a harsh review of Greider's book. He thought it was too conspiratorial, that it failed to recognize that there existed "good citizenship reasons" for Volcker's policy turn, and that much of what Greider explained with reconstructions of behind-the-scenes events was perfectly comprehensible by pulling up publicly available flow-of-funds data and reading them through the lens of his financial Keynesianism.[23]

As Samuel Knafo points out, it is too easy – and all too common – to look back at the turmoil of the 1980s and to imagine that it was functional to what came after.[24] From such a perspective, financialization is like a phoenix rising from the ashes of the industrial crisis. But that is to downplay the severity of the crisis. The wave of bank failures that washed over the American economy was without comparison. During the 1930s, the number of bank failures had never surpassed a hundred; at the peak of the 1980s crisis, almost 300 banks failed in one year.[25] In combination with numerous mergers and acquisitions, the total number of banking organizations decreased sharply.[26]

All of this had been perfectly predictable – it was exactly why Burns had been reluctant to step on the brake with full force. And although Volcker disavowed any suggestion that he was forcing other agencies in the US government to adjust their policies in specific ways, that was nonetheless the objective point of his move. As he explicated his line of thinking in this respect:

it would be unwise to expect monetary policy alone, however conducted, to carry the full load of reconciling our economic goals. Inflation is difficult to eliminate because of forces deeply imbedded in the structure of our economy, our social policies, and our political life. To my mind, monetary aggregate targets are a useful – even a necessary – gauge of appropriate monetary policy action in bringing inflation under control. But they do not in themselves alter the real problems and hard choices imposed by the economic structure itself.[27]

Such broader adjustments would not just have to include measures to bring down the average standard of living, but also policies to protect the nodal points of the financial system.

The point was not to send the American economy into free-fall, but to stabilize it. Volcker did not expect the American government to sit idly by while the system collapsed. In any case, when it comes to bailouts, rather than the infliction of austerity, the Federal Reserve itself had a direct role to play. As he put it to the Federal Open Market Committee in 1982:

> If it gets bad enough, we can't stay on the side or we'll have a major liquidity crisis. It's a matter of judgment as to when and how strongly to react. We are not here to see the economy destroyed in the interest of not bailing somebody out.[28]

During the next years, the Federal Reserve would lead authorities in providing bailouts when and where needed. It relaxed criteria for bank mergers, and worked with other agencies and regulators to organize capital infusions and lending facilities to support mergers.[29] The Treasury reins were held by Donald Regan, who had previously led the growth of Merrill Lynch into a huge, diversified financial supermarket that constantly pushed against the institutional dividers of the New Deal, and had been appointed with a clear brief to promote the consolidation of the financial services industry.[30] Volcker's support was critical to the pivotal bailout of Continental Illinois in 1984, which could not be managed under regulatory subterfuge and attracted the full light of day.[31] Officials in the FDIC came to refer to the Federal Reserve as the "Evil Empire" because it seemed so unconditionally devoted to bailing out large banks.[32]

At all times, Volcker was concerned to make sure that his tightening policies would not destabilize the market for Treasury debt. He recognized not only the Federal Reserve's responsibility for ensuring an orderly market to allow the Treasury to sell its debt without difficulty, but also the fact that the Treasury market had come to play an absolutely central role in the repo market where shadow banks sourced short-term funding.[33] Without a generous supply of Treasury debt of stable value, the repo market would stop working, and the balance sheets of large banks would start to come apart, destabilizing the system as a whole.

Again, what Volcker's actual thoughts and feelings might have been is probably irrelevant. The point is that an overriding concern with system-level stabilization could go hand-in-hand with a realistic perspective on the system's operations. The stabilization imperative required turning the heat up on everyone and standing ready to put out fires as needed. Volcker's commitment to the public cause did not prevent him from understanding that some groups were going to receive government support they had done nothing to earn. Charles Schultze, Carter's CEA chair who had been caught between old and new perspectives with his "momentum" inflation, also expressed that Volcker's victory over inflation had been worth the price of severe recession.[34]

Stabilizing expectations

Inside the Federal Reserve, there had long existed voices who wanted to impose more discipline. But these had been drowned out by more powerful factions that insisted on the institution's role in facilitating broad-based credit growth and backstopping new markets where needed. Johnson had appointed liberal Board governors to reinforce that tendency. One of those appointments, Andrew Brimmer, was a progressive economist and the first African American to serve on the Board. He had been a driving force behind the formulation of the Emergency Credit Assistance program, a set of organizational protocols for intervening quickly with liquidity support when new sources of instability emerged.[35]

During the 1970s, that program was used with growing frequency. It was used first in 1970, when the failure of the heavily indebted Penn Central railroad threatened to disrupt financial markets.[36] But in 1974 the Federal Reserve used those same protocols to spend a far greater amount of money to bail out the Franklin National Bank. The bank was sizeable, but not enormous – it was America's twentieth largest bank. Where would all this end? Who exactly could expect a bailout?

In his quest for financial discipline, Volcker would not have to go to war with factions in his own institution: he had come into the job with a clear mandate, amidst widespread acknowledgment that the existing way of handling financial instability was pushing the US economy into ever more dangerous territory. More worrying were developments in the FDIC, the regulator primarily responsible for resolving bank failures.

When a bank became insolvent, the FDIC could either pay depositors and close the bank, or support its sale.[37] Takeover was typically the cheapest and therefore preferred option, and the FDIC and the Federal Reserve would jointly manage the merger.[38] A third option – supporting a bank's balance sheet so that it could continue doing business – was more expensive and only available under exceptional circumstances, namely, if a bank was considered essential to the economy of the community in which it operated.[39]

During the 1950s and the 1960s, the FDIC had never invoked this "essentiality doctrine." But as the number of bank failures increased during the 1970s, the FDIC used this provision to bail out banks whose continued operation was important for the stability of local communities. On that basis, it bailed out Unity Bank in 1971, a small Boston bank in a heavily underserved African American community.[40] In subsequent years the FDIC supported other banks on similar grounds.[41] This represented, in the word of Irvine Sprague, who headed the FDIC from the mid-1970s to the mid-1980s, a break with the FDIC's more "narrow role of acting only after the bank had failed, and then merely to dispose of the remains through a payoff or sale."[42]

These banks were not too big to fail in the sense that we now understand that term: they were very important to the economic fortunes of their local communities, but their failure would not have had severe knock-on effects for the wider economic system. In other words, the FDIC originally entered the "bailout business" not primarily to protect the balance sheets of large New York money center banks, but to advance social objectives.[43] At the same time, the FDIC became reluctant to extend guarantees when *only* system risk considerations were at stake.[44] Such priorities converged with the objectives of the reinvestment movement, which identified the reluctance of financial institutions to serve low-income neighborhoods as one of the key obstacles to their development.

To Volcker's mind, this presented a clear problem. Local banks were always going to be important to their local communities. If the FDIC was going to bail out each and every local bank, it would undo the effects of his program. The Federal Reserve needed the FDIC to fall in line with the Federal Reserve's approach.

The issue came to a head soon after Volcker's policy turn. First Pennsylvania Bank had invested heavily in Treasury securities and, following the Volcker shock, saw their value drop while the cost of its funding increased. When the FDIC expressed reluctance to arrange a bailout, the Federal Reserve put major pressure on it to do so. Volcker communicated that he would keep the bank in business by providing liquidity until the FDIC stepped in.[45] It forced the first clean bailout of the post-Volcker shock era to be organized, whereby an institution was able to continue under its own flag with a massive injection of public funds. It was the stability of the financial system, not of local communities, that was "essential."[46]

During the next years, many more banks failed.[47] A key moment was the bailout of Continental Illinois in 1984. The bank was heavily leveraged and exposed to uninsured short-term funding, and it had overinvested in debt issued by the governments of Global South countries.[48] It was unambiguously too big and interconnected to fail.[49] As news of its bad loans spread, creditors started cashing out. The Federal Reserve provided a large loan, but it failed to turn things around. It was only once the government guaranteed all of the institution's creditors that confidence was restored.[50] This is where the term "too big to fail" originates. During a Congressional hearing, a Representative said: "Mr. Chairman, let us not bandy words. We have a new kind of bank. It is called too big to fail."[51]

Another critical moment in the development of too-big-to-fail as a policy regime occurred in the same year, when the Comptroller of the Currency declared that the nation's largest banks were simply too big to fail and that their creditors were effectively ensured by the government, without limit. By explicitly assigning too-big-to-fail status to the nation's eleven largest banks, it created a quantitative benchmark. If a bank could be at least as big and dangerous as number eleven on the list, it would also be able to enjoy full public guarantees.[52]

The American government's assurance that it would not let key firms go under did not mean that everyone was able to sit easy. Regaining the trust of financial markets required more than such a macro-level blank check. The Treasury market would remain highly volatile until well into the decade, and it would require ongoing handholding and expectation management.[53] When in 1982 a government securities dealer failed, the Federal Reserve quickly opened a number of new financing facilities to enable other government debt dealers to cover for the bankrupt firm.[54]

Later the same year, another government securities dealer, Lombard Wall, failed. In the ensuing bankruptcy proceedings, a court ruling determined that its repo collateral was subject to an "automatic stay," in effect denying creditors from taking ownership of the collateral that had been pledged by the bankrupt firm.[55] This threatened the legal basis of the repo funding model and so the Federal Reserve's ability to perform stabilizing operations through the repo market.[56] Volcker was deeply concerned that "a repo market that has been narrowed by the withdrawal of participants that are unprepared to accept the risks inherent in the Lombard Wall decision could *limit the ability of the Federal Reserve to act promptly and in the large volumes necessary to achieve monetary policy objectives.*"[57]

Volcker lobbied heavily, and successfully, for legislation to exempt securities pledged in a repo deal from the automatic stay rule.[58] During the 1980s, repo markets grew dramatically, and it became a central conduit through which the Federal Reserve stabilized the shadow financial system. Leon Wansleben summarizes the systemically central role of the repo market in Minskyan terms:

> the formalized, standardized, and publicly subsidized nature of repo allowed for new kinds of relationships in money markets. For lenders, it offered a routine way to deposit funds, akin to holding savings on a bank account for retail customers; and correspondingly for borrowers, the existence of strongly institutionalized repo markets suggested that the validation of their risk-taking activities was a matter of course.[59]

Separating the inflation cousins

The Federal Reserve's policies supported a rapid increase of asset values. As the financial sector woke up from Volcker's gut punch, it was presented with a world of opportunities. The Volcker shock had done nothing to disable banks' liability management strategies, and the deregulation of the Carter and Reagan administrations in fact made it far easier for banks to source funds in the open market. Levels of leverage grew rapidly, and much of this credit growth financed a burgeoning stock market. After the capital gains reduction in 1978, new stock issues had shot up, and they did so again after another reduction in 1981.[60] The Carter administration had introduced the 401(k) to subsidize pension savings, and Reagan had relaxed the rules for making tax-deductible contributions, turning it into a "a universal savings vehicle."[61] The number of Americans with an Individual Retirement Account, and the value of savings held in those accounts, exploded.[62]

The stock market rally of the mid-1980s underpinned many schemes for which the era would become notorious, such as the predatory dealmaking and buy-out culture portrayed in books like *Barbarians at the Gate* and movies like *Wall Street*.[63] Many practices that have all the appearances of corruption, such as corporate stock buybacks, were made legal at that time.[64]

Despite several years of stormy market conditions and rapid asset price growth, inflation did not re-emerge. That asset prices and consumer prices were different things had been clear for a while: what politicians and policymakers of all stripes wanted was credit growth and rising asset prices without price inflation. The problem was that they had no way of achieving this. Volcker thought of price inflation and asset inflation as "cousins" – different but closely related things.[65] And so he remained cautious, continuing to accept a high price for his still fragile achievement and keeping interest rates high even as unemployment was slow to come down.[66]

The handover of Federal Reserve leadership from Paul Volcker to Alan Greenspan marked a shift in approach. In an important sense, continuity dominated. As became clear almost immediately with the Federal Reserve's response to the 1987 stock market crash, the Greenspan Fed was fully committed to ensuring that the financial safety net functioned smoothly and could be efficiently extended as and when needed.[67] And Greenspan was even more of an inflation hawk than Volcker – which is why he persisted with the kind of overtight policies he had inherited from Volcker.

However, Greenspan's worldview was different, and the conception of asset and consumer price inflation as "cousins" had no place in it. Volcker still had a broadly institutional understanding of how money worked, and it prevented him from imagining that financial markets could expand indefinitely without this at some point showing up as general economic instability. By contrast, Greenspan's conception of money was orthodox to the core, fully structured by the parable of the village fair. For him, money was a simple measure, and inflation could be measured by tracking the prices of a basket of commodities consumed by the average family – period.

Like others, Greenspan couldn't initially look at financial market gyrations without some apprehension. But such concern had no integral place in his worldview, where asset prices and consumer prices occupied different compartments. As reality appeared to confirm that worldview during the next decade, Greenspan would gradually abandon reservations and extend the financial safety net as system risk considerations dictated. It was an acceptable price to pay for broad-based prosperity, and it seemed to have no bearing on the Federal Reserve's ability to safeguard the neutrality of America's money supply.[68]

Greenspan would be a key force behind the bailout of the savings and loan industry. The deregulation of that sector at the start of the decade had created as many new problems as it had solved old ones. These institutions now had to pay much higher rates on deposits even as many of their assets were still long-term and locked in at low rates.[69] Their backs against the wall, they threw caution to the wind, investing in junk bonds and other schemes at odds with the wholesome image of the sector.

The Reagan administration was unwilling to deal with the growing problem. But the number of failures continued to grow and eventually pushed the Federal Savings and Loan Insurance Corporation into insolvency, so forcing the Bush administration to act.[70] The Financial Institutions Reform, Recovery, and Enforcement Act of 1989 authorized use of public funds for restructuring thrifts and it subsumed them under the authority of the FDIC.[71] But the resources that the Act made available were insufficient and further action was soon required.

This was a pivotal moment in the development of the bail-out state. Congress balked. Many legislators were concerned about the electoral optics of rewarding irresponsible behavior by financial institutions, and there existed considerable appetite for restricting the government's ability to organize bailouts or even to ban them altogether.[72] The first version of the bill would not have allowed any exceptions to the rule of least-cost resolution of failing firms, for all intents and purposes tying the hands of financial authorities.[73]

In testimony before Congress, Federal Reserve Governor John LaWare articulated the danger that the representatives of the American people were courting. By refusing to let financial authorities bail out banks when needed, Congress was exposing the American public at large to the threat of system failure, he argued. He likened the failure of a too-big-to-fail bank to:

> a meltdown of a nuclear generating plant like Chernobyl. The ramifications of that kind of a failure are so broad and happen with such lightning speed that you cannot after the fact control them. It runs the risk of bringing down other banks, corporations, disrupting markets, bringing down investment banks along with it. That is the kind of situation in which we have to be able to intervene to protect the innocent, the people who have nothing to do with the situation that creates the collapse, but who are sucked into the maelstrom.[74]

Congress's refusal to acknowledge that the financial sector held the American public to ransom would lead the country to ruin.

What was no longer thinkable, even for politicians otherwise flinching at the prospect of appearing to be in the pockets of the financial industry, was the idea that the fortunes of the American people and the banking sector might be disentangled, let alone that this was the right moment to do so. That would have required an ability to see past the urgency of the moment and a willingness to reconnect to the legacy of radicalized Keynesianism that saw public planning and resourcing as the only real alternative to the socialization of private risk. Following Humphrey–Hawkins, however, Democrats had spent the 1980s suppressing such ideological currents in hopes of regaining their electability.

A compromise was brokered that allowed for exceptions to the rule of least-cost resolution in cases of "system risk" considerations – an expression that would go on to serve as code for the number of hostages a bank has been able to take and the degree of blackmail power it enjoyed as a result.[75] Even as it allowed politicians to claim they had held the line on bailouts, it gave regulators a great deal of discretionary authority. The FDIC Improvement Act of 1991 in effect consolidated the too-big-to-fail doctrine, providing banks with a powerful set of incentives to step up their efforts to secure too-big-to-fail status.[76]

7

Asset-Driven Growth

Three successive rounds of defeat in the presidential elections had led to a great deal of anxious introspection in the Democratic Party. Already in 1982, the newly created House Democratic Caucus Committee on Party Effectiveness published a report stressing the need to reorient the Party's program away from redistribution and towards growth, in particular through investment in the high-tech sector.[1] In 1985 the Democratic Leadership Council (DLC) was founded, and its prominence grew after the defeat of Dukakis in the 1988 presidential election.

New Democrats shared a conviction that "old" Democratic politics in the New Deal mold had run its course, and that a new politics needed to make active use of the flexibility and innovation of the market.[2] As the Democrats' 1992 election program put it: "We reject both the do-nothing government of the last 12 years as well as the big government theory that says we can hamstring business and tax and spend our way to prosperity."[3]

In reality, Reagan's supply-side economics had essentially been a more bravado version of the tax cutting that had been pursued by Keynesians since the war.[4] Until the 1970s,

Republicans had been known as the balanced budget party.[5] Reagan too had long cared about balancing the budget as much as about cutting taxes.[6] But, seeing the power of Proposition 13, he committed to running on massive tax cuts for the American people, looking to the Laffer curve to square the objective of aggressively cutting taxes with the goal of balancing the budget.[7] Reagan's plan for a sweeping general income tax cut had a degree of popular appeal that the Keynesian Swiss cheese approach, with its ambitions for applying precise incentives, had never enjoyed. In fact, it had taken considerable pressure from business to force the tax cuts back into a Keynesian mold.[8]

The "do-nothing" accusation was more apt when it came to the Reagan administration's industrial policy, which soon became a series of few-strings-attached corporate subsidies.[9] The actual objectives of public–private partnerships were often not even clearly specified,[10] leading even as conservative a character as Bob Dole to express concern that they would end up being "just another boon to big business."[11] Such concerns were held so widely that most of Reagan's attempts to introduce comprehensive legislation in this area during the 1980s faltered.[12]

While the New Democrats contrasted their own economic policy thinking to that of the Reagan administration, they were even more fond of contrasting their project to the 1970s. Aided by a lack of historical memory or perhaps active amnesia, they never even so much as acknowledged the long history of Keynesian supply-side thinking. They invented a past where tax-and-spend liberalism had reigned supreme and caused galloping inflation until it had been unseated by the right.

The 1970s were held up as a cautionary tale of what could happen when the American people came to harbor unrealistic expectations. As a reading of DLC founder Al From's account of that era makes clear, the New Democrats saw inflation as the main threat to the public interest in a strong economy, and they viewed wage pressures and deficit spending as the key drivers of inflation.[13]

Like each previous generation of Democrats since the New Deal, New Democrats "discovered" that a purely distributional politics was no longer viable and that economic growth was needed to solve social problems.[14] But they nonetheless gave this idea a radical twist. Wage growth could only ever be sustainable when it was an *outcome* of economic growth. Any public policy that took lowering unemployment or increasing wages as its direct objective was bound to fan inflation. In the new way of thinking, the only acceptable earnings increase was the result of human capital formation.[15] It was the era of the knowledge economy, and the power of training and education featured prominently in the New Democrats' fantasy of the transubstantiation of labor into capital.[16]

Only high productivity increases could justify high wage rises. Old industries were largely considered a lost cause in that respect.[17] With economic competition increasingly global, trying to protect the jobs and pay levels of unionized, low-skilled industrial workers was a losing game. Protecting the living wages of low-skilled workers was simply not a viable proposition in a global economy. Good jobs with high wages could only be produced by new industries, driven by new technologies, high levels of investment, and high rates of productivity growth.[18]

New Keynesians

In the new thinking, the government's role was to encourage the emergence of such new growth sectors, which would produce higher wages not through the faux solidarity of taxing and public spending but on the back of productivity increases.[19] By investing in human capital, education, and infrastructure, the government could provide the framework for the emergence of growth synergies and productivity increases that could accommodate wage increases. New Keynesians accepted the critique of Keynesian inflationism, but they retained a broad concern with market imperfections and built on that a rationale for supply-side interventions.[20] All government spending was to be approached with consideration for how it would affect the economy's supply-side structure.

The Clinton administration had a supply-side program from day one.[21] The 1992 campaign program had drawn on Robert Reich's work on the role of human capital in growing the economy and improving international competitiveness, and Clinton put Reich in charge of his economic policy transition team.[22] As Clinton formulated the administration's economic mission to Reich: "Macroeconomics is important, but micro is critical – productivity, education, job training, management–labor relations. So the whole thrust will be new and different."[23]

But this still required spending, of course. Clinton's supply-side revitalization program was challenged not just by Republicans, but also by key members of his own administration. Robert Rubin had been appointed head of the newly created National Economic Council, a new agency created to coordinate the implementation of Clinton's program across different departments and agencies and outranked the bastion of old-school Keynesianism, the Council of Economic Advisers.

Rubin had enjoyed a long career on Wall Street and, as a former bond trader, he was highly attuned to the possibility that fiscal adventures could fuel inflation and undermine market confidence.[24] The success of the administration's economic program, Rubin argued, was dependent on private investment picking up. Additional federal borrowing for public spending would jeopardize that prospect. The new administration had inherited large deficits, and Rubin encouraged Clinton to get out in front of the problem by cutting back on public expenditure.[25]

Rubin was supported by other key players in the economic policy team of the new administration, including his protégé Larry Summers and Treasury Secretary Lloyd Bentsen. People like Summers had come to fully accept the logic of the NAIRU, which marked the transition from the neo-Keynesianism of the postwar era to the New Keynesianism. The problem was that there was no way to know in advance what the level of the NAIRU was – only the markets knew. And if you ever under-shot, you would set off a self-reinforcing spiral of inflationary expectations. So, it was of utmost importance to always err on the side of caution and to stay above that unknown number. Greenspan reinforced the Rubin side, impressing on Clinton the importance of managing the markets' expectations about the future course of inflation.[26]

Pushback came from Labor Secretary Robert Reich and CEA chair Laura Tyson, who felt that, without the possibility of spending on public infrastructure, the distinctiveness and progressive credentials of the Clinton economic program would become hard to discern.[27] But the Rubin team had the upper hand. A world of growth synergies and wage increases was certainly on offer, they assured Clinton. But imprudent management of the public finances would kill the goose of private investment before it could lay its golden eggs.

As Lukas Haffert and Philip Mehrtens show, the commit-ment to fiscal austerity is not to be seen as a neoliberal import.[28] New Keynesianism offered its own, distinctive model of fiscal consolidation: getting control of deficits in order to open up spending capacity over the longer term. In the New Keynesian playbook, fiscal restraint is a *precondition* for growth and public investment. Generosity could only follow from prior restraint.[29]

The model of "austerity now, investment later" guided Clinton's attempt to appease the Rubin camp while keeping alive his supply-side program. But the absence of an objec-tive economic timeline meant that anything was up for political negotiation. By the time the Omnibus Budget and Reconciliation Act of 1993 was a reality, much of the investment that Clinton had scheduled for future years had been whittled down.

In scaling back its spending plans, the Clinton administration offered up social programs, including employment and poverty programs targeted at what it itself had so prominently identified as the urban problem.[30] Other things stayed, including an extensive range of public–private partnerships and enterprise zones ("Empowerment Zones") that were meant to elicit private investment through capital gains exemptions and weakened enforcement of industrial standards.[31] The less politically viable plans for substantial public investment seemed, the more important it was to position remaining programs as *incentives* that could be *leveraged* with private capital.

The lack of fiscal stimulus meant that an already long recession dragged on. Unemployment had come down from its mid-1980s peak but appeared to have stabilized at an unacceptably high level. It was a major factor allowing Republicans to take control of Congress with the 1994 midterm elections, which drove the final nail into Clinton's hopes for eventually increasing public spending.[32]

Reich lamented that Clinton had built himself a "conceptual prison."[33] He had made many appointments to signal that he could be trusted on economic matters and had broken with "old" Democratic ways. Those advisers would consistently veto "new" Democratic policies when they required public spending, and over time Clinton internalized their concerns. Initially Clinton had been reluctant to abandon his supply-side investment program, famously expressing his outrage at the idea that the success of his administration was somehow in the hands of "a bunch of fucking bond traders."[34] But his later comment that "I have a jobs program and my jobs program is deficit reduction" was a clear statement of changed priorities.[35]

The Federal Reserve came to enjoy an extraordinary degree of institutional autonomy. That the management of the nation's money should not be a matter for the American people or their elected officials became the common sense of the public sphere. Even as he grew frustrated with Greenspan's single-minded concern with inflation, Clinton felt he had no choice but to reappoint him – any other course of action would have exposed his administration to accusations of political interference with the management of the markets.[36]

The most radical intervention that Clinton permitted himself in relation to the Federal Reserve consisted in the appointment of economists with avowed liberal political affinities, including future Federal Reserve chair and Treasury Secretary Janet Yellen. Her colleague Alan Blinder soon found himself at the center of a media storm after he stressed in a speech at Jackson Hole that the Federal Reserve needed to balance its inflation and employment targets. That was of course its literal, official mandate. But by the mid-1990s, the employment objective had been fully pushed out of the frame by the inflation objective.[37] Blinder soon resigned, correctly perceiving that there was no longer any place for more old-fashioned Keynesians in the administration.

The asset economy

After a series of steep rate rises, Greenspan's grip relaxed. He stopped raising and then began cautiously lowering interest rates. As growth picked up and unemployment dropped, inflation did not return. And so, he stayed the course.[38] By the time Clinton was up for re-election, the economy was showing signs of dynamism not seen for a long time.[39]

To the Clinton administration, it confirmed the essential correctness of their program.[40] And so it continued down the same path, ensuring that any new expenditure was matched by cutbacks elsewhere,[41] and going beyond what any old-school Republican could have dreamt by passing the Balanced Budget Act.[42] The recipe of fiscal austerity subsequently morphed into a fantasy of a government without debt. In the presidential election of 2000, Al Gore ran on an economic program that included a plan to pay down the entire federal debt during the next decade.

Many on the left have viewed this as capitulation to neo-liberalism. But that doesn't allow us to make sense of the tremendous excitement the new regime elicited. This was not the dour austerity of the Eisenhower years. New Democrats viewed themselves as joyously reaping the rewards that came with growing up and accepting that the American govern-ment, like any other organization or household, needs to pay its bills.

Even Blinder came around to this way of thinking. In the book on the 1990s experience that he and Janet Yellen co-authored, they drew the lesson that fiscal austerity does not have to be an obstacle to economic growth but is in fact a cru-cial precondition for stimulating private investment.[43] What this pro-investment climate did, in the estimation of the New Democrats, was to encourage productivity-boosting invest-ment in high-tech sectors, above all new information and communication technologies associated with the boundless promise of the internet. This was at the heart of announce-ments of a New Economy, an idea that Gore had picked up from Silicon Valley gurus.[44]

It took to a new level the paradoxical combination of credu-lity and skepticism embedded in the economic style. Whereas simple measures having a direct and obvious beneficial effect in people's everyday lives were subjected to endless cost-benefit analysis, the projections supplied by finance capital – supported by Silicon Valley narratives about growth syner-gies, network effects, and the power of information technology – were taken at face value.

New Keynesians viewed the separation of asset price and consumer price dynamics not as a historically specific way of organizing the economic world, but as the victory of economic reason. Social scientists too started to see a financialized world, even if they contrasted it, critically, to an era when the American economy had made real, useful things.

In reality, the 1990s were neither uniquely productive nor especially unproductive. Measures of productivity increased along their secular, steadily upwards path, neither displaying the magic of the information economy nor post-industrial stagnation. What kept inflation at bay was the fact that wages flatlined. The Reagan administration had severely weakened the legal position and political power of organized labor, and unionization rates had plummeted. While striking a broadly labor-friendly pose, the Clinton administration actively built on that Reagan legacy.

In a political context where the employment guarantee had become unthinkable, the predictable effect of Clinton's grand bargain with Republicans to end "welfare as we know it" was to make a larger number of poor Americans compete for a given number of jobs. Moreover, the management of the reserve army became intricately tied up with the dramatic growth of the prison population. This was the other face of the New Democrats' Third Way philosophy. The shiny exterior of technological solutionism encased a core of intensified, often race-based exploitation.

Greenspan's famous "irrational exuberance" comment was the last gasp of the concern that a credit-fueled dynamic of asset price growth was a potentially dangerous source of instability.[45] He quickly sounded the retreat and went back to lowering rates.[46] The fact that roaring financial markets did not cause inflation did not remain a simple empirical fact – it morphed into a worldview. Expressing the view that credit expansion could be a potential cause of inflation was increasingly viewed as a sign of economic illiteracy. The idea that capital gains were anything other than the present value of future growth, involving at least partly the redistribution of existing claims on property, had become unthinkable in mainstream discourse.

The middle-class Americans who benefitted from strong growth of their home values and stock portfolios tended to reinvest their earnings, so further driving up the prices of assets rather than consumer goods.[47] Legislative and regulatory changes had made defined-benefit plans unwieldy and expensive to run, and the forward march of the defined contribution 401(k) was unstoppable.[48] By the end of the century, half of the American population had money in the stock market. "Baby boomers dreamed of retiring at 50 while Gen Xers invented their very own version of the American Dream: wealth without working at all."[49]

But the main route whereby ordinary Americans enjoyed the fruits of the bailout state and the asset economy was via increases in the value of their homes.[50] Until the 1990s, homeownership had been a middle-class phenomenon; it was premised on the ability to save from one's wage to serve a mortgage. The government and the financial sector helped by allowing such households to leverage those savings and so to build up property. Now, with capital gains seemingly a certain prospect, homeownership *itself* became the ticket to the middle class – *especially* as stable employment and a living wage had become distant prospects for many. What Keynes had characterized as a "serious situation" had become the basis for continuing the Keynesian project.

The asset state

In the wake of the bailout of the thrift crisis, mortgage lending had become comprehensively securitized.[51] The government put major pressure on Fannie Mae, Freddie Mac (created in 1970 to promote competition in the subsidized mortgage sector) and the other government-sponsored enterprises to support home purchases by lower-income groups. They responded by lowering lending standards, requiring smaller down payments and lower credit scores for mortgage insurance, and by expanding opportunities for securitization.[52] But the profit motive played a central role in the public-to-private transmission channel, and it was often not clear where social policy ended and private greed began. Fannie Mae and Freddie Mac, in Ralph Nader's words, "managed to pick up the roughshod tactics of the private corporate world and at the same time cling tightly to the federal government's deepest and most lucrative welfare troughs."[53]

The relationship of African Americans to the housing and mortgage system underwent a structural shift – from exclusion to what Keeanga-Yamahtta Taylor has termed "predatory inclusion."[54] Whereas in previous decades mortgage providers had redlined specific geographical areas to identify the groups they would not lend to, they now used similar techniques to identify the groups they could charge high rates and fees – and were therefore often *particularly* eager to lend to.[55] The profitability of such business was justified in terms of the higher level of risk associated with such loans, even as the fully securitized mortgage lending system meant that such risks could in fact be easily passed on.

As part of the Clinton administration's general rollback of social programs, federal spending on public housing and assistance for low-income housing collapsed.[56] At the same time, the value of tax breaks for homeowners grew dramatically.[57] The welfare state did not disappear or wither, as neoliberals had intended and progressives had feared. Instead, public expenditure was comprehensively reoriented from the socialization of demand to the subsidization of ownership.

Previous supply-side make-overs of Keynesianism had already ensured that Democrats understood that governments should primarily incentivize private actors, refraining as much as possible from directly doing things themselves. Such subsidization now increasingly took the form of complex public–private financing constructions to ensure public funds were spent in full accordance with the priorities of private interests, who were given endless opportunity for rating and vetoing government actions.[58]

The boundaries between finance and other policy areas became blurry. And the more the markets constrained public authority, the more naïve it appeared to imagine that government could do anything without endorsement from a consortium of banks. The management consultants who perfected the jargon of the economic style guided the roll-out of public–private partnerships as far as the eye could see. The welfare state was transformed into "a confusion of public–private partnerships and back-door financing techniques."[59] As even inexpensive but vital social programs were gratuitously undone, the value of "tax expenditures" for the propertied class grew dramatically.[60]

Although these submerged institutions thrived on opacity,[61] we should not overstate the intrinsic difficulty of conceptually unraveling the daisy-chains of contractual obligations whereby public authority was harnessed to private interests. The far more significant problem was that critical observers were captivated by another way of seeing, one that was preoccupied with expanding markets and a retreating state. Whenever they encountered evidence for the undiminished importance of public resources, they took this to indicate the persistent vitality of institutions organizing social protection.[62] What they did not see sharply was the qualitative *transformation* of the fiscal structure of the state and comprehensive *repurposing* of public expenditure. The priorities of public budgeting were increasingly shaped by the financialized economy in which it operated.

The success of the Clinton administration added to the disorientation among critics whose mental framework said that an assault of markets on public things should have shown up as mass immiseration.[63] That Third Way politics was exceptionally rich in rhetoric was evident to even its most ardent supporters, but even after those layers had been peeled back, there remained an undeniable core of middle-class prosperity. The idea of trickle-down economics has always been a cruel joke when it comes to wages. But in the area of asset politics the trickle-down formula has enjoyed much greater plausibility. The logic of bailouts has been at the basis of a new middle-class politics that revolved around access to capital gains.[64]

Even as Reich withdrew from the political fray with a sense of betrayal and resignation, the second Clinton administration viewed itself as fully living up to the promise that the president had made to his old friend. The rising tide would occur through direct participation in the returns on capital, not by draining capital of its dynamism or by stunting growth.

Clinton-era economic policy developed a deep skepticism towards any public scheme designed to improve the lives of Americans in their capacity as wage earners. That wage growth conflicted with other objectives of macroeconomic management had been clear for a long time. But, as wage growth was the main route through which most of the American population could attain a higher standard of living, Keynesian economists in the Democratic administrations of the 1960s and 1970s could still think of it as a legitimate objective, fraught and contradictory as it was. Kennedy would not have imagined that his "rising tide" could be achieved without wage growth.

By Clinton's time, the outlook had changed: any wage increase that was not an unforced outcome of market-driven productivity growth, extended by employers on the basis of their own interests in recruiting the best human capital and incentivizing employees to perform at peak ability, was considered unwelcome, an inflationary tax on economic growth. Generalized wage growth came to be seen as the enemy of the rising tide.

The middle-class politics of the 1990s rested almost solely on widespread asset price increases. Edward Wolff summarizes the middle-class logic of the asset economy thus: "while household income virtually stagnated for the average American household from 1989 to 2007, median net worth and especially median financial resources grew strongly."[65] New Democrats and New Keynesians, it seemed, had finally found the holy grail of Keynesianism: non-inflationary growth.

The Great Moderation

The revitalization of middle-class politics came at a price: the growth of inequality, as well as its concentration along racial lines.[66] The consolidation of a core middle class went hand-in-hand with rapid polarization at the top and the bottom of the socio-economic structure.[67] Households who were unable to participate in the asset economy were fully dependent on a fragmenting labor market that offered neither stable employment nor decent wages.

The Clinton administration's embrace of fiscal discipline largely relieved the Fed of having to police the government on that score. It allowed Greenspan to focus fully on backstopping financial markets and promoting asset inflation without fear of price inflation. The "Greenspan put" placed a floor under asset markets, providing liquidity assistance and regulatory forbearance whenever markets threatened to dip dangerously.[68] As Christopher Leonard summarizes, Greenspan "chose to control price inflation, ignore asset inflation, and then step in and bail out the system when asset prices collapsed."[69]

That this did not produce any major conflict with Greenspan's self-image as a libertarian, presumably detesting nothing more than unearned public handouts, was a sign of just how deeply such derisking operations had become embedded in the routine operations of financial governance, and how easy they were to overlook for those who were minded to do so. Indeed, Greenspan managed to restore some of Martin's innocence, to all appearances genuinely believing that the institution he headed up was working first and foremost to ensure the neutrality of the nation's money supply by leaning against the economic winds, without bias or favor.

The foundational asymmetries at the heart of financial governance were certainly legible to financial markets actors, however – that was the only way the new regime of expectations could work. To them, it was clear that the central bank provided more fuel at times of headwind than it applied the brakes when banks had the wind in their backs.[70] The managers of the American economy did not of course deny that financial bubbles occurred every now and then. Their point was not that irrational exuberance could *never* happen, just that policymakers or politicians were not in a position to second-guess the markets on this issue. On the rare occasions that markets failed to self-correct in time, the only thing to do was to "mop up after" the event.[71] Bubbles were "epiphenomena that could be dealt with on an ad hoc basis" because they did not "lead to major changes in advanced economies' macroperformance."[72]

Constraining financial markets was a fool's errand, akin to a neurotic's feverish attempts to gain control over every minute detail while missing out on the rewards of a fully lived life. If that sounds like the height of neoliberal delirium, we should remember that this way of seeing the world was being actively legitimated in the academy. In New Keynesian models, the governance of money is an ethereal game of expectations management – Keynes' beauty contest, somehow producing not speculative instability but a neutral monetary standard.

These models conspicuously excluded credit-driven asset prices and balance sheet leverage as constitutive components of economic reality. Such phenomena were considered derivative – not, as in Minsky's model, the main drivers of the capitalist economy, but primarily indexes reflecting economic fundamentals. To the extent that the movement of asset prices presented a problem that needed managing, it would show up as consumer price instability, that is, as inflation.[73]

Ben Bernanke would become the embodiment of the new consensus.[74] His research on the Great Depression had taught him about the dangers of financial instability and the over-riding priority of stabilization as the objective of financial policymaking. He had interpreted the meltdown of that decade through the lens of a fully domesticated Keynesianism, which thought of banks as credit intermediaries and assumed rational foresight. Bernanke's work offered, as Charles Kindleberger put it in a letter to him, "a most ingenious solution to a non-problem": financial instability only becomes an intellectual surprise after one has adopted the implausible postulates of New Keynesianism and thoroughly eradicated balance sheet leverage and the speculative drivers of investment from one's worldview.[75]

Bernanke built on his early work to develop a general theory of how central banks should largely *ignore* stock markets or asset prices and focus on inflation targeting alone.[76] As a member of the Federal Reserve Board, he brought into popular circulation the phrase the Great Moderation, expressing the conviction that problems of financial instability had been largely overcome and that the expectational fine-tuning abilities of the Federal Reserve were the best guarantee for stable, non-inflationary growth.[77] And he would be chair of the Federal Reserve when, several years later, that institution was faced with the worst financial crisis since the 1930s. As Bernanke's memoir of his own time as Federal Reserve chair makes clear, this set of convictions comfortably survived his own involvement in the rescue operations that were required following the near-collapse of the American financial system in 2007–8.[78]

Expanding the bailout state

The piece of New Deal regulation that survived the longest was the Glass–Steagall separation of deposit taking and stock trading. Previous administrations had not been responsive to lobbying on this particular reform, and their ability to stave off such efforts had been facilitated by the fact that the financial sector did not pose a united front. Commercial banks and investment banks were very interested in playing on the other's terrain but also had a vested interest in maintaining barriers to entry in their own sphere.

But with an administration drunk on the magic of finance, the climate changed.[79] Increasingly, the notion that banks should not be mixing their management of the American public's deposits with the aggressively profit-driven business of securities trading seemed at best quaint, more likely fundamentally misguided.

It is often argued that the repeal of Glass–Steagall through the Financial Services Modernization Act of 1999 only formalized a fait accompli. But, as Richard Barton argues, that is to greatly understate the significance of that legislative change.[80] It made it far easier and cheaper for institutions to merge their lines of business, and the result was a rapid growth of integrated financial conglomerates. Enormous in size, their operations were knitted deeply into the fabric of America's financial infrastructure.[81]

These banks were not just too big or interconnected to fail. They were also "too big to discipline adequately": regulators simply did not have the resources or knowledge to police banks of such size and complexity adequately, and so they came to rely heavily on banks' own risk models and on information generated by banks' internal governance processes.[82] As regulation and business became even more deeply interwoven, supervisory authorities became invested in the survival of the institutions they regulated. When instability hit, regulators had every reason to grant banks as much forbearance as possible.[83] Financial support and regulatory accommodation came with ever fewer strings attached.[84] Large institutions could simply count on a degree of leniency that small banks could not.[85]

All this created huge incentives for banks to become as big as possible and to get their fingers in as many different pies as they could. The number of banking institutions had already dropped significantly since the early 1980s, but even as profit levels were up, wave after wave of mergers meant that the historically fragmented institutional landscape of American finance became dominated by an ever-smaller number of ever-larger institutions that enjoyed tremendous blackmail power.[86]

Too-big-to-fail morphed from "a status conferred by government regulators on large banks that were economically important but insolvent" to "a status achieved by a complex of large banking firms on the basis of its direct and indirect control over the day-to-day operations of core financial markets."[87] It was no longer a discrete, stand-alone policy of mopping up after the fact, but a preemptive institutional regime around which large banks, and other actors in their orbit, could form expectations and build their strategies.[88]

As much as they would talk about moral hazard when the situation called for it, politicians did not necessarily view this state of affairs as a problem. These financial behemoths could finance the American Dream and secure the continued delivery of non-inflationary growth – it was on such grounds that Clinton, Greenspan, and Rubin approved the creation of the financial giant Citigroup even before the relevant laws had been repealed.[89] And when crisis hit and regulators were forced to bail out, nothing prevented those same politicians from rhetorically validating the feelings of angry taxpayers by denouncing bailouts and the moral hazard that gave rise to them.[90]

8

Bailouts and Austerity

Following the dot-com meltdown in 2001, Greenspan started lowering interest rates to maintain home values and so to cushion the impact of the stock market crash.[1] The large universal banks that had been created following the repeal of Glass–Steagall were crucial in driving the growth of credit, confirming in the eyes of many the essential correctness of earlier decisions.[2] The Bush administration doubled down on the growth of mortgage credit, underscoring the conspicuous continuity between conservative and progressive discourse of homeownership.[3] The homeownership rate had grown rapidly during the 1990s, so that the gains of the property price boom of early 2000s were widely distributed.[4]

By the Bush administration's own admission, it was entirely unconcerned with issues of affordability. As Treasury Secretary John Snow put it, "The Bush administration took a lot of pride that homeownership had reached historic highs . . . what we forgot in the process was that it has to be done in the context of people being able to afford their house."[5] Property appreciation was not built on wage growth; it was a substitute for it.[6] To the Bush economic policy team, spreading opportunity in homeownership was a natural complement to their signature fiscal policy of tax cuts for the upper class.

Inflation did not return, and so the Federal Reserve was happy to let mortgage credit grow. But there were signs of trouble. The rate of homeownership rate still increased, but markedly more slowly than during the previous decade.[7] A growing proportion of new credit was for refinancing or upgrading, doing little but push up the prices of existing homes.[8] At the lower end of the market, new entry was increasingly dependent on the possibility of drastically lowering lending standards, and it was associated with highly exploitative terms. Encouraged by regulators and legislators, the share of "subprime" lending in the total mortgage market grew rapidly, accounting for about one-fifth of all mortgages by 2004.[9]

Since 2004, the Federal Reserve had been increasing rates to take some pressure out of the mortgage bubble. But it had been entirely uninterested in acting, alone or in concert with other regulators, on growing evidence that subprime lending was fast becoming a predatory industry. The sector no longer served to open up homeownership to vulnerable constituencies, and instead offered hugely profitable ways to generate fees from the issuance of mortgages that were supported by little servicing capacity.[10] Such subprime lending was far more prevalent among African American groups than it was for whites, even after controlling for income, education, and other variables.[11]

Deploying the bailout state

In mid-2007, it became clear that many subprime debts would never be repaid. The scale of the problem had taken considerable time to become apparent. Because of the way such debt had been sliced, diced, and repackaged to create securitized assets, it had spread far and wide. Reversing the attempt to raise rates that it had embarked on since 2004, the Federal

Reserve started cutting interest rates. But the infection ran deep, and toxic debt could be hiding anywhere.

Bush was resolved not to go down in history as the president who had let the Second Great Depression happen, and bailouts were on the table right from the start.[12] Regulators worked with banks to develop a variety of ad hoc schemes to contain pressure where needed. They swapped bad debt with Treasury bills that banks could then use as collateral to access financing,[13] essentially "let[ting] banks and investment banks borrow against securities no one wanted to buy," in the words of Hank Paulson, Treasury Secretary in the Bush administration.[14] When investment bank Bear Stearns experienced a run on its repo liabilities, the Federal Reserve recognized the possibility of the fire spreading and engulfing the critically important repo market as a whole, and so it provided large guarantees to facilitate its takeover by J.P. Morgan.[15] Volcker commented that the Federal Reserve's actions "extend[ed] to the very edge of its lawful and implied powers."[16]

The Housing and Economic Recovery Act was passed to provide a huge amount of additional government guarantees for the US mortgage market. But by September of 2008, the challenges that Fannie Mae and Freddie Mac faced had become so severe that direct intervention was required. Paulson, who had spent more than three decades working at investment bank Goldman Sachs and considered himself "a firm believer in free markets,"[17] had no compunction proposing "that we seize control of the companies, fire their bosses, and prepare to provide up to $100 billion of capital support for each."[18] That is the path the administration went down, supplementing it with bespoke lending facilities and a program for buying mortgage-backed securities.[19]

Next up was Lehman Brothers, which was highly exposed to the subprime market and suffering heavy losses. The Federal Reserve and the Treasury initially tried to take the same approach as they had with Bear Stearns, that is, supporting a takeover with government guarantees. But no buyer showed up.[20] Lehman's troubles ran deep, and only government recapitalization of the firm could have made it an appealing proposition for a buyer. At that point in time, such a move seemed a bridge too far. The Federal Reserve and the Treasury had long trampled on the specific precepts of the Bagehot doctrine by lending against assets whose value was fundamentally uncertain. But explicitly taking public ownership stakes in a failing firm in order to protect existing owners was a different, and potentially much more politically hazardous, proposition.

The subsequent failure of Lehman exposed the depth and breadth of the sources of instability, forcing the Federal Reserve to abandon any remaining caution and to step up the level of support it offered for banks' balance sheets.[21] Congress approved a massive bailout package, the Toxic Asset Relief Program, better known by its acronym TARP.[22]

It was under these tumultuous circumstances that Barack Obama was elected to be the next American president. Many progressives drew parallels with Roosevelt, who had also come into office amidst an economic crisis of generational significance, and they declared the start of a second New Deal. Hopes for political change and a return to an original Keynesianism were further animated by Obama's racial background as well as the fact that he had some distance from the rhetorical style of Clintonism.[23]

But Clintonism had become the air that Democrats breathed. Following defeat of Hillary Clinton in the Democratic presidential primaries, Obama recruited much of his staff from her past advisers.[24] Biden was the figure most conspicuously marking the continuity of Democratic politics from the Carter through the Clinton to the Obama administration. He became the driving force behind a series of appointments that seemed designed to dash the hopes that progressives had projected onto Obama's candidacy.

The National Economic Council was filled with "a team of Rubins,"[25] and Larry Summers was appointed as its head. Tim Geithner, another Rubin protégé, was appointed Treasury Secretary.[26] Others, including prominent regulators such as the (Republican) chair of the FDIC Sheila Bair, made a strong case for Volcker as Treasury Secretary, but at this point in time his neutrality and distance from the big banks had become a clear liability. Obama was interested primarily in making appointments that would reassure the markets.[27] Thus, he populated his administration with "folks who understand the financial markets."[28]

And a great deal of understanding for the financial markets they would display. The starting assumption of Obama's economic team was that the Clinton administration's program had been successful because it had abandoned the kind of ambitious supply-side programs that people like Reich, and initially Clinton himself, had been most interested in. The roaring nineties had happened, in their view, because the Clinton administration had won the confidence of financial markets.

The lesson that Clinton had needed to learn after coming into office – the need to placate bond traders – was understood by Obama from day one. His administration's management of the crisis and the recovery was fully shaped by the belief that any attempt to improve the lives of ordinary people needed to go through and obtain authorization from the financial markets.

Half-hearted stimulus

The Obama administration's first order of business was to pass a stimulus bill. The American Recovery and Reinvestment Act (ARRA) offered almost $300 billion in tax cuts and half a trillion predominantly devoted to infrastructure spending, much of which was invested through public–private partnership intended to spur investment in "green" technologies.[29]

As incomprehensibly large as such amounts of money sound, prominent members of Obama's economic policy team, including CEA chair Christina Romer, considered the package far too small. Intervening decisively to prevent the financial crisis from developing into a new Depression, they argued, required a much larger public stimulus. It would result in sizeable budget deficits, but that was precisely what the economy needed, they urged. Such proposals were vetoed by Summers, Geithner, as well as Budget Director Peter Orszag, who viewed any larger intervention as threatening financial confidence and insisted that the administration needed to avoid any hint of wanting to return to tax-and-spend liberalism.[30]

The stimulus bill conspicuously did not include any significant relief for homeowners. Even as it became clear just how comprehensively the mortgage lending sector had become organized around tricking people into taking on debt they could not afford, and even as it became clear that racial minorities had been the main victims of such schemes, the idea of targeting public support directly at homeowners was just considered too radical.

There was, of course, ample opportunity to do so. As Jack Rasmus notes, "With the government – Fannie and Freddie – holding trillions of dollars in mortgage notes there was no reason why the government couldn't simply renegotiate principal and interest for homeowners facing foreclosure or in negative equity."[31] Even amidst a frontal challenge to the belief that the benefits of asset inflation could be extended indefinitely, what never found a mainstream hearing, even among Democrats, was the idea that the crisis had its roots in "the way the anti-inflation commitment had since the 1970s ruled out the public expenditures that would have been required just to start addressing the crisis of inadequate housing in US cities," in the words of Leo Panitch and Sam Gindin.[32]

At the time of the rescue of the savings and loans sector two decades earlier, it had no longer seemed possible to help people without going through the banks. But now helping banks was seen as the *only* real task, self-evidently superior to any ill-advised plan to tie the rescue packages to conditions regarding their use, let alone demands that banks change their business model in more fundamental ways. To the extent that the ARRA targeted assistance specifically to Main Street, it did so by offering tax breaks to small businesses.[33] But the amount ($30 billion) was small, and a general lack of interest in effective implementation meant that only a fraction ($4 billion) ever made it to the small businesses.[34]

Fundamentally, the Obama team just did not really believe that it could or should make the lives of ordinary people better by using the federal budget. Anything it would do in that space was just for the sake of optics. As much as the disconnect between wages and asset prices was apparent as the deeper cause of the crisis, it was just not something that the Obama administration ever made any plans to tackle.[35] The fortunes of the American middle class centrally hinged on the possibility of getting *credit* flowing again – that's where action was needed. And, in keeping with the New Keynesian faith, such action needed to take the form of public restraint, the responsible management of the public finances.

Leveraging public money

Whereas the 1990s boom had been built on a severe rationalization of American business and the consolidation of the financial sector, the bailouts that followed the 2007–9 crisis had required virtually nothing of capital.[36] It is impossible to read accounts of the era and escape the impression that the people in charge of economic policy had come to live in a bubble of their own. They seemed incapable of contemplating that the American people could have interests that were not fully encapsulated in the needs of America's too-big-to-fail complex.

Even Congress was not fully part of that bubble, and legislators soon expressed shock, feigned or genuine, at how little the massive bailout they had approved was doing to help ordinary people. Congress had not made approval of TARP funds conditional on any specific use, or indeed on any specific treatment of those who ultimately owed the mortgage debt. It was an open invitation for banks to take advantage of the expanded protections on securitized loan products while still foreclosing on mortgages.[37] It also gave the crisis leadership team the leeway to shift the program from asset purchases to recapitalization, the type of assistance for banks – partial nationalization without any concomitant increase in public control over bank activities – that had been considered a step too far during the Lehman crisis.

As Bernanke explains, trying to spend the funds as originally envisaged would simply have taken too long – the problem consisted precisely in the fact that nobody knew where exactly the bad debt was hiding.[38] The only thing they could do was to reduce general uncertainty by protecting the critical nodes of the system. But this gave rise to another issue. The $700 billion in TARP funding might have been enough for a targeted bailout, but as a general capital infusion to buffer market confidence, it was in fact a very small amount, not nearly enough to derisk all the areas that had been afflicted by severe uncertainty about asset values.[39] The only way for it to work was by serving as a baseline of security, a springboard for repairing the balance sheets of financial institutions. The taxpayers' money needed to be leveraged.[40]

An example of how such leveraging worked was the Public–Private Investment Program, designed in close collaboration with some of Wall Street's most powerful investment managers including BlackRock, who "would later manage funds under the program and stand to profit from it the most."[41] In this program, a fund manager would raise an initial sum, and on that basis the Treasury would provide a loan. The fund manager could then go to the Federal Reserve and obtain another, much larger loan.[42] With those commitments locked in, only an especially bad fund manager would be unable to source further commitments.

According to Neil Barofsky, the Treasury's special inspector general appointed to oversee the TARP program, this "'leverage on leverage' gave Wall Street a huge potential upside for profits while leaving the taxpayer on the hook for massive potential losses."[43] The government was not imposing public authority on banks. Instead, it had shown up with the public purse to participate in a game designed by banks. Like many similar programs, this one was "designed by Wall Street, for Wall Street."[44]

Barofsky reports being struck by the high level of trust that Treasury and Federal Reserve officials had in the motivation and abilities of Wall Street banks. There existed widespread faith among regulators that Wall Street banks would not take undue advantage of the rescue programs because of the "reputational risk" such behavior would entail.[45] As a result, the rescue program "replicate[d] . . . the very same flaws that had just crippled the global financial system: lax regulatory oversight, overreliance on conflicted credit-rating agencies, incomplete risk models, and an inherent trust in investors' good decision making."[46] But it wouldn't be accurate to describe this as a return to the status quo: banks had been given new, additional government guarantees shielding them from downside risk.[47]

Politicians were upset about the shift to capitalization, and even more upset as it became clear just how little banks were doing to help homeowners.[48] As one member of Congress expressed it:

We have been lied to; the American people have been lied to. We have been bamboozled; they came to us to ask for money for one thing, then used it for another. . . . they are not lending it but using it for acquisitions, using it for salaries.[49]

His anger may have been entirely real. But it also came after earlier having turned a blind eye. A dialectic of willful ignorance and righteous anger had been consolidated as the affective style of bailout capitalism.

In response to such Congressional concerns, the government announced mortgage modification and refinancing programs, which provided banks with financial incentives to adjust home loans.[50] It soon became apparent that financial institutions just did not have the infrastructure to undertake this work. Their organizations were designed for issuing and servicing large volumes of standardized loans, not for bespoke loan modifications.[51]

Nor did lenders have any real reasons to change this situation. The incentives that the program offered were simply no match for the profits that could be made from repossessing homes.[52] At each point, the administration responded to problems of implementation by increasing the voluntary nature of the program. Oversight was weak, and enforcement almost absent.[53] The programs were completely ineffective in stemming let alone reversing the foreclosure trend.[54]

The median American home lost a quarter of its value,[55] and more than a third of all mortgages went "underwater," meaning that families owed more on a home than it was worth.[56] More than 10 million American families eventually lost their homes,[57] and half of those were African American or Latinx.[58] By 2013, the cumulative percentage of home loans in foreclosure had reached 10 percent for the white population and was starting to level off. By contrast, for African American and Latinx groups, the percentage of loans in foreclosure was almost three times as high and was still rising rapidly.[59] Many minority households who had bought homes in the run-up to the crisis were dealt a blow from which they would not be able to recover and that permanently cost them a place in the middle class.[60]

When irregularities and fraudulent behavior in the foreclosure procedures of the main banks came to light, prominent voices called for a broad mortgage moratorium. The Obama administration rejected such proposals out of hand, citing the likelihood that it would introduce moral hazard into the system.[61] That was rich, of course: the same administration that was working overtime to ensure that Wall Street firms would not have to worry about their liquidity, now sounded the alarm about what might happen if it relaxed the financial discipline on homeowners. Perhaps it was aware of the hypocrisy. But since the administration had first announced plans to help struggling homeowners, the political atmosphere had changed.

Wholehearted austerity

Minimal as the Obama administration's efforts to encourage home loan modification had been, they had given right-wing commentators a powerful talking point. When CNBC reporter Rick Santelli expressed outrage that the Obama administration was "rewarding bad behavior,"[62] he threw a match into a powder keg of popular resentment. The Tea Party movement that sprang up demanded the return to an uncorrupted republic, whose government would not think to use taxpayer money to fund unearned handouts and bailouts. To this end, it demanded austerity: a tightening of the public belt.

The role of right-wing billionaires in funding the Tea Party is well-documented. But that the movement was spawned not by the trillions lavished on Wall Street but by the scraps for struggling homeowners reflected a deeper change. During the 1970s, the recognition that the state had become heavily involved in picking winners and losers had fueled demands for the democratization of the public finances. The intervening decades, shaped so deeply by the fantasy of universal capital gains through the a-political management of money, had pushed such ideas beyond the political pale. In the new ideological climate, popular misgivings about the state's role in determining economic fortunes gave rise to demands for the imposition of strict limits on its size.

The righteous anger of those who sought to recover the original promise of American freedom had no affinity with fine distinctions, and public opinion was unable to tell the difference between bailouts and fiscal stimulus, both appearing as manifestations of the same pernicious government overreach.[63] During the next years, the Tea Party would play a central role in pushing the Republican Party to the far right,[64] squashing what little remained of the administration's interest in using the public budget to improve the lives of ordinary people.

To be sure, the Obama administration had been highly receptive to the concern with austerity right from the start. The short-term splurging necessitated by extraordinary circumstances had produced a lot of bills that needed to be paid, and the money would have to be found by conservative management of the American purse.[65] It had created a bipartisan National Commission on Fiscal Responsibility and Reform, which duly warned that public debt and deficit spending would crowd out private investment, push up interest rates, and bring back inflation.

The administration wasted no time acting on the Commission's recommendations, which included deep cuts in social programs and a return to Clinton-era budget rules that required every new public expenditure to be balanced by cuts elsewhere.[66] The precise extent to which such proactive – gratuitous, some said – austerity contributed to the popular discontent from which right-wing radicalism would draw such strength is hard to say. But the administration's actions were fully premised on the belief that it made sense to require collective fasting after organizing an obscene feast for bankers, and to sacrifice widely held concerns about the state of the job market on that same altar.

The one area where the Obama administration was still strongly committed to using public resources to alleviate non-bank private hardship was unemployment, which was high and slow to come down. Time and again, the administration's attempts to extend unemployment benefits met with fierce resistance from Republicans. To extract minor concessions in this area, the administration conceded to Republican demands to make permanent the enormous tax cuts that the Bush administration had gifted the wealthiest American households, creating yet more bills that would need to be paid.[67]

Reflecting the relentless ascendancy of sabotage and hostage taking as techniques of power,[68] a radicalized Republican Party discovered that it could use the federal government's debt ceiling as a source of political leverage. In the past, raising the government's debt ceiling had been a matter of course – it was in no one's interest if the American government was forced to declare bankruptcy. But Republicans were willing to bet the house to limit the reach of the bailout state. When government borrowing was about to breach the ceiling, they would repeatedly make approval of a higher ceiling conditional on draconian cuts in a wide range of social programs.[69]

Again, to suggest that Tea Party Republicans were torpedoing programs that Obama was trying to defend would be an overstatement. The administration readily accepted that no significant funding could be directed towards job programs, small business subsidies, or indeed even infrastructure, casually rebuffing pleas from the powerful construction industry for increased federal spending.[70] In the view of the administration, the fact that such supply-side policies were not available only reinforced the cardinal importance of wielding the one sure-fire supply-side policy that it did have: deficit reduction.

9

Locked in Place

As it always had in the past, fiscal austerity meant weak growth. Business investment remained low, and unemployment high. Already by mid-2010, most foreclosures were no longer in the subprime category – most commonly, they occurred as a result of job loss.[1] To make everything worse, no one could be certain that the recession had bottomed out. The possibility that it might yet double-dip into a depression on the scale of the 1930s remained entirely real until well into the decade. For many years, pundits, politicians, and policymakers had worried about nothing but inflation. But now, the possibility of a prolonged deflation loomed.

As the Obama administration reverted to austerity policies reminiscent of the Hoover administration, it fell to the Federal Reserve to keep the economy going. Bernanke formulated the Federal Reserve's new role as follows:

> With the outlook distinctly mediocre and with no new initiatives from Congress, monetary policy became "the only game in town" for battling unemployment, to use the phrase that Paul Volcker coined in connection with fighting inflation.[2]

Volcker had discerned that the Federal Reserve was the only game in town when it came to fighting *inflation*; in his time, Bernanke understood that the Federal Reserve was the only game in town to fight *deflation*.

From around the turn of the century, the Federal Reserve had actively thought about how to deal with potential deflationary trends. As the Great Moderation seemed unbreakable, policy-makers had started wondering whether the economy's curious immunity to inflation was in part due to as-yet-unidentified deflationary forces that, under different circumstances, might manifest themselves in less agreeable ways.

It was also the time when the economic success of the Clinton administration generated a great deal of interest in proposals to pay down the entire national debt – an obvious problem for an institution that conducted its operations through the market for Treasury debt. Worries that the supply of Treasury debt would dry up were soon put to rest by the Bush admin-istration's commitment to war and tax cuts. But a scenario in which a deflationary movement would be exacerbated rather than counteracted by fiscal authorities still seemed realistic enough to merit in-depth consideration.

What were central bankers supposed to do in such a sce-nario? In a general sense, the answer was obvious: extend the safety net and flood the market with liquidity. That lesson from the 1930s had been thoroughly absorbed. But what would that look like in a situation where interest rates were already close to their natural lower bound (zero)?[3] There were some ways to increase the leeway for interest rate policy, such as paying interest on the cash reserves that banks held with the Federal Reserve, a policy that it would implement during the next decade.[4] But far greater firepower might well be needed.

An answer was found in "quantitative easing": directly purchasing large amounts of assets to support their prices. In developing this approach, the Federal Reserve could draw on the recent experience of the Japanese economy, which had stagnated during the 1990s and had been propped up by large-scale asset purchases by its central bank. The policy was labeled "unconventional," but it was so only for those who had bought into the New Keynesian fantasy of monetary policy as a game of self-anchoring expectations. In reality, the Federal Reserve's interest rate magic had always been the tip of an iceberg – the visible part of an elaborate constellation of guarantees, subsidies, and backstops that provided stability by constantly shifting resources away from critical too-big-to-fail nodes onto to the rest of the system. Quantitative easing would be a scaled-up, and inevitably more visible way of doing this.

Such discussions made occasional reference to the Federal Reserve's role in supporting the Treasury's debt funding efforts during the New Deal and World War II, holding that up as an example of the kinds of practices that the Federal Reserve might have to return to. But, as we have seen, the idea that the Federal Reserve had ever actually extricated itself from such responsibilities is highly misleading. The Federal Reserve never revoked its commitment to preventing financial instability by expanding the safety net. Instead, it found ways to counteract the inflationary effects of its support infrastructure by tightening elsewhere.

Volcker had made full use of the Federal Reserve's institutional independence, and his reset had renewed the Federal Reserve's ability to balance the inflationary and deflationary effects of its policies. The dramatically reduced power of unions and social movements had installed a semi-permanent, depressurizing leak at the heart of the economic system, and after the heyday of the asset economy in the 1990s, it became clear that this could become a problem in its own right. The Obama administration's response to the crisis had widened the leak further. The Federal Reserve's contingency plans for asset purchases were not motivated by the need to support the

Treasury's ability to borrow and spend but by the possibility of the opposite scenario, one where the country's fiscal machinery just stopped working.

The backstop state

The most significant system-level event of the financial crisis had been the freezing of the wholesale repo market, where shadow banks raise funds by issuing short-term debt. Lenders require such short-term IOUs to be collateralized because (in contrast with the IOUs I receive from my bank when I deposit money into my checking account) they are not automatically guaranteed by the government. During the subprime crisis, this market stopped working: the value of any asset that could potentially contain a sliver of subprime debt had come under suspicion, and from one moment to the next lenders were reluctant to roll over existing loans – the equivalent of a run on the bank. As funding dried up, banks were forced to cut down on credit, putting further downward pressure on asset prices and exacerbating the deleveraging dynamic. The contraction of bank balance sheets and the downward pressure on asset values reinforced each other.

Only US Treasury debt was still considered safe collateral.[5] But there was no guarantee that the creditworthiness of the American government would not also eventually be swept up in the turmoil. That possibility of comprehensive meltdown was what justified the bailouts, but the Federal Reserve did not wait long – that is, until March of 2009 – to initiate the first round of quantitative easing, purchasing more than a trillion dollars of agency debt and Treasury debt.[6] The American government became what Daniela Gabor calls a "collateral factory," providing the repo market with the same degree of public insurance that the FDIC has long provided for funds held in checking accounts.[7]

Quantitative easing was presented as a temporary measure, but during the next years, as the specter of a Second Great Depression refused to disappear, the Federal Reserve would extend and expand its asset-buying programs again and again.[8] The Federal Reserve was monetizing government obligations not to support the public budget, but to support the private creation of credit and to keep asset values afloat.[9] A century earlier, financial elites had barred the Federal Reserve from holding government debt, because they worried that it would mix money and democracy in dangerous ways. But they were now the main beneficiaries of a credit system that defied any public/private divide.[10]

The collateral factory served a global role. At an earlier point, many had hypothesized that a crisis with its roots in the American financial system would finally knock the dollar off its pedestal as the world's most undisputed symbol of value. But the crisis wrought as much devastation elsewhere as it did at home, and any remaining possibility of a major shift in global financial power disappeared as European countries embraced the austerity recipe with unrivaled intensity. The dollar's public–private partnership went global, and the Federal Reserve sat at the pinnacle of a global web of organizations that kept the blood coursing through the veins of the world economy.[11]

It did not take long for the Federal Reserve to recognize that asset purchases offered no magical fix.[12] After the first years of quantitative easing, concerns that the Federal Reserve was simply monetizing public debt could be heard – the ultimate insult to central bankers' self-image of independent experts whose knowledge and authority transcended politics.

From 2011, the Federal Reserve adjusted its approach to quantitative easing by concentrating its purchases on the long end of the Treasury market. The objective was to take away the option of lazy rentiership by lowering long-term Treasury yields and pushing investors to put their money towards riskier types of investment.[13] It accelerated the stock market recovery and set off a massive boom in asset prices that lasted for the better part of the next decade. The most affluent households benefitted handsomely, and the wealth effect for the rest of the population was minimal.[14]

Quantitative easing developed a perversely symbiotic relationship with the legislative agenda and regulatory reform initiatives that had been pursued since the crisis, which had all been billed as preventing the need for future bailouts. The Dodd–Frank Act of 2010 had created a Financial Stability Oversight Council, which could formally designate Systemically Important Financial Institutions and was tasked with coordinating their management across various agencies.[15] In the Federal Reserve, Bernanke created the Office of Financial Stability Policy and Research, which was tasked with pulling together all the expertise and capabilities scattered across the Federal Reserve and the rest of the regulatory system to lead an integrated system risk management approach.[16] System risk management was rebadged as "macroprudentialism," a regulatory ethos that vowed to no longer assess the health of financial institutions on an individual basis, but with explicit reference to their impact on overall system stability.

Macroprudential risk management used "stress testing" to model the ability of financial institutions to withstand the impact of various hypothetical adverse events. Such stress testing programs had been pioneered by Geithner's Treasury to assist with the administration of TARP funding, and it proved a useful basis for identifying vulnerabilities and calibrating support accordingly. From there, it evolved into an early warning system for financial instability. Macroprudentialism embedded this logic deeply in the operations of financial institutions.[17] The Federal Reserve placed its officers inside the largest banks,[18] where they worked with corporate officers to both identify and manage vulnerabilities, creating "a deeply incestuous relationship rife with conflicts of interest."[19]

Authorities became invested in the success of the large financial firms they regulated like never before:

> the Treasury and the Fed were in effect making it a government objective to restore bank revenue to healthy levels. The logic was inescapable. If financial stability, along with inflation control and employment, was now a key objective of economic policy, then bank profits were one of the key intermediate variables. More profit meant more strength on bank balance sheets and more stability.[20]

"Macroprudentialism" in effect became a politely coded reminder to regulators that the economic prospects of the American public were in fact held hostage by the too-big-to-fail banks. And for banks, that acknowledgment was always an incentive to ensure they cleared the too-big-to-fail threshold.

As Matthias Thiemann has demonstrated, system risk management since the Global Financial Crisis has been characterized by a systemic bias. Authorities worked to limit banks' downside exposure, but they did little to stop banks from taking full advantage of upside exposure. During downturns, regulators would work closely with banks to cover off new sources of vulnerability as they emerged. During the upswing, their efforts to prevent banks from building up highly leveraged positions were limited and perfunctory, even when it was clear that such strategies were bound to develop into sources of instability at a later date.[21]

All of this was premised on the availability of a plentiful supply of safe assets – debt issued or guaranteed by the American government and rendered fully liquid by the asset-purchasing operations and lending facilities of its central bank – that could serve as the base money of the shadow banking system. The result was a system of monetary financing without fiscal ambitions – financial stabilization undertaken with no purpose other than the expanded reproduction of the too-big-to-fail banking complex itself.[22] The monetization of public debt served as a method not for supporting the Treasury's borrowing capacity or for keeping the nation's debts affordable, but for supporting the balance sheets of too-big-to-fail banks.[23] This was "modern money," but it harnessed public power to private interests rather than the other way around.[24]

Losing the middle class

Quantitative easing never delivered the goods. The escalation of the asset economy served to keep asset values afloat and so prevented the Great Recession from turning into a Second Great Depression. But it was unable to rekindle the spirit of financial democratization of the 1990s and early 2000s. Wall Street traders referred to the boom of the 2010s as the "everything bubble"[25] – everything in their field of vision, that was. Past that perceptual horizon, many things were not floating but sinking.

Before the crisis, the logic of asset inflation had been characterized by all the inequity that attends trickle-down logics. But capital gains *had* in fact trickled down. After the crisis this was barely the case any longer. Of course, the wheel within the wheel would have been much squeakier than in the past anyway, given the many rounds of asset inflation that had already taken place. With each round, more and more central stimulus was needed to ensure the same trickle at the end. But the Obama administration's refusal to bail out underwater homeowners had disengaged the trickle-down mechanism altogether. The disparity of wealth growth was stunning.

Many working-class households in regional areas would spend years rebuilding their finances. The unrelenting stagnation of real wage levels meant that, despite the waves of foreclosures that depressed home values in such areas, it remained extremely difficult for many households to gain a foothold in the property market. Increasingly, they resigned themselves to renting.[26] The Obama administration lowered lending requirements, but it failed to provide much momentum. It was not until the very end of Obama's tenure that real estate lending was back to its pre-crisis level.[27]

Homeownership rates among the lower middle class dropped dramatically, as did their net worth, leading the Federal Reserve to speak of a "wealthless recovery."[28] Minorities were affected severely,[29] and the decline in homeownership rates was particularly pronounced among younger generations.[30] The days when one could find a house and get a loan on the basis of nothing but a median salary were over. Many families that until that point had been able to hold on to a place in the middle class were now dropping out.

Unlike the rest of the population, the top 10 percent of American households had fully rebuilt their wealth by the middle of the decade.[31] The home values of the upper middle class had declined by far less to begin with, and now the housing market for the bourgeoisie was booming. Stock prices had recovered much sooner than house prices, and this had benefitted the top 10 percent of the population greatly, the next 40 percent moderately, and the bottom half, which holds virtually no stock, not at all.

As long as the middle class seemed robust, attention to the steady growth of inequality had remained subdued. Since the 1990s, the progressive class has viewed the fortunes of the rich as unseemly, closer to a character flaw than social criticism. What mattered, they said, was that the tide was rising. But when it stopped doing so during the Great Recession, it became harder to summarily reject the possibility that obscene wealth and grinding poverty could in some way be connected.

The Federal Reserve's quantitative easing policy was easily identified as an example of how wealth begat more unearned wealth. Both the far left and the far right, Bernie Sanders no less than Rand Paul, resented the Federal Reserve.[32]

In 2014, an otherwise deeply and bitterly divided House of Representatives found common purpose in passing the Federal Reserve Transparency Act.[33] The bill stood no chance of passing the Senate or President Obama, but the symbolism was powerful. In 2015, during Humphrey–Hawkins testimony to Congress, Yellen commented: "I want to be completely clear that I strongly oppose the Fed bill. Audit the Fed is a bill that would politicize monetary policy."[34] Of course, the argument that Paul and others made was that the Federal Reserve had already politicized itself – so why shouldn't it be subject to public scrutiny?

Locked in place

The Federal Reserve didn't disagree that quantitative easing had some unpleasant side effects – it just didn't have any better medicine to give its patient. It was always developing plans to begin unwinding its enormous balance sheet at an appropriate time, while also reassuring the markets that it would do so slowly and gradually. Bernanke regularly foreshadowed that at some point in the future the Federal Reserve would gradually reduce its long-term bond holdings.[35] But when it actually tried to do so, the markets would panic and force the Federal Reserve to sound the retreat – as with the so-called taper tantrum in 2013.[36] Subsequent episodes followed the same logic, and they underscored just how heavily the markets had come to depend on Federal Reserve support.[37]

Simply resigning to indefinite QE was not an option, at this time at least. It had become impossible not to notice that each round of asset purchases did less and less to help ordinary people and sired more and more new millionaires and billionaires. The structural impossibility of the Federal Reserve's position became even more apparent under the reign of Janet Yellen, a labor market economist more politically to the left than Bernanke. She understood all too well that the challenges facing monetary policy were so great because fiscal policymakers were failing to show up for duty. Monetary policy *shouldn't* be the only game in town.

Cautiously, the Yellen Fed tried to draw attention to the inherent difficulty of managing an economic system where social spending and living wages were beyond the pale.[38] Occasional reminders that the Federal Reserve should be able to return to a depoliticized model of inflation-targeting, as during the Greenspan heyday, became controversial statements. That arguments for central bank independence and monetary orthodoxy were now allied to arguments for fiscal *stimulus* demonstrated just how extreme the austerity agenda of the Obama era had been.

But at the end of the day, it was also the weakness of the labor market that gave Yellen cause to insist on extreme caution when it came to unwinding the central bank's balance sheet.[39] After all, for now monetary policy *was* the only game in town. The most powerful actor in the global political economy had become fully locked into a policy pattern of which the limitations were increasingly visible. Katharine Pistor's critical definition of monetary sovereignty captures this paradoxical state of affairs: the capacity to backstop a financial system over the direction of which you are unable or unwilling to exercise substantial control.[40] By the standards of democratic theory, that is of course a deeply miserable form of sovereignty.

Social scientists portrayed this situation as a conflict between the financial sector and the real economy. But misgivings about lackluster growth were expressed even by the winners of the financialized economy, the asset management industry. As institutional funds had grown and their fiduciary obligations had become more tightly regulated, they had engaged investment managers to achieve the requisite degree of diversification.[41] By the start of the twenty-first century, these firms had become prominent players, and following the GFC they came to own a substantial cross-section of the American economy.

These firms had an obvious interest in public austerity – it was what powered the constantly growing need for public–private partnerships. When politicians talked about the need to mobilize private capital to create public things, they in effect referred to the standing collaborations between asset managers and their associates in the executive and regulatory branches. More and more, the benefits of such arrangements were not limited to direct subsidies. Asset managers demanded that the government use its regulatory capacity to comprehensively derisk their investments and provide iron-clad guarantees of future returns – upside exposure without downside.[42] This meant yoking the future tax-collection capacity of local government to asset managers' demands for revenue, often just to get basic things done.[43]

Public austerity also produced the new sources of social disadvantage that asset managers were well-positioned to take advantage of – what we might call, borrowing a term from Devin Fergus, "financial fracking."[44] The exclusion of homeowners from the Obama bailout packages was a major boon for the asset management industry. With the encouragement and assistance of authorities desperate to revive local housing markets and lure capital into regional economies, they bought up large numbers of foreclosed properties and converted them into rental housing.[45] Many working families forced to rent would have seen some of their rental payments return as pension winnings. But this was of course not a closed loop – the bulk of such payment streams trickled up.

But, profitable as family rental housing and infrastructure projects were, they could absorb only so much of the "wall of money" that required investment. Asset managers have a massive "dry powder" problem: funds under management that are yet to be invested.[46] One way to think of an asset manager is as a truly enormous mother ship, slow and unwieldy, which sends out numerous small expeditions to explore conditions in its wider environment and uses the feedback from these forays to adjust course and make decisions about further future explorations. Too many expeditions returned with little to report.

That, of course, was the other face of austerity – plenty of social needs that cried out for capital, but progressively fewer that were backed up by an ability to repay. Investment management was occasionally akin to drawing blood from a stone. Experiencing first-hand the difficulty of securing returns on capital in a society where purchasing power was concentrated in fewer and fewer hands, asset managers joined the growing chorus of voices expressing unease about the American government's inability to direct resources where they were needed.

Diagnosing stagnation

During the second Obama administration, theories of secular stagnation made a comeback. None other than Larry Summers led the charge, with a speech at the Economic Forum of the International Monetary Fund at the end of 2013. What Hansen had called "sick recoveries which die in their infancy," became in Summers' hands "protracted stretches of growth that are well short of previous trends or estimates of potential along with incompatibility between full employment and financial stability."[47] As we have seen, a core tenet of New Keynesian thought is that there can exist no long-term incompatibility between full employment and financial stability. But even the iterative downward adjustment of expectations through convoluted econometric models could not shield Summers from the sense that something was awry.

Hansen's original theory had been closely allied to the insistence on aggressive fiscal stimulus. Supply-side considerations were present from the start, as we have seen, but

primarily in a supportive role, as a way to make fiscal stimulus and growth possible without generating inflation. When
stagnation worries made a return in the capital formation
debates during the 1970s, the focus was almost entirely on
the supply side. Summer's return to Hansen's original formulation of the theory was motivated by a sense that the
endless multiplication of supply-side subsidies would only do
so much.

Summers considered that an ambitious program of public
investment in infrastructure was called for – "it is difficult to
imagine a better moment to stop paint chipping off school
buildings or to fix LaGuardia Airport."[48] Of course, he himself
had played a key role in blocking such a plan only several years
earlier, at what had unquestionably been the most opportune
time to execute it. Joseph Stiglitz pointed out that Summers'
intervention appeared to be an excuse for his own past mistakes, not just his role in the formulation of the Obama stimulus
but also his role as a champion of the financial deregulation
that had led to the crisis in the first place.[49] Summers objected,
citing political constraints. But, noting that "thinking about the
future" is more useful than "litigating the past," he was mostly
just happy that he and an old-school, left-wing Keynesian like
Stiglitz had belatedly found common ground in advocating for
aggressive demand stimulus.[50]

During the next years, Summers became an unlikely advocate of expansionary fiscal policy. He even expressed some
sympathy for the idea of a job guarantee, although was quick
to conclude that it was not realistic and that American workers
would be better served by a "combination of wage subsidies,
targeted government spending, support for workers with
dependents, and increased training and job-matching programs."[51] But when, several years later, the Biden government
tried to implement exactly the kind of remedy that Summers
seemed to prescribe, he changed his tune again. Summers saw
the re-emergence of inflation before others did.

Taking to the airwaves to battle the idea of fiscal stimulus kept him busy enough during lockdown, but it did not provide an answer to the question of what might be done in a situation where Keynesian stimulus was desperately needed but always bound to be inflationary. At the end of his New Keynesian rope, Summers called on the social sciences to contribute an explanation for the secular force that eluded the demand and supply models of economics. Tweeting his excitement about the arch-conservative book *Men Without Work* – which laments the "male flight from work" not just as an economic problem but equally as a moral and civilizational crisis inducing "sloth, idleness, and vices perhaps more insidious"[52] – he hypothesized that "There is some social phenomenon which I suspect explains non work, non marriage, deaths of despair, general alienation and, I suspect, the rise of reactionary populism. It should be a major task of social science to understand it."[53]

Concerns about the biological and moral quality of the human beings who populate the economy are by no means alien to the Keynesian mindset.[54] But for most of the Keynesian century it had enjoyed rather more benevolent associations. When Hansen had emphasized the role of declining population growth, he lamented primarily the end of steady inflows of migration. And while Minsky ridiculed neo-Keynesians' interest in human capital, their focus was on skills, education, and training – nothing too sinister. But Summers' attempts to work out what mechanism had taken the wind out of capitalism's sails went down the path of conservative cultural lament. New Keynesianism had become a vehicle for political reaction.

Minsky considered stagnationism to be the Achilles' heel of Keynes' thinking. It reflected a tendency to mistake symptom for cause and to substitute observation for explanation. Anyone taking it too seriously would inevitably end up with some very questionable ideas, much like the ones that Summers was now broadcasting. According to Minsky, the *General*

Theory's residual attachment to "stagnationist and exhaustion-of-investment-opportunity ideas" had prevented Keynes from committing fully to "a cyclical perspective in which investment, asset holdings, and liability structures are guided by speculative considerations."[55] Had Minsky been more of a Marxist, he might have said that Keynes should have paid closer attention to Marx's critique of classical political economy, which says that it is impossible to abstract the forces of production from the institutions that define property relations.

Stagnationism was also at the heart of Thomas Piketty's work, which documented in great detail the increase in inequality that had taken place over the previous decades.[56] His famous formula "r > g" expresses the proposition that, unless counteracted by political interventions, the rate of return on capital will tend to outrun the general rate of growth. In one sense, this is just a tautology: the owners of capital are the main beneficiaries of a capitalist system. But the idea that this could be an unregulated, laissez-faire system is extremely misleading. It obscures the constant institutional and political interventions that are required to ensure that the system works and the "r > g" formula holds.

What Summers, Piketty, and many others misdiagnosed as economic stagnation reflected the fact that the bailout state was no longer capable of driving growth yet seemed equally impossible to wind down. It was locked in place.

Of course, the kinds of policies that could change that situation were not inherently invisible. Economists who were closer to everyday practices of capital valorization could not avoid exploring that terrain. In 2019 the BlackRock Investment Institute published a paper addressing the problem that there was no more policy leeway for monetary policy to deal with a future downturn. It was co-authored by Stanley Fischer, a prominent New Keynesian economist who had worked harder than many of his colleagues to keep alive the idea that monetary policy has an active role to play in securing economic growth, and who had served as vice chair of the Federal Reserve from 2014 to 2017. The paper rejected fiscal expansion for all the usual reasons, emphasizing the likelihood that monetary financing of government deficits would set in motion new spirals of inflationary expectations. Instead, it recommended "going direct": "the central bank finding ways to get central bank money directly in the hands of public and private sector spenders."[57]

The similarity of the paper's proposals to MMT arguments was impossible to ignore. So, the authors went out of their way to mark the difference by stressing the need to protect central bank independence. Of course, the whole problem with quantitative easing consisted in the fact that, once in place, support was almost impossible to wind down – the markets were hooked. The only thing that central bank independence evidently still meant for Fischer and his co-authors, then, was its autonomy from social demands and democratic pressure. Any pretense that it might also mean independence from banks and markets was gone.

10

The Future of Bailouts

In early 2020, the global Covid pandemic broke out. The intense uncertainty that swept the world economy meant that markets for short-term funding froze. Shockingly, even Treasury debt came under tremendous pressure.[1] The fact that even the Treasury bill – normally the risk-free benchmark for financial markets – was no longer considered sufficiently cash-like meant that the entire risk calculus of financial markets was being upended. Stock markets and bond prices fell in tandem, creating an "unhedgeable risk."[2] The Federal Reserve responded by dramatically expanding its repo facilities, opening them up to new financial institutions such as mutual funds, widening the range of acceptable collateral, and signaling that it would provide unlimited support.[3]

As the scale of the pandemic became clear, economic policymakers soon realized they were faced with a highly unusual task: to bring the economy into a state of induced coma. To do this, they needed to bypass the normal mechanisms of payment and get cash in people's hands directly. The Coronavirus Aid, Relief and Economic Security (CARES) Act provided direct cash payments, tax relief, foreclosure moratoria, and incentives for employers not to lay off employees.[4] These measures created an extraordinary budget deficit (about double the size that it had reached after the 2007–8 crisis), and it fell to the Federal Reserve to buy all this debt.[5]

Before the GFC, the total size of the Federal Reserve balance sheet stood at a little less than a trillion. It had emerged from that crisis with a balance sheet twice that size. During the decade of quantitative easing, its asset holdings grew to a total of 4.5 trillion. The Federal Reserve had started to reduce this, somewhat, but before any meaningful shrinkage could occur, the pandemic doubled the Federal Reserve's asset holdings to around 9 trillion.[6]

Such explicit monetary financing of government deficits – a situation where the Federal Reserve was again yoked to the government's financing needs, as before 1951 – is of course not what Yellen and Powell had had in mind when, in previous years, they had emphasized the role for fiscal policy. What they had pushed for was a correction of overtight policy that would allow the Federal Reserve to *shrink* its balance sheet.

But as spectacular as all the public spending was, it was nowhere near enough. The Federal Reserve was perhaps no longer the only, but certainly still the main game in town. The American economy as a whole needed a floor, and it was no longer enough for the Federal Reserve to simply buy up larger and larger amounts of Treasury securities and agency debt.[7]

Federal Reserve officials had major misgivings about proposals to expand support to a wider range of assets, as it could further politicize Federal Reserve policy.[8] But they couldn't escape the obvious fact that the argument also worked in the opposite direction: if the Federal Reserve had already compromised its commitment to sound central banking on behalf of Wall Street, becoming doctrinaire amidst a global pandemic reeked of hypocrisy. The stature of politically progressive Federal Reserve governors like Lael Brainard, whose philosophy of risk socialization was closer to Brimmer's than to Volcker's, grew dramatically.[9] Powell, whose appointment had once signified Trump's rejection of Yellen's liberal politics, did not object.

The Federal Reserve had trampled on the Bagehot doctrine in all kinds of ways during the previous decades, but there was one cardinal rule it had never broken: it had always reserved access to its programs to financial institutions. Getting directly involved with the allocation of credit to economic sectors and firms would have made too much a mockery of central bankers' pretensions to neutrality. But it now started doing just that, providing direct support to corporations, small businesses, local government, and other segments of the American economy under pressure.[10]

The BlackRock report discussed at the end of the last chapter had warned that, unless new institutional safeguards were put in place, "the response to the next downturn will inevitably blur the lines currently dividing monetary and fiscal policy."[11] It was exactly what was happening now. The Federal Reserve's corporate bond purchasing program, co-designed with BlackRock as well as other asset managers such as Pimco, clearly broke with the narrow application of system risk considerations.[12] Many firms on the list of beneficiaries could be seen as sufficiently large or interconnected that their failure would bring down a wider part of the system; but many more could not reasonably be seen to fit that description.[13]

Almost overnight, MMT went from being an obscure school of thought to receiving mainstream attention. It had long said that if governments can afford to bail out banks, they can afford to pay for programs that the American public needs – childcare, health services, the greening of investment, even a social wage or basic income. And now the American government was moving in exactly that direction, expanding its safety net to constituencies that were not too big to fail, doing so without causing inflation or indeed any of the other horrors that were supposed to ensue if financial discipline was loosened.

Adam Tooze summarizes economic policy during the pandemic in the following words:

> Governments around the world issued debt as not seen since World War II, and yet interest rates plunged. As the private sector shut down, the public sector expanded. As government deficits grew, the monetary system responded elastically. Government spending made up for the loss of private incomes and spending.[14]

This was Lerner's Keynes in action – governments spending and borrowing to plug the leaks of the capitalist economy. In an interview, responding to the question, "Has the Fed done all it can do?", Powell said, "Well, there is a lot more we can do. We're not out of ammunition by a long shot. No, there's, there's really no limit to what we can do with these lending programs that we have."[15]

It vindicated the core proposition of MMT: that there exist no scientific, purely technical principles dictating limitations on public spending and lending, that it was all a matter of political will and priorities. But MMT's eagerness to prove that point has always made it prone to oversimplifying the issue. Just because a state of affairs can be exposed as political or ideological does not automatically make it more amenable to prompt change – sometimes even less so. As Tooze points out, it was only because the threat of democratic control over the nation's financial apparatus was so remote that the extraordinary measures taken during the pandemic were even contemplated.[16]

Politicization and democratization are different things. The machinery of the bailout state was operated not by a democratic public or its elected representatives, but by technocrats who thought of their tight connections to the financial industry not as conflicts of interest but as indispensable infrastructure for effective policy design and implementation. The overwhelming majority of the dollars they pumped into the system flowed through the too-big-to-fail banking complex, where every dollar was quickly leveraged with many more dollars, oiling America's wealth machinery and pushing up asset values. As it percolated down, all the middlemen got their cut, and by the time it finally landed in the budget of the average household only cents on the initial dollar were left.

Two years after the start of the pandemic, it was clear that the economic policy response had caused an extraordinary wealth explosion that benefitted the already wealthy far more than anyone else. The Federal Reserve's corporate bond purchases had spurred massive corporate borrowing, which firms had used to finance an extraordinary wave of stock buybacks, so further bolstering their borrowing capacity.[17] Since the GFC, the number of so-called "zombie firms" (corporations unable to cover payment on their debt through normal revenue streams) had grown steadily, and their business model had come to rely heavily on such practices.[18]

That the trickle-down effect of wealth growth had all but dried up was particularly evident in the housing market, long the mainstay of middle-class hopes for capital gains. Between December 2019 and June 2022, US home prices increased by a staggering 45 percent.[19] But the gains were concentrated heavily among the most expensive homes in large cities. Property inflation had reached its endpoint.

Worries that government support would do more to push up prices than expand homeownership can be traced back all the way to the New Deal.[20] The experience of mid-twentieth-century capitalism had put them to rest, but the Great Recession had reawakened such anxieties. Increasingly, the wheel within the wheel worked not to spread wealth, but to concentrate it. During the pandemic, concentrating capital gains in the hands of the bourgeoisie is all it did.[21]

It was undeniably the case that the extension of the bailout state had also helped the rest of the American population.

Whereas the response to the 2007–9 crisis had been downright punitive, pandemic policies kept many average households just liquid enough that they could survive. But that was very different from thriving. The real contrast was not with the period after, but *before* the Global Financial Crisis, when rampant inequality had seemed an acceptable price to pay for a viable, asset-driven middle-class politics. Progressive hopes that the deal might still be on offer had been disappointed over the preceding decade, and they were now exposed as downright delusional.

The return of inflation

The growth of America's billionaire class did not go unnoticed. But, as reports of the stupendous concentration of wealth started coming in, something else came along to capture the public's attention: after four decades, inflation made a comeback. Whatever one's feelings about the fact that billionaires were doubling and tripling their fortunes, inflation was a far more acute threat to the economic fortunes of the average family.

The year 2020 had appeared to be a real "told-you-so" moment for MMT: an aggressive expansion of American society's financial safety that did not appear to cause inflation.[22] But when the Biden administration announced its intentions to build on the CARES Act with further legislation, critics lined up to predict that the size of the stimulus would fuel inflation.

Ignoring the critics, Biden's American Rescue Plan expanded unemployment and food stamp benefits, provided direct payments to all American households ($1,400, straight into people's bank accounts), and increased a range of tax credits targeted at lower-income groups. Even in housing, which occupied a marginal position in the package, the bill did far more than Obama's 2009 stimulus bill had. Combined with the Infrastructure Investment and Jobs Act, passed towards the end of 2021, the administration provided a total of $3 trillion worth of stimulus – far surpassing the numbers that, just a decade earlier, Obama's advisers had considered beyond the pale.

As inflationary pressure gathered force, the rhetorical tables turned. Before too long, the airwaves were dominated by nervous chatter of the danger of a wage–price spiral. Led by Summers, inflation hawks availed themselves of the public image of the 1970s that had been consolidated since the 1990s. The Clinton-era New Democrats had thoroughly edited the public memory of that decade, erasing the political possibilities it had offered and magnifying the middle-class injuries attributed to inflation. By the time they were done, the decade was remembered as a bonfire of unrealistic expectations and consumerist hedonism, fueled by political irresponsibility and the near-collapse of law and order.[23]

The public health emergency meant that low-wage workers suddenly became less dispensable, and the combination of falling unemployment and resurgence of local labor militancy pushed up wages in select sectors. But this never came close to tipping over into an ability of workers to command wage increases that factor in anticipated price increases – the defining element of a wage–price spiral. Nevertheless, mainstream media outlets worked hard to conjure that very threat, inventing a genre of reporting that speculates about expectations. *Any* wage increase could set off the spiral, and so it was always legitimate to wonder whether the Federal Reserve could be underestimating the risk and if it was doing enough to preempt it. *Especially* during an inflationary crisis, wage levels could not be allowed to increase.

Others, including more traditional Keynesian economists like Blinder, counseled caution. They contended that declarations of a new wage–price spiral driven by unmoored expectations were premature, and poor guides to policy responses. Blinder had long argued that New Keynesians had gone too far in accepting the idea that trade-offs between employment levels and inflation rates were imaginary except in the shortest run. In his view, as long as it was not clear that inflation was more than a transitory phenomenon, the American government had a responsibility to make use of whatever policy room remained to spare millions of people the harsh fate of unemployment.

As inflationary pressures proved less fleeting than Blinder and the other members of his team had hoped, he maintained a tortuously balanced perspective that evolved from "Don't worry too much about the inflation surge" through "The Fed should raise interest rates, but gently" to "Inflation isn't transitory, but it isn't permanent either" – all titles of his regular columns in the *Wall Street Journal*.[24] In mid-2023 he looked back and defensively mused that "Team Transitory had a point about inflation,"[25] but that it had not factored in the impact of Russia's war on Ukraine or the severity of supply-chain disruptions.

Blinder's special pleading contrasted starkly with the aggressive energy that Summers and aides like Jason Furman brought to their attempts to goad the Fed into increasing unemployment by raising interest rates. These grown-up whiz kids had always mistrusted empathy as a guide to action, and they considered Blinder's belief that "being a Keynesian sometimes means worrying more about unemployment than about inflation" as nothing but unhelpful sentimentality against which rational policymakers needed to steel themselves.[26] And they had a point. By the logic of Blinder's own beloved Phillips curve, what Summers and Furman were advocating made perfect sense: the way to reduce inflation is by increasing unemployment.

Powell's Federal Reserve too understood the logic. Before the pandemic, he had participated in the mainstreaming of worries about the impact of prolonged fiscal austerity on economic growth. His rate hikes in the years leading up to the crisis were motivated not by any actual inflation fears, but by the aim to give the Federal Reserve some leeway to respond to the next crisis. And during the pandemic, he had worked closely with liberal governors like Brainard to press the Federal Reserve's machinery into the service of pandemic recession-fighting.

But when inflation reared its head, he knew who to take his marching orders from. The Federal Reserve started increasing interest rates. The objective was, as Powell put it, "to get wages down."[27] To protect people from pernicious cost-of-living increases, their standard of living needed to be brought down.

A new supply-side Keynesianism?

Other economists, further removed from the mainstream, focused more squarely on the sheer absurdity of shouldering wage earners with the responsibility for solving a problem they had not caused. They argued that it was above all the ability and willingness of corporations to increase their mark-ups and profits that was responsible for inflation.[28] The solution was obviously not to starve the economy of demand, but to target corporate profits with controls on prices and profit margins. These critics sought to revitalize a Keynesian supply-side economics. The reasoning is familiar, at least for readers of this book: if it is possible to identify the specific supply-side components of price pressures, we can target those, obviating the need to put the economy as a whole in a bind.

Such arguments were not made in a political vacuum.[29] The Biden administration was open to Keynesian ideas in a way that no administration since the 1960s had been. Even as the Federal Reserve stepped on the brake, the Biden administration was unwilling to do the same. The 2022 CHIPS and Science Act represented a significant investment in the American high-tech sector – the kind of supply-side initiative that neither Clinton nor Obama had got around to. The

Inflation Reduction Act of 2022 funded almost a trillion dollars in green investments and health care subsidies by enhancing tax collection capabilities but also by reforming prescription drug pricing. By the standards of Washington, it was a highly creative approach to taxing and pricing that synced with the supply-side spirit progressives were touting.

The new supply-side Keynesianism has been highly successful in demystifying the inflation phenomenon. Many people of my own generation (X) have only a very limited ability to think about prices in terms of market power or to question official lines about price stability, never having had the reason or the opportunity to do so. Younger generations have often had both, and the ability of supply-side Keynesians to disrupt mainstream discourse on these issues has been a very important factor enabling the growth of such critical awareness.

Nevertheless, the excitement surrounding the new supply-side progressivism was at least in part bound up with an exaggerated projection and perception of novelty. As this book has shown, supply-side Keynesianism is as old as Keynesianism. The search for the "real" causes of inflation has a long history that is fraught with paradoxes. Its appeal consists in the possibility of debunking orthodox arguments in a scientific way. But this has often been a case of winning the battle while losing the war. Over the longer run, such thinking has lured progressives into solving the problems of capital, trapping them into a political project that generates steadily diminishing returns.

The formulation of the Phillips curve had originally been intended as a means to undercut conservative arguments for general deflation. But it was never able to provide an alternative understanding of inflation as a *systemic* phenomenon. Amidst growing systemic turmoil, the idea of the unemployment–inflation trade-off became an easy target for neoliberal arguments, which in turn served as highly effective triggers for the Keynesian auto-immune responses that this book has foregrounded.

In the post-Covid debates, the difficulty of coming to terms with the system-level dimension of inflation was especially visible in the anxious insistence that the Biden stimulus could not possibly have played a role in fanning inflation – as if acknowledging that possibility would automatically entail a commitment to austerity politics. But of course, there is every reason to think that, had consumer demand not been as robust, corporations would have had much greater difficulty raising prices. Controls on profits and prices can be useful weapons to fight that trend. But that's a political strategy, not a technical solution mandated by superior expertise alone.

Inflation expresses the existence of social tensions that cannot be harmonized within the existing institutional order. The Keynesian program has therefore invariably led progressives to places where questions of economic policy verge on political ones. Too often, progressives have looked to Keynesianism as a set of strategies to *forestall* the need for political engagement, as a language to transform their objectives into claims that *can* be accommodated within the existing institutional order.

It will be some time before we can generate an accurate reading of Bidenomics. There is, however, little reason to think that it reflects a swing of the historical pendulum, a paradigm shift that will outlive the political circumstances that gave rise to it. Those include the previous decade's prolonged recession, the growth of political radicalism among racial minorities, resurgent labor militancy, and the growing awareness among younger generations that access to a middle-class life is determined no longer primarily by educational and professional choices but by parental wealth. The social protests during the pandemic demonstrated the limits of playing these constituencies off against each other, all against the background of right-wing radicalization and geopolitical shifts.

The fact that even Biden, the ultimate centrist whose long political career encapsulates all the conservative affinities of middle-class politics, could be pushed to embrace a Keynesian agenda demonstrates not the power of ideas, but changing political realities. That is not to rule out that Biden might have learned some lessons from how the previous decade had unfolded, largely under his watch. During the Trump years, Obama's reputation had taken a hit, and a continued perpetration of fiscal austerity on the American population would have carried the clear danger that Biden could go into history as the second coming not of Herbert Hoover but of Heinrich Brüning, the German Chancellor whose policies had paved the way for fascism's rise to power in the 1930s.

The inclusion of key representatives from the asset management industry in the Biden administration gave institutional reality to the lessons from the previous decade, bringing issues of employment, growth, and corporate profits back into mainstream policy circles.[30] They had come to own a slice of everything, and were required to think more broadly, from the standpoint of a policymaker as much as that of a profit-maximizing capitalist.[31] There may be political openings there, but any actual pathways towards a sustainable green transition and any actual advancement of an ambitious social justice agenda will depend entirely on persistent political pressure.[32]

Leveraged buy-ins

From the perspective of a certain brand of orthodox Marxism, there is a simple lesson to draw here: the Keynesian reluctance to challenge the private ownership of capital imposes hard limits on any attempt to reform capitalism and make it work for the general interest. The only viable supply-side program is national ownership and public control. Without that, you're just swimming against the capitalist tide, twisting and turning yourself into knots to get ahead but inevitably failing to develop momentum.

There is an obvious element of truth here. Considering himself a member of the reform-minded bourgeoisie, neither revolutionary nor conservative, Keynes offered a critique of capitalism that accepted its core institutional features.[33] His belief that the rentier would go quietly as steady economic growth rendered that character superfluous erred on the side of naivety, as did his conviction that this development would solve the most serious economic challenges of capitalism.

But benchmarking contemporary capitalism against a model of true communist ownership does little to help us see where we are in the present. The main weakness of Keynesianism is one that it *shares* with Marxism: an insufficiently developed understanding of the role of money, credit, and banking as active forces in shaping the development of capitalism. I have already argued this point at length when it comes to the dominant, mainstream Keynesian paradigms. But to get the contours of a specifically *financial* Keynesianism into sharper focus, we need to recognize that heterodox Keynesianism, or post-Keynesianism, has not always fared better.

Indeed, Marxist and post-Keynesian analyses of what has happened to the American political economy over the past fifty years are remarkably similar. Adopting the "Keynesianism to neoliberalism" periodization, this style of left-wing analysis views the period since the early 1980s as a period of "financialization" that has allowed the speculator and the rentier to gain the upper hand over productive capitalists.[34] It holds the explosion of finance responsible for a growing rift between those who produce a nation's wealth and those who appropriate it, between makers and takers. On the one side there is a rapidly shrinking number of property-owning "haves" who hold society's purse strings, and on the other there exists an increasingly indebted, propertyless stratum class of "have-nots." As Dirk Bezemer and Michael Hudson put it, the era of the Great Moderation was in reality the "Great Polarization," pitting creditors against debtors.[35]

However, the idea that social lines of division have come to coincide with the creditor/debtor divide is misleading. It's not the haves that lend and the have-nots that borrow. To the contrary, property and debt go hand in hand. Credit is predominantly created not for the needs associated with poverty, nor even for consumption by the middle class, but to finance investment – homeownership, primarily.[36] The central divide is not between those who are in debt and those who are not, but between those who can leverage their wage or assets to position themselves for savings, subsidies, and capital gains on the one hand, and those who cannot.[37]

Contemporary ownership is at its core a balance sheet phenomenon, in a sense that was not true of the pre-World War I world in which Keynes grew up. In that world, property was often still political, rarely financed by or encumbered with debt, and owners were therefore likely to be creditors. Keynes viewed the rentier as a bizarre symptom of two worlds intersecting – an old order of aristocratic, inherited wealth with a new, financialized system that enabled such wealth to lead an abstract life, earning returns without the need for any real-world investments or practical entanglements. Contemporary rentiers are very different creatures: they are debtors.

The middle-class societies that emerged in Western countries during the twentieth century are composed of a vast number of interlocking balance sheets. That situation cannot be modeled as if society has one big balance sheet, with people occupying places on either side of the sheet, as creditors or debtors. To imagine that individual household balance sheets can be "netted out" in that way is to reduce the idea to an empty formality, simply a way of showing that a society's credits equal its debts.[38] Minsky's purpose in viewing capitalist society through the lens of the balance sheet ran counter to that: he wanted to understand *how* contemporary society makes promises to itself. What institutional protocols regulate the process whereby a society projects itself into the future?

His answer centered on the role of investment and leverage. Economic units expose themselves to the short-term payment pressures of debt in order to finance a potentially beneficial long-term position. This produces particular sources of vulnerability. If economic units did not "lock up" their borrowed liquidity by investing, payment problems and market downturns could simply not happen. Managing instability requires derisking operations, and over time such support mechanisms become part of the system's baseline settings. As the system stabilizes, bailouts become backstops.

If we do not acknowledge the central role of leveraged investment, the past fifty years become incomprehensible. It means that we will only be able to see unleashed financial markets producing a mountain of credit and debt – sheer collective irrationality. This book has drawn a different picture. Relying on finance to manage political tensions is not an invention of neoliberalism, but rooted deeply in the logic of welfare capitalism. And so is the socialization of risk exposure for qualifying constituencies. Following the Volcker reset, the extension of public support for private interests *accelerated*. During the putative era of retreating governments and free markets, a sprawling infrastructure of public–private channels was built out to support too-big-too-fail firms and their clients.

Others too have questioned the idea of a sharp break between Keynesianism and neoliberalism, arguing that the promises of financial capitalism took the place of the declining promises of welfare capitalism.[39] But unless we foreground the role of leverage and debt-financed assets, that idea can in fact be quite misleading. As Etienne Lepers demonstrates, credit expansion has never served as a functional substitute for fiscal policy.[40] It has been as a source of income replacement for those who previously depended on social programs, and it has not facilitated the kind of public investments that we associate with a Keynesian state standing above the fray of economic competition, acting on behalf of an enlightened capitalist self-interest. It's the other way round: fiscal policy settings increasingly function as parameters in a Minskyan economy of interlocking balance sheets, and in that sense fiscal policy itself has been transformed into a branch of monetary policy.[41]

This is quite different from the well-worn argument that government expenditure is subordinated to or constrained by financial markets – a key plank of the neoliberalism literature.[42] That is to reproduce the excuses and rationalizations used by politicians when they are in the austerity phase of the policy cycle. The fiscal state has always depended on private financing to some extent, but what is new is that the government has become deeply *implicated* in the production of financial wealth. The American state is not responding to the demands of a social group outside itself. Instead, its *own* core operations have become integrated with the reproduction and concentration of wealth. The welfare state has become a wealthfare state.[43]

Less than a century ago, the rapid growth of the public purse represented a major threat to capitalist private property. The new colossus was never reversed or undone – instead, it was conquered and colonized. The fiscal state has been repurposed, reorganized around the subsidization of asset ownership.[44] Keynesian stabilization policies now serve "to give life to rentiers rather than to abet their euthanasia," as Minsky put it in his book on Keynes.[45]

Implicated

Does that mean we should renew the Keynesian critique of the parasitical rentier? That's the gambit of many post-Keynesian and Marxist authors,[46] as well as a growing number of intra-establishment critiques.[47] But the analysis that this book has presented indicates an immediate problem with such a perspective: too many of us are beneficiaries of the rents produced by the bailout state.

Of course, for many the return on investment is shrinking rapidly. But while that adds urgency to the need for critique, it does not make the rentier angle any more viable. It's just not in any obvious way a critique that can be leveled against the 1% on behalf of the 99%, or even against the top 10% on behalf of the 90%. Of course, it's not clear where exactly we would draw the boundaries, who exactly is in or out – but that's the point. Trying to draw clear lines inevitably evolves into a scientistic game without political purchase. Beyond misleading precision, a major question looms: if we were to adopt a truly global perspective, that is, the scale on which capitalism operates, could many citizens of OECD countries truly claim to be on the wrong side of the maker/taker divide? The answer, of course, is no.

To those exposed to the structural violence of global capitalism, even mid-century Keynesianism never looked particularly democratic or egalitarian. But, when faced with the tyranny of free-market thinking, progressives find it almost impossible to resist looking back to a time when Western welfare capitalism offered an imperfect but meaningful haven of economic security and social democracy. However, taking the outcome of past struggles as a future objective results in an incoherent politics, inevitably assuming the ready availability of things that were hard-won. Before too long, awareness fades that the society depicted in the AFL-CIO poster (shown in chapter 1) was not a coherent, self-contained model, a capitalism "fit for purpose," as its proponents like to call it, but a messy, unstable compromise that required constant reinforcement and renegotiation. Capitalism offers no baseline level of security or freedom – no natural "living wage" – that can be taken for granted. In that sense, the welfare state was the original bailout state.

That obviously does not mean we should refrain from criticizing the dramatic growth of inequality within Western countries themselves. But a simple opposition between a democratic interest in real economic growth and the unproductive opulence of the top layers misses the political problem of implication: how the growth of extreme wealth has been built on a broader middle-class politics. The wish to draw clear battle lines and to project an easily discernible enemy is understandable, given that the political stakes are so high and almost call out for rhetorical dramatization. But as an analytical frame it doesn't get us very far. It occludes how a century of middle-class politics has scrambled such boundaries.

Critics of neoliberalism have often focused on its most avant-garde manifestations, nurtured by eccentric billionaires who see progress as the natural province of people who look and think like them. The age of Trump supplies plenty of plausible reasons to cast the present as a well-defined confrontation between democracy and reaction. Research into neoliberalism's intellectual origins has revealed the intimate connections of free-market radicalism to a variety of racist ideologies. It's a bottomless barrel of course, and it's all been so shocking that many are now wondering if neoliberalism has self-destructed and given way to something else altogether.[48]

That constant sense of shock is part of the problem. It maintains the innocence allowing us to imagine that such findings tell us less about the society we've built than about those who are trying to undo it. And that leads us to respond to pressure on our way of life by defending it instead of examining it. The evolution of the American political economy over the past four decades has taken place while democratic political institutions were still intact. That may not be the case for much longer, of course. But even if a future Trump administration, or a similar creature of authoritarian populism, manages to undo democracy in America, we will still be faced with the question of how democratic institutions enabled their own euthanasia.

Whereas the "Keynesianism to neoliberalism" narrative is driven by a concern with all the ways that the system is prevented from working properly, the focus in this book has been on all the ways in which the system has been made to work. That history also contains an endless number of nefarious schemes and outright abuses of power. But to focus solely on heightening the visibility of such events often means reinforcing the constitutive blind spots on which contemporary society works. In the end, the reason the bailout state stays in place is that it feeds on our insecurity, the fact that the thinner the rewards become, the more anxiously we seek to stop our grip on its coattails from slipping further.

Keynesianism for the twenty-first century

Keynes' main difference with classical political economy consisted in his awareness that the abstract forms that property could assume in a monetary society undermined the possibility of modeling money as a neutral institution. But Keynes never committed to the idea that capitalism was *essentially* a financial structure, as Minsky would later argue. That made him, on the one hand, receptive to overtures from mainstream economists who sought to tame his thought by translating it back into a language that had no real place for money as an active force in the making of history. And it was why, on the other hand, his thought revolution could revert to the most banal critique of money, centered on its ability to multiply itself without having to touch the soil tilled by real human activity – an image that traded heavily on ancient antisemitic tropes.

Truly understanding the core of the Keynesian revolution, according to Minsky, meant abandoning any and all attempts to define the motor of capitalist growth in abstraction from the property and financing relations that organized it. Minsky made those institutions visible by modeling society as a dynamic, interlocking network of payments flows and balance sheet interconnections. During the heyday of the Fordist manufacturing economy, he insisted that the American economy be studied on the model of Wall Street high finance. Separating the productive and parasitically extractive aspects of capitalism would have required freezing the economy in time – impossible, because stable institutional arrangements invite destabilizing strategies. And, unless we are willing to let the economy as a whole go down out of sheer spite, maintaining stability requires risk socialization. Rentiers, in this world, are just derisked asset owners, not characters in a world-historical morality play.

According to Minsky, *financial* Keynesianism was yet to be tried as a practical policy program. Such a Keynesianism would not simply have stabilized the economic system, but it would also have addressed the contradictions – inflation, above all – that had arisen from such arrangements. As he put it, somewhat enigmatically:

> Because of the essential continuity of our economic structure since the 1930s, there has never been a Keynesian revolution in economic policy. The institutional structure has not been adapted to reflect the knowledge that the collapse of aggregate demand and profits, such as occasionally occurred and often threatened to occur in pre-1933 small government capitalism, is never a clear and present danger in a Big Government capitalism such as has ruled since World War II.[49]

Progressives employing a properly financial Keynesianism would not be constantly preoccupied with the need to prove that the state is required to stabilize the capitalist economy. They would acknowledge that the stabilization imperative has already sunk deep into the muscle memory of policymaking, regardless of the political affiliations of the people at the controls. And they would work to adapt the institutional structure in light of such awareness.

Such a politics might include price controls, tax subsidies, publicly funded infrastructure, and any number of other things that have typically been included in the Keynesian program. But we will be stepping into old traps if we do not acknowledge that the obstacles it will encounter are political in nature. Intellectuals can help here by providing terrain reconnaissance, but we misunderstand our own role if we think of the knowledge we produce as ways to bypass political confrontation.

Minsky, not Lerner, is the best guide to capitalism's financial terrain – banks, not governments, are in the driver's seat. That suggests a notion of "modern money" that is indebted to but does not align seamlessly with how that idea has come to prominence in recent years, and I will leave it to others to decide whether my position is consistent with the MMT framework. But what summary dismissals of MMT by many on the left certainly fail to acknowledge is that the straightforwardness of its proposals is born not from naivety but precisely from a clear-eyed perception that money holds no secret. There exist no hidden, quasi-natural economic laws, known only to self-styled experts, that prevent us from making the economy more democratic.

There is ultimately little to be gained or learned from engaging the fake complexity of mainstream policy debates on their own terms – they're rhetorical traps, invitations to reformulate our objectives in ways that undermine their viability. As Stephanie Kelton has so effectively insisted, the question "How are you going to pay for that?" is rarely asked in good faith. When we are responsive to the provocations from Summers and other establishment representatives, we get caught in a game where we do the work of undermining the case for a truly modern, democratic money – by making complex what is simple, turning excuses into reasons, transforming symptoms into causes. When we resurface from the rabbit hole, what initially seemed to be political openings now face us as unwelcome policy conundrums.

Trying to prescribe the outcome of a movement to make money democratic is to miss the point of advocating democracy. But it's clear where it needs to start: with a recognition that people like Summers understand nothing about money that is somehow beyond our grasp or ken. Any viable progressive politics must set its sight on the practices whereby society produces financial claims on property, and it must aim at a fundamental reconstruction of that structure. Otherwise, progressive elites dialing in from tropical beachside resorts to tell us exactly how many livelihoods must be destroyed to make money safe, may well become the norm – and then a nostalgic memory of a more civilized past.

Postscript

Although this book breaks with some currently prominent trends in Marxist political economy in a less hesitant way than my previous work did, it can plausibly be read as a materialist answer to the Hegelian overtones of my first book.[1] The trajectory that led from there to here has been shaped by the research I undertook for my previous books, especially *Capital and Time*.[2] Insofar as the latter book suggested that Minsky's insights were legible only through the lens of postfoundational social theory, it left something important unsaid. As this book has made clear, I consider Minsky perfectly capable of standing on his own conceptual feet. Once the prevailing interpretation of his work as a critique of overindebtedness wears thin, he will, I hope, come to be recognized as one of contemporary capitalism's most compelling critics, on par with Marx, Weber, and Keynes. What Marx did with the commodity, Minsky did with the asset: use it as a lens to critically reconstruct our understanding of capitalist society.

The centuries-long transformation of property from a political institution into an abstract financial claim has amplified both prospects of democratic progress and opportunities for deepening hierarchy. Conservatives see that clearly, and they design their political programs accordingly. Progressives, by contrast, often suppress awareness of modernity's double-edged sword, preferring to hold on to assumptions of historical progress by moderating them.

Conversation partners have occasionally noted that I seem far more riled by the innocent idealism of progressives than by the hard-nosed realism of conservatives and neoliberals. I have tried to adjust my expression in that respect, but I remain convinced that it speaks to a very real problem: the left's ineffectual moralism, the constant tendency to put our considerable intellectual firepower not towards understanding but towards disavowing our own implication.

That left-wing moralism has a way of turning on itself is readily apparent in the constant emergence of progressive leaders who work to sabotage the energies that propelled them to power. But that is a symptom – worth noting, but offering little opportunity for transformation. Engaging with it too closely produces the kind of obsessive, slightly unhinged response that my interlocutors noted in me.

More significantly, the problem manifests as the persistent difficulty that progressives have in relating constructively to their own history. Mesmerized by what Western economies delivered for their white middle classes during the early post-war period, the progressive program has become captive to an idealized past. Aiming to refute neoliberal claims for the necessity of free markets, it narrates history to show that events since the 1970s might have unfolded differently. But while the progressive mindset is always concerned to point up space for political agency, it often has little interest in understanding the agency that it has already exercised, its own role in producing the present it laments.

We are all Keynesians, but trying to rehabilitate Keynesianism as a policy program in the narrow sense of the word – a technical, expertise-driven response to political problems, to be wielded by an appropriate set of elites – is a sure way to end up on the wrong side of history. Inhabiting the Keynesian worldview with greater purpose and political orientation requires re-engaging the modernist impulses out of which it arose. In one sense, Minsky did exactly that, replacing a static world of economic laws and rational actors with a dynamic model of financial flows that compose volatile webs of interdependence, constantly remake the future by revaluing the past, and are not readily transparent to their political communities. In another sense, however, he made Keynes more of an economist, abstracting the core of his thought from its many connections to culture, psychology, and politics. A Keynesianism appropriate to the twenty-first century, where the most obscene concentrations of power and wealth are built every day on humanity's most extraordinary achievements and capabilities, will need to occupy that terrain in its own way.

The Bailout State began life as what I thought was going to be the least challenging chapter in a separate, more wide-ranging book on the ambivalent – fraught, but by no means straightforwardly antagonistic – relationship between capitalist property and democratic politics. That project languished during the first years of the pandemic, and it got its start in earnest during a 2021–2 fellowship held jointly at the Berggruen Institute in Los Angeles and the Center on Science, Technology, and Public Life at the University of Southern California. Thanks to Yakov Feygin, Andy Lakoff, Leila Lorenzo, Emily Anderson, and Nils Gilman for their hospitality. I am also grateful for support from the University of Sydney (through a Research Accelerator Prize), its Faculty of Arts and Social Sciences (through the FutureFix program and study leave), and the Australian Research Council (through its Special Research Initiative and Discovery Projects scheme).

At Sydney, I have benefitted from collaboration and conversation with Lisa Adkins, Gareth Bryant, Melinda Cooper, Monique McKenzie, Damien Cahill, Adam Morton, Frank Stilwell, Fiona Allon, Dallas Rogers, Laurence Troy, Sophia

Maalsen, Martin Duck, Oliver Levingston, Claire Parfitt, John Clegg, Matt Costa, David Primrose, and Austin Smidt. Some early speculative thoughts on the bailout state appeared in a volume on Covid politics edited by Vanessa Lemm and Miguel Vatter, for which series editors Sonja van Wichelen and Marc de Leeuw organized an energizing launch. Finance and Society – the network, conference, and journal – has offered a highly stimulating intellectual environment. Thanks to Amin Samman for his unique ability to combine critical thinking with the creation of critical infrastructure. Others who helped me develop the ideas presented here include Sam Knafo, Onur Özgöde, Randy Germain, Janet Roitman, Chris Desan, Matthias Thiemann, Christian Borch, Ewald Engelen, Mareike Beck, Susan Zieger, Eli Cook, Leon Wansleben, Michel Feher, Jim Stanford, Marieke de Goede, Nathan Coombs, Sahil Dutta, Perry Mehrling, Devika Dutt, Joscha Wullweber, Ben Braun, Scott Aquanno, Mark Paul, Daniela Gabor, Katharina Pistor, Mona Ali, and Stefano Sgambati.

Stefan Eich went over and beyond, generously providing me with several rounds of incisive feedback. Discussing our different perspectives on Keynes' relationship to Keynesianism and on Minsky's contribution has allowed me to see, and I hope articulate, much more sharply what is at stake. Sam Chambers and Dick Bryan gave the manuscript searching readings that helped me to clarify key issues and saved me from some embarrassing mistakes. Gavin Fridell, Michelle Chihara, Matthew Sussman, Aaron Wistar, and Mike McCarthy provided input at important moments and nudged me to keep my eye on the storyline. An account of the community from which this book has emerged would be incomplete without mention of the late Leo Panitch, whose work with Sam Gindin has been an enduring influence on my worldview. Louise Knight saw a book where there was only an idea, and I am grateful to her for putting her faith in it at an early stage. She sourced a number of exceptionally helpful reviews that have greatly improved the final product. Inès Boxman, and now Olivia Jackson, as well as the rest of the Polity team have been a pleasure to work with. Thanks to Jane Fricker for her careful copy-editing.

The book was completed in the evening hours of an anxious hospital stay. I dedicate it to Anik, who fights like no one else, and to Bhavani, who fixes things like no one else.

Notes

Preface

1 "The World Enters a New Era: Bail-outs for Everyone!", *The Economist*, September 25, 2022.

2 Jeanna Smialek, "Is This What Winning Looks Like?", *New York Times*, February 7, 2022.

3 Leo Panitch and Sam Gindin, *The Making of Global Capitalism: The Political Economy of American Empire*, Verso, 2013.

4 Adam Tooze, *Crashed: How a Decade of Financial Crises Changed the World*, Penguin, 2018; Adam Tooze, *Shutdown: How Covid Shook the World's Economy*, Viking, 2021.

Chapter 1: How Did We Get Here?

1 I define "middle class" as the group of households whose income is not entirely absorbed by the necessities of everyday life and are therefore able to save and invest, but who do not have access to an existing stock of wealth that allows them to escape the need to work for a living.

2 https://twitter.com/ojblanchard1/status/1550375191645126657?lang=en

3 Quoted in Roshan Abraham, "More People Must Lose Jobs to

Fight Inflation, Larry Summers Bravely States from Tropical Beach," *Vice*, January 11, 2023.

4 Quoted in Matt Novak, "Larry Summers Says Now is not the Time for 'Moral Hazard Lectures' about Bailouts," *Forbes Magazine*, March 12, 2023.

5 Ibid.

6 John Maynard Keynes, *The General Theory of Employment, Interest and Money*, Harcourt, Brace and Company, 1936.

7 Thomas Piketty, *Capital in the Twenty-First Century*, Harvard University Press, 2014.

8 Perry Mehrling, *The Money Interest and the Public Interest: American Monetary Thought, 1920–1970*, Harvard University Press, 1998.

9 Quoted in Sarah Quinn, "'The Miracles of Bookkeeping': How Budget Politics Link Fiscal Policies and Financial Markets," *American Journal of Sociology*, 123(1), 2017, p. 58.

10 Quoted in Steven Rattner, "Volcker Asserts U.S. Must Trim Living Standard," *New York Times*, October 18, 1979.

11 Keynes, *The General Theory of Employment, Interest and Money*, p. 159.

12 The neoliberalism literature is vast. For overviews, see Damien Cahill and Martijn Konings, *Neoliberalism*, Polity, 2017; Julie Wilson, *Neoliberalism*, Routledge, 2017; Manfred B. Steger and Ravi K. Roy, *Neoliberalism: A Very Short Introduction*, Oxford University Press, 2021.

13 Jeffrey M. Chwieroth and Andrew Walter, *The Wealth Effect: How the Great Expectations of the Middle Class Have Changed the Politics of Banking Crises*, Cambridge University Press, 2019; Lisa Adkins, Melinda Cooper and Martijn Konings, *The Asset Economy: Property Ownership and the New Inequality*, Polity, 2020.

14 For recent approaches with a similar emphasis on the role of progressives in the making of the neoliberal era, see Patrick Andelic, *Donkey Work: Congressional Democrats in Conservative America, 1974–1994*, University of Kansas Press, 2019; Elizabeth Popp

Berman, *Thinking like an Economist: How Efficiency Replaced Equality in U.S. Public Policy*, Princeton University Press, 2021; Lily Geismer, *Left Behind: The Democrats' Failed Attempt to Solve Inequality*, PublicAffairs, 2022; Brent Cebul, *Illusions of Progress: Business, Poverty, and Liberalism in the American Century*, University of Pennsylvania Press, 2023; Brian Judge, *Democracy in Default: Finance and the Rise of Neoliberalism in America*, Columbia University Press, 2024.

15 Stephanie Kelton, *The Deficit Myth: Modern Monetary Theory and the Birth of the People's Economy*, PublicAffairs, 2020; L. Randall Wray, *Modern Money Theory: A Primer on Macroeconomics for Sovereign Monetary Systems*, Palgrave Macmillan, 2015; L. Randall Wray, *Making Money Work for Us: How MMT Can Save America*, Polity, 2022; William Mitchell and Thomas Fazi, *Reclaiming the State: A Progressive Vision of Sovereignty for a Post-Neoliberal World*, Pluto Press, 2017.

16 Abba P. Lerner, "Functional Finance and the Federal Debt," *Social Research*, 10(1), 1943, p. 39.

17 Ibid., p. 39.

18 John Maynard Keynes, *Collected Writings Vol. 27*, Cambridge University Press, 2012, p. 270.

19 I refer to Minsky's Keynesianism specifically as "financial Keynesianism," a label he preferred to "post-Keynesianism" (see Ricardo Bellofiore, "Financial Keynesianism," in Jan Toporowski and Jo Michell, ed., *Handbook of Critical Issues in Finance*, Edward Elgar, 2012, p. 105). Minsky was certainly part of the wider constellation of "post-Keynesian" authors who resisted the formation of the neo-Keynesian synthesis. But especially when it comes to thinking about money, post-Keynesians have appropriated Minsky primarily as a critic of overindebtedness, which is far too limited a perspective on his work. For interpretations of Minsky similar to the one offered here, see Perry Mehrling, "The Vision of Hyman P. Minsky," *Journal of Economic Behavior and Organization*, 39(2), 1999; and Daniel H. Neilson, *Minsky*, Polity, 2019. I take financial Keynesianism to have significant

overlap with what has recently been referred to as "critical macro-finance" (Daniela Gabor, "Critical Macro-Finance: A Theoretical Lens," *Finance and Society*, 6(1), 2020; Fabian Pape, "Rethinking Liquidity: A Critical Macro-Finance View," *Finance and Society*, 6(1), 2020; Samuel Knafo, "Macro-Finance and the Financialisation of Economic Policy," *Finance and Society*, 6(1), 2020).

Chapter 2: What Keynes Missed

1 As Keynes put it, "the only reason why an asset offers a prospect of yielding during its life services having an aggregate value greater than its initial supply price is because it is *scarce*; and it is kept scarce because of the competition of the rate of interest on money" (Keynes, *The General Theory of Employment, Interest and Money*, p. 213).

2 Stefan Eich, *The Currency of Politics: The Political Theory of Money from Aristotle to Keynes*, Princeton University Press, 2022; Jakob Feinig, *Moral Economies of Money: Politics and the Monetary Constitution of Society*, Stanford University Press, 2022; Aaron Sahr, "Claims to Sovereignty: MMT as a Challenge to Money's Technical Imaginary," in Benjamin Braun and Kai Koddenbrock, ed., *Capital Claims: The Political Economy of Global Finance*, Routledge, 2022; Samuel A. Chambers, *Money Has No Value*, De Gruyter, 2023.

3 Hyman P. Minsky, *Stabilizing an Unstable Economy*, McGraw Hill, 2008 [1986], p. 114.

4 The neo-Keynesian consensus was only able to differentiate itself from orthodox theories of money to the extent that it conceived of liquidity as *itself* a commodity that could be analyzed in terms of neoclassical demand and supply logics. As depicted in the IS-LM model, the equilibrium interest rate reconciling the demand for and supply of money had a real-world impact by constraining the equilibrium options available to the real economy. Mehrling has referred to this as "monetary Walrasianism," which "brought in money, not as the critical infrastructure of a decentralized

market economy but rather as a separate sector of the economy sitting alongside the 'real' sector" (Perry Mehrling, "The Money Muddle: The Transformation of American Monetary Thought, 1920–1970," *History of Political Economy*, 30(Supplement), 1998, p. 304).

5 Keynes, *The General Theory of Employment, Interest and Money*, p. vii.
6 Lerner, "Functional Finance and the Federal Debt," p. 43.
7 Ibid., p. 38.
8 Ibid., p. 39.
9 Ibid., p. 39.
10 Ibid., p. 41.
11 Abba P. Lerner, "Money as a Creature of the State," *American Economic Review*, 37(2), 1947.
12 Keynes, *The General Theory of Employment, Interest and Money*, p. 378.
13 Eich, *The Currency of Politics: The Political Theory of Money from Aristotle to Keynes*, p. 5.
14 Hyman P. Minsky, *John Maynard Keynes*, McGraw-Hill, 2008 [1975], p. 21.
15 Minsky, *Stabilizing an Unstable Economy*, p. 111.
16 Keynes had considered and rejected that idea. As he explained in the *Treatise on Money*, bank money was not "money proper" – it was "simply an acknowledgment of a private debt" (John Maynard Keynes, *A Treatise on Money*, Cambridge University Press, 1930, p. 5). Real money needed the government's stamp on it.
17 "in principle every unit can 'create' money – the only problem for the creator being to get it 'accepted'" (Minsky, *Stabilizing an Unstable Economy*, pp. 78–9).
18 Josh Ryan-Collins, Tony Greenham, Richard Werner and Andrew Jackson, *Where Does Money Come From?*, New Economics Foundation, 2012; Richard A. Werner, "A Lost Century in Economics: Three Theories of Banking and the Conclusive Evidence," *International Review of Financial Analysis*, 46(July),

2016. Neo-Keynesians themselves have in fact wondered how real these multiplier and fractional reserve logics are, and whether we are not just dealing with an aggregate effect that is a little like an optical illusion. In that vein, James Tobin ("Commercial Banks as Creators of 'Money'," in Deane Carson, ed., *Banking and Monetary Studies*, Richard D. Irwin, 1963) rejected the idea that banks are "special" in that sense, arguing that their economic function – the maturity transformation of credit – could also be undertaken by other institutions who had mastered the relevant risk management techniques.

19 L. Randall Wray, *Money and Credit in Capitalist Economies: The Endogenous Money Approach*, Edward Elgar, 1990; Victoria Chick and Sheila Dow, "Post-Keynesian Theories of Money and Credit: Conflicts and (Some) Resolutions," in Geoffrey Colin Harcourt and Peter Kriesler, ed., *The Oxford Handbook of Post-Keynesian Economics, Volume 1: Theory and Origins*, Oxford University Press, 2013.

20 The problem manifests in another way too. The post-Keynesian critique stresses that banks actively produce money and create credit, and that this is never a neutral process. At the same time, however, the post-Keynesian critique of contemporary capitalism relies heavily on the idea that the creation of debt relations can never be productive in a deeper sense: finance does not make new useful things of real value (Steve Keen, "Predicting the 'Global Financial Crisis': Post-Keynesian Macroeconomics," *Economic Record*, 89(285), 2013; Dirk Bezemer and Michael Hudson, "Finance is not the Economy: Reviving the Conceptual Distinction," *Journal of Economic Issues*, 50(3), 2016). This last line of reasoning tacitly reinvokes the intermediation conception of banks, using it as a benchmark to criticize the creation of credit for unproductive purposes. This disarticulation of the empirical meaning of the word "productive" from its moral meaning introduces an element of arbitrariness into post-Keynesian thought.

21 Stefano Sgambati, "Rethinking Banking: Debt Discounting

and the Making of Modern Money as Liquidity," *New Political Economy*, 21(3), 2016.

22 Stephanie Bell, "The Role of the State and the Hierarchy of Money," *Cambridge Journal of Economics*, 25(2), 2001; Geoffrey Ingham, *The Nature of Money*, Polity, 2004; Perry Mehrling, *The New Lombard Street: How the Fed Became the Dealer of Last Resort*, Princeton University Press, 2011; Christine Desan, *Making Money: Coin, Currency, and the Coming of Capitalism*, Oxford University Press, 2014; Katharina Pistor, "From Territorial to Monetary Sovereignty," *Theoretical Inquiries in Law*, 18(2), 2017; Anush Kapadia, *A Political Theory of Money*, Cambridge University Press, 2024.

23 Perry Mehrling, "Financialization and its Discontents," *Finance and Society*, 3(1), 2017, p. 7.

24 Kai Koddenbrock, "Money and Moneyness: Thoughts on the Nature and Distributional Power of the 'Backbone' of Capitalist Political Economy," *Journal of Cultural Economy*, 12(2), 2019, p. 111.

25 Keynes often seemed to argue that deflation was a basic economic property of a pure, laissez-faire capitalism. On other occasions he described deflationism as a pernicious political ideology. Perhaps he felt that these amounted to different ways of saying the same thing. But they are different propositions that describe different aspects of capitalist development.

26 Minsky, *Stabilizing an Unstable Economy*, p. 165.

27 Paul A. Samuelson and Robert M. Solow, "Analytical Aspects of Anti-Inflation Policy," *American Economic Review*, 50(2), 1960, drawing on A.W. Phillips, "The Relation between Unemployment and the Rate of Change of Money Wage Rates in the United Kingdom, 1861–1957," *Economica, New Series*, 25(100), 1958.

28 Minsky, *Stabilizing an Unstable Economy*, ch. 11.

29 Quoted in Robert P. Bremner, *Chairman of the Fed: William McChesney Martin Jr., and the Creation of the Modern American Financial System*, Yale University Press, 2004, p. 5.

Chapter 3: How Welfare Capitalism Worked

1 Walter Bagehot, *Lombard Street: A Description of the Money Market*, Scribner, Armstrong & Co., 1877.

2 Gretchen Ritter, *Goldbugs and Greenbacks: The Antimonopoly Tradition and the Politics of Finance in America, 1865–1896*, Cambridge University Press, 1997.

3 Elizabeth Sanders, *Roots of Reform: Farmers, Workers, and the American State, 1877–1917*, University of Chicago Press, 1999, p. 258.

4 Robert F. Bruner and Sean D. Carr, *The Panic of 1907: Lessons Learned from the Market's Perfect Storm*, John Wiley & Sons, Inc., 2007.

5 J. Bradford DeLong, "Fiscal Policy in the Shadow of the Great Depression," in Michael D. Bordo, Claudia Goldin and Eugene N. White, ed., *The Defining Moment: The Great Depression and the American Economy in the Twentieth Century*, University of Chicago Press, 1998, p. 67.

6 Ibid., p. 75.

7 Robert M. Collins, *The Business Response to Keynes, 1929–1964*, Columbia University Press, 1981, pp. 24–5.

8 Dennis J. Ventry, "The Accidental Deduction: A History and Critique of the Tax Subsidy for Mortgage Interest," *Law and Contemporary Problems*, 73(1), 2010, p. 245.

9 Collins, *The Business Response to Keynes, 1929–1964*, p. 27.

10 Paige Lancourt, *Benefiting Business: The Fragmented Federal Response to American Deindustrialization*, PhD thesis, University of California Santa Cruz, 2022, p. 58; Collins, *The Business Response to Keynes, 1929–1964*, pp. 32–3.

11 Lancourt, *Benefiting Business: The Fragmented Federal Response to American Deindustrialization*, p. 55; Collins, *The Business Response to Keynes, 1929–1964*, p. 29.

12 Sarah L. Quinn, *American Bonds: How Credit Markets Shaped a Nation*, Princeton University Press, 2017, p. 127.

13 Julian E. Zelizer, "The Forgotten Legacy of the New Deal: Fiscal

Conservatism and the Roosevelt Administration, 1933–1938," *Presidential Studies Quarterly*, 30(2), 2000, p. 333.

14 Herbert Stein, *The Fiscal Revolution in America*, University of Chicago Press, 1969, p. 80.

15 Collins, *The Business Response to Keynes, 1929–1964*, p. 43; Stein, *The Fiscal Revolution in America*, pp. 74–5.

16 Collins, *The Business Response to Keynes, 1929–1964*, p. 40.

17 Stein, *The Fiscal Revolution in America*, p. 44.

18 Quinn, *American Bonds: How Credit Markets Shaped a Nation*, p. 131.

19 Ibid., p. 145.

20 Quoted in Quinn, "'The Miracles of Bookkeeping': How Budget Politics Link Fiscal Policies and Financial Markets," p. 58.

21 Kevin Fox Gotham, "Separate and Unequal: The Housing Act of 1968 and the Section 235 Program," *Sociological Forum*, 15(1), 2000, pp. 18–19.

22 Quinn, *American Bonds: How Credit Markets Shaped a Nation*, pp. 142–4; Mehrsa Baradaran, *The Color of Money: Black Banks and the Racial Wealth Gap*, Belknap Press, 2017, p. 106.

23 Alvin Hansen, "Economic Progress and Declining Population Growth," *American Economic Review*, 29(1), 1939.

24 Cebul, *Illusions of Progress: Business, Poverty, and Liberalism in the American Century*, pp. 41–2.

25 Ibid., p. 40.

26 Ibid., p. 4.

27 Stein, *The Fiscal Revolution in America*, p. 104.

28 Zelizer, "The Forgotten Legacy of the New Deal: Fiscal Conservatism and the Roosevelt Administration, 1933–1938," pp. 353–4.

29 Margaret Weir, "Full Employment as a Political Issue in the United States," *Social Research*, 54(2), 1987, p. 385.

30 Walter S. Salant, "The Spread of Keynesian Doctrines and Practices in the United States," in Peter A. Hall, ed., *Keynesianism Across Nations*, Princeton University Press, 1989, pp. 45–6.

31 Stein, *The Fiscal Revolution in America*, p. 169.
32 Kenneth Garbade, *After the Accord: A History of Federal Reserve Open Market Operations, the US Government Securities Market, and Treasury Debt Management from 1951 to 1979*, Cambridge University Press, 2021, p. 1.
33 Aaron Wistar, *Disorderly Markets: The Federal Reserve, the Banking Lobby, and the Government Securities Market, 1920–1961*, PhD thesis, University of California Santa Cruz, 2021, p. 62.
34 Ibid., p. 51.
35 Garbade, *After the Accord: A History of Federal Reserve Open Market Operations, the US Government Securities Market, and Treasury Debt Management from 1951 to 1979*, p. 2; Wistar, *Disorderly Markets: The Federal Reserve, the Banking Lobby, and the Government Securities Market, 1920–1961*, pp. 69–70.
36 Wistar, *Disorderly Markets: The Federal Reserve, the Banking Lobby, and the Government Securities Market, 1920–1961*, pp. 56–7.
37 Stein, *The Fiscal Revolution in America*, p. 249.
38 Ibid., p. 278; Robert A. Degen, *The American Monetary System: A Concise Survey of its Evolution since 1896*, Lexington, 1987, p. 114.
39 Quoted in Degen, *The American Monetary System: A Concise Survey of its Evolution since 1896*, p. 117.
40 David Stein, "Containing Keynesianism in an Age of Civil Rights: Jim Crow Monetary Policy and the Struggle for Guaranteed Jobs, 1956–1979," in Gary Gerstle, Nelson Lichtenstein and Alice O'Connor, ed., *Beyond the New Deal Order: U.S. Politics from the Great Depression to the Great Recession*, University of Pennsylvania Press, 2019, p. 140.
41 Robert L. Hetzel and Ralph Leach, "The Treasury-Fed Accord: A New Narrative Account," *FRB Richmond Economic Quarterly*, 87(1), 2001, p. 58.
42 Tracy Alloway, "The Shadow is Born: How the Fed Helped Spawn a $23.7 Trillion Market," *Bloomberg*, November 7, 2022.

43 Lev Menand, *The Fed Unbound: Central Banking in a Time of Crisis*, Columbia Global Reports, 2022, p. 111.

44 Alloway, "The Shadow is Born: How the Fed Helped Spawn a $23.7 Trillion Market"; Kenneth Garbade, "The Evolution of Repo Contracting Conventions in the 1980s," *Economic Policy Review*, 12(1), 2006, p. 28.

45 For his contemporaneous statements, see Hyman P. Minsky, "Central Banking and Money Market Changes," *Quarterly Journal of Economics*, 71(2), 1957, and Hyman P. Minsky, "Financial Crisis, Financial Systems, and the Performance of the Economy," in Irwin Friend, Hyman P. Minsky and Victor L. Andrews, ed., *Private Capital Markets; A Series of Research Studies Prepared for the Commission on Money and Credit*, Prentice-Hall, 1964.

46 Alloway, "The Shadow is Born: How the Fed Helped Spawn a $23.7 Trillion Market."

47 Helen Lachs Ginsburg, "Historical Amnesia: The Humphrey–Hawkins Act, Full Employment and Employment as a Right," *Review of Black Political Economy*, 39(1), 2012, p. 126; Andrew Yamakawa Elrod, *Stabilization Politics in the Twentieth-Century United States: Corporatism, Democracy, and Economic Planning, 1945–1980*, PhD thesis, University of California Santa Barbara, 2021, p. 92.

48 Alan Brinkley, *The End of Reform: New Deal Liberalism in Recession and War*, Vintage, 1996; Jefferson Cowie and Nick Salvatore, "The Long Exception: Rethinking the Place of the New Deal in American History," *International Labor and Working-Class History*, 74(1), 2008.

49 Samir Sonti, "The Strange Career of Institutional Keynesianism," in Romain Huret, Nelson Lichtenstein and Jean-Christian Vinel, ed., *Capitalism Contested: The New Deal and its Legacies*, University of Pennsylvania Press, 2021.

50 Michael Dennis, "The Idea of Full Employment: A Challenge to Capitalism in the New Deal Era," *Labor*, 14(2), 2017, p. 70.

51 Michael Kalecki, "Political Aspects of Full Employment," *Political Quarterly*, 14(4), 1943.

52 Hyman P. Minsky, "The Strategy of Economic Policy and Income Distribution," *Annals of the American Academy of Political and Social Science*, 409(September), 1973, p. 94.

53 Nancy Beck Young, *Why We Fight: Congress and the Politics of World War II*, University Press of Kansas, 2013, pp. 228–9.

54 Eccles cited in Wistar, *Disorderly Markets: The Federal Reserve, the Banking Lobby, and the Government Securities Market, 1920–1961*, p. 167.

55 Ginsburg, "Historical Amnesia: The Humphrey–Hawkins Act, Full Employment and Employment as a Right", p. 127; Wistar, *Disorderly Markets: The Federal Reserve, the Banking Lobby, and the Government Securities Market, 1920–1961*, p. 174.

56 Margaret Weir, "Innovation and Boundaries in American Employment Policy," *Political Science Quarterly*, 107(2), 1992, p. 255.

57 Ibid., p. 256.

58 Edmund F. Wehrle, "Welfare and Warfare: American Organized Labor Approaches the Military-Industrial Complex, 1949–1964," *Armed Forces and Society*, 29(4), 2003, p. 533; Robert M. Collins, *More: The Politics of Economic Growth in Postwar America*, Oxford University Press, 2000, p. 43.

59 Wehrle, "Welfare and Warfare: American Organized Labor Approaches the Military-Industrial Complex, 1949–1964," p. 527.

60 Ginsburg, "Historical Amnesia: The Humphrey–Hawkins Act, Full Employment and Employment as a Right," p. 127.

61 Dennis R. Judd, "Symbolic Politics and Urban Policies: Why African Americans Got So Little from the Democrats," in Adolph Reed, ed., *Without Justice for All: The New Liberalism and Our Retreat from Racial Equality*, Routledge, 1999, p. 126.

62 Desmond S. King and Rogers M. Smith, *Still a House Divided: Race and Politics in Obama's America*, Princeton University Press, 2011, pp. 146–7; Gotham, "Separate and Unequal: The Housing Act of 1968 and the Section 235 Program," p. 19.

63 Judd, "Symbolic Politics and Urban Policies: Why African Americans Got So Little from the Democrats," p. 130.

64 David Freund, *Colored Property: State Policy and White Racial Politics in Suburban America*, University of Chicago Press, 2007, pp. 9–10.

65 King and Smith, *Still a House Divided: Race and Politics in Obama's America*, p. 146.

66 Dorothy A. Brown, "Homeownership in Black and White: The Role of Tax Policy in Increasing Housing Inequity," *University of Memphis Law Review*, 49, 2019, p. 224.

67 Ibid., pp. 213–14.

68 King and Smith, *Still a House Divided: Race and Politics in Obama's America*, p. 147; Judd, "Symbolic Politics and Urban Policies: Why African Americans Got So Little from the Democrats," p. 126.

69 Julia Ott, "'Leave Something for the Risk-Takers': How the Democrats Rebuilt Structural Racism and Hastened the Great Polarization, 1964–1978," in Rudiger L. von Arnim and Joseph E. Stiglitz, ed., *The Great Polarization: How Ideas, Power, and Policies Drive Inequality*, Columbia University Press, 2022, p. 233.

70 Gary A. Dymski, "Racial Exclusion and the Political Economy of the Subprime Crisis," *Historical Materialism*, 17(2), 2009, p. 152.

71 Ibid., p. 152.

72 Michael McCarthy, "Turning Labor into Capital: Pension Funds and the Corporate Control of Finance," *Politics & Society*, 42(4), 2014, p. 457.

73 Michael R. Glass and Sean H. Vanatta, "The Frail Bonds of Liberalism: Pensions, Schools, and the Unraveling of Fiscal Mutualism in Postwar New York," *Capitalism: A Journal of History and Economics*, 2(2), 2021, pp. 428–9.

74 Baradaran, *The Color of Money: Black Banks and the Racial Wealth Gap*, p. 109; Glass and Vanatta, "The Frail Bonds of Liberalism: Pensions, Schools, and the Unraveling of Fiscal Mutualism in Postwar New York", p. 228. This is not to say that the postwar era simply reproduced pre-existing racial divides. It brought down

barriers for some immigrant groups, and it expanded the definition of whiteness to include new groups such as those of Italian and Polish descent (Baradaran, *The Color of Money: Black Banks and the Racial Wealth Gap*, p. 126).

75 Stein, "Containing Keynesianism in an Age of Civil Rights: Jim Crow Monetary Policy and the Struggle for Guaranteed Jobs, 1956–1979," p. 133.

76 Quoted in Nick Timiraos, *Trillion Dollar Triage*, Little, Brown, 2022, p. 31.

77 Quoted in Anthony T. Ross, *"The Ownership Society": Mortgage Securitization and the Metropolitan Landscape Since the 1960s*, PhD thesis, University of Michigan, 2015, p. 94.

78 Edwin Dickens, "U.S. Monetary Policy in the 1950s: A Radical Political Economic Approach," *Review of Radical Political Economics*, 27(4), 1995.

Chapter 4: The Promise of Growth

1 Stein, "Containing Keynesianism in an Age of Civil Rights: Jim Crow Monetary Policy and the Struggle for Guaranteed Jobs, 1956–1979," p. 129.

2 Collins, *More: The Politics of Economic Growth in Postwar America*, p. 51.

3 Josh Mound, "Stirrings of Revolt: Regressive Levies, the Pocketbook Squeeze, and the 1960s Roots of the 1970s Tax Revolt," *Journal of Policy History*, 32(2), 2020, p. 109.

4 Kenneth T. Andrews and Sarah Gaby, "Local Protest and Federal Policy: The Impact of the Civil Rights Movement on the 1964 Civil Rights Act," *Sociological Forum*, 30(S1), 2015, p. 509.

5 Quoted in Collins, *More: The Politics of Economic Growth in Postwar America*, p. 52.

6 Aaron Major, *Architects of Austerity: International Finance and the Politics of Growth*, Stanford University Press, 2014, p. 131.

7 Quoted in Cebul, *Illusions of Progress: Business, Poverty, and Liberalism in the American Century*, p. 41.

8 Weir, "Innovation and Boundaries in American Employment Policy," p. 257.
9 Cebul, *Illusions of Progress: Business, Poverty, and Liberalism in the American Century*, p. 106.
10 Major, *Architects of Austerity: International Finance and the Politics of Growth*, p. 133.
11 Samuelson and Solow, "Analytical Aspects of Anti-Inflation Policy."
12 Daniel J.B. Mitchell and Christopher L. Erickson, "The Concept of Wage-Push Inflation: Development and Policy," *Labor History*, 49(4), 2008, p. 418; Norikazu Takami, "The Baffling New Inflation: How Cost-Push Inflation Theories Influenced Policy Debate in the Late-1950s United States," *History of Political Economy*, 47(4), 2015; Samuel Milner, "Assuming Direct Control: The Beguiling Allure of Incomes Policies in Postwar America," *Journal of Policy History*, 31(1), 2018, p. 49.
13 W. Elliott Brownlee, "Tax Policy in the United States: Was There a 'Neo-Liberal' Revolution in the 1970s and 1980s?", in Gisela Huerlimann, W. Elliot Brownlee and Eisaku Ide, ed., *Worlds of Taxation*, Palgrave Macmillan, 2018, p. 161.
14 Elizabeth Popp Berman and Nicholas Pagnucco, "Economic Ideas and the Political Process: Debating Tax Cuts in the U.S. House of Representatives, 1962–1981," *Politics and Society*, 38(3), 2010, p. 351.
15 Quoted in Collins, *More: The Politics of Economic Growth in Postwar America*, p. 52.
16 As Kennedy had put it, "only full employment can . . . achieve the more prosperous, expanding economy which can bring a budget surplus" (quoted in Cebul, *Illusions of Progress: Business, Poverty, and Liberalism in the American Century*, p. 106).
17 Major, *Architects of Austerity: International Finance and the Politics of Growth*, p. 135; Brownlee, "Tax Policy in the United States: Was There a 'Neo-Liberal' Revolution in the 1970s and 1980s?", p. 160.

18 Quoted in Cebul, *Illusions of Progress: Business, Poverty, and Liberalism in the American Century*, p. 107.

19 Brownlee, "Tax Policy in the United States: Was There a 'Neo-Liberal' Revolution in the 1970s and 1980s?", p. 161.

20 Berman and Pagnucco, "Economic Ideas and the Political Process: Debating Tax Cuts in the U.S. House of Representatives, 1962–1981," p. 351.

21 Quoted in Cebul, *Illusions of Progress: Business, Poverty, and Liberalism in the American Century*, p. 106.

22 Heller quoted in Major, *Architects of Austerity: International Finance and the Politics of Growth*, p. 136.

23 Ibid., pp. 132–3.

24 Milner, "Assuming Direct Control: The Beguiling Allure of Incomes Policies in Postwar America," p. 49.

25 Lancourt, *Benefiting Business: The Fragmented Federal Response to American Deindustrialization*, pp. 72–3.

26 Michel Feher, "Actualizing, Enterprising and Appreciating Selves: The Three Guises of Human Capital," unpublished ms., 2023, p. 3.

27 Ibid., pp. 5–6.

28 Collins, *More: The Politics of Economic Growth in Postwar America*, p. 53.

29 Ben S. Bernanke, *21st Century Monetary Policy: The Federal Reserve from the Great Inflation to COVID-19*, W.W. Norton & Company, 2022, p. 18.

30 Quoted in Wyatt C. Wells, *Economist in an Uncertain World: Arthur F. Burns and the Federal Reserve, 1970–78*, Columbia University Press, 1994, p. 20.

31 Bernanke, *21st Century Monetary Policy: The Federal Reserve from the Great Inflation to COVID-19*, p. 18.

32 Judge Glock, *The Dead Pledge: The Origins of the Mortgage Market and Federal Bailouts, 1913–1939*, Columbia University Press, 2021, p. 8.

33 Robert Z. Aliber, "The Commission on Money and Credit: Ten Years Later," *Journal of Money, Credit and Banking*, 4(4), 1972.

34 Eugene N. White, *The Comptroller and the Transformation of American Banking 1960–1990*, Comptroller of the Currency, 1992; Phillip L. Zweig, *Wriston: Walter Wriston, Citibank, and the Rise and Fall of American Financial Supremacy*, Crown Publishers, Inc., 1995, p. 147.

35 Ott, "'Leave Something for the Risk-Takers': How the Democrats Rebuilt Structural Racism and Hastened the Great Polarization, 1964–1978," p. 237.

36 Major, *Architects of Austerity: International Finance and the Politics of Growth*, p. 158.

37 Collins, *More: The Politics of Economic Growth in Postwar America*, p. 51.

38 Major, *Architects of Austerity: International Finance and the Politics of Growth*, p. 162.

39 Ibid., pp. 162–3.

40 Ibid., p. 169.

41 Ibid., pp. 173–4.

42 Robert M. Collins, "The Economic Crisis of 1968 and the Waning of the 'American Century'," *American Historical Review*, 101(2), 1996, p. 421.

43 Zweig, *Wriston: Walter Wriston, Citibank, and the Rise and Fall of American Financial Supremacy*, p. 46.

44 Minsky, "Financial Crisis, Financial Systems, and the Performance of the Economy," p. 197.

45 Ibid., pp. 179–80.

46 Martijn Konings, *The Development of American Finance*, Cambridge University Press, 2011, ch. 10.

47 Zweig, *Wriston: Walter Wriston, Citibank, and the Rise and Fall of American Financial Supremacy*, p. 141.

48 Onur Özgöde, "The Emergence of Systemic Risk: The Federal Reserve, Bailouts, and Monetary Government at the Limits," *Socio-Economic Review*, 20(4), 2022, p. 2052.

49 Samuel Knafo, "The Power of Finance in the Age of Market Based Banking," *New Political Economy*, 27(1), 2022, p. 42.

50 Ibid., p. 42.

51 Quinn, "'The Miracles of Bookkeeping': How Budget Politics Link Fiscal Policies and Financial Markets," p. 59; Dustin Ryan Walker, *Unleashing the Financial Sector: Home Loan Deregulation and the Savings and Loan Crisis, 1966–1989*, PhD thesis, University of California Santa Barbara, 2018, p. 33.

52 Konings, *The Development of American Finance*, ch. 10.

53 Garbade, *After the Accord: A History of Federal Reserve Open Market Operations, the US Government Securities Market, and Treasury Debt Management from 1951 to 1979*, pp. 347–50.

54 Minsky, "Financial Crisis, Financial Systems, and the Performance of the Economy," pp. 197–8.

55 Garbade, *After the Accord: A History of Federal Reserve Open Market Operations, the US Government Securities Market, and Treasury Debt Management from 1951 to 1979*, pp. 340–1; Jospeh S. Mascia, "From Sandpaper to Silk: The Treasury's Recent Refundings in Retrospect," *Financial Analysts Journal*, 26(6), 1970, pp. 98–9.

56 Garbade, *After the Accord: A History of Federal Reserve Open Market Operations, the US Government Securities Market, and Treasury Debt Management from 1951 to 1979*, p. 425.

57 Leon Wansleben, *The Rise of Central Banks: State Power in Financial Capitalism*, Harvard University Press, 2023, p. 153; Garbade, *After the Accord: A History of Federal Reserve Open Market Operations, the US Government Securities Market, and Treasury Debt Management from 1951 to 1979*, pp. 3–4, 491.

58 Major, *Architects of Austerity: International Finance and the Politics of Growth*, pp. 132–3.

59 Özgöde, "The Emergence of Systemic Risk: The Federal Reserve, Bailouts, and Monetary Government at the Limits," p. 2056.

60 Ross, *"The Ownership Society": Mortgage Securitization and the Metropolitan Landscape Since the 1960s*, p. 91.

61 Gotham, "Separate and Unequal: The Housing Act of 1968 and the Section 235 Program," p. 20.

62 Alexander von Hoffman, "Calling upon the Genius of Private Enterprise: The Housing and Urban Development Act of 1968

and the Liberal Turn to Public–Private Partnerships," *Studies in American Political Development*, 27(2), 2013, p. 166.

63 Keeanga-Yamahtta Taylor, *Race for Profit: How Banks and the Real Estate Industry Undermined Black Homeownership*, University of North Carolina Press, 2019, p. 12.

64 Hoffman, "Calling upon the Genius of Private Enterprise: The Housing and Urban Development Act of 1968 and the Liberal Turn to Public–Private Partnerships," p. 165.

65 Taylor, *Race for Profit: How Banks and the Real Estate Industry Undermined Black Homeownership*, p. 61.

66 Ibid., p. 56.

67 Quinn, "'The Miracles of Bookkeeping': How Budget Politics Link Fiscal Policies and Financial Markets," p. 71; Gotham, "Separate and Unequal: The Housing Act of 1968 and the Section 235 Program," p. 22.

68 Ross, *"The Ownership Society": Mortgage Securitization and the Metropolitan Landscape Since the 1960s*, p. 2.

69 Ibid., pp. 10–11.

Chapter 5: The Inflation Decade

1 Benjamin C. Waterhouse, "Mobilizing for the Market: Organized Business, Wage-Price Controls, and the Politics of Inflation, 1971–1974," *Journal of American History*, 100(2), 2013, p. 455.

2 Patrick J. Akard, *The Return of the Market: Corporate Mobilization and the Transformation of U.S. Economic Policy, 1974–1984*, PhD thesis, University of Kansas, 1989, p. 152.

3 Wells, *Economist in an Uncertain World: Arthur F. Burns and the Federal Reserve, 1970–78*, p. 35.

4 Akard, *The Return of the Market: Corporate Mobilization and the Transformation of U.S. Economic Policy, 1974–1984*, p. 65.

5 Ibid., p. 65.

6 Waterhouse, "Mobilizing for the Market: Organized Business, Wage-Price Controls, and the Politics of Inflation, 1971–1974," p. 466.

7 Allen J. Matusow, *Nixon's Economy: Booms, Bust, Dollars, and*

Votes, University Press of Kansas, 1998, p. 1; Jefferson Cowie, "Nixon's Class Struggle: Romancing the New Right Worker, 1969–1973," *Labor History*, 43(3), 2002, p. 257.

8　Collins, *More: The Politics of Economic Growth in Postwar America*, p. 126.

9　Timiraos, *Trillion Dollar Triage*, pp. 36–7.

10　Waterhouse, "Mobilizing for the Market: Organized Business, Wage-Price Controls, and the Politics of Inflation, 1971–1974," p. 463; Timothy Barker, "'Don't Discuss Jobs Outside This Room': Reconsidering Military Keynesianism in the 1970s," in Jennifer Mittelstadt and Mark R. Wilson, ed., *The Military and the Market*, University of Pennsylvania Press, 2022, pp. 143–4.

11　Akard, *The Return of the Market: Corporate Mobilization and the Transformation of U.S. Economic Policy, 1974–1984*, p. 66; Waterhouse, "Mobilizing for the Market: Organized Business, Wage-Price Controls, and the Politics of Inflation, 1971–1974," p. 477.

12　Cowie, "Nixon's Class Struggle: Romancing the New Right Worker, 1969–1973," p. 275.

13　Collins, *More: The Politics of Economic Growth in Postwar America*, p. 127.

14　John T. Woolley, "Exorcising Inflation-Mindedness: The Transformation of Economic Management in the 1970s," *Journal of Policy History*, 10(1), 2011, p. 140.

15　Wells, *Economist in an Uncertain World: Arthur F. Burns and the Federal Reserve, 1970–78*, p. 150.

16　Burns to the House Committee for the Budget in 1975, quoted in ibid., p. 163.

17　Harvey L. Schantz and Richard H. Schmidt, "The Evolution of Humphrey–Hawkins," *Policy Studies Journal*, 8(3), 1979, p. 369.

18　Akard, *The Return of the Market: Corporate Mobilization and the Transformation of U.S. Economic Policy, 1974–1984*, pp. 8, 69–70.

19　Dan Immergluck, *Credit to the Community: Community*

Reinvestment and Fair Lending Policy in the United States, Routledge, 2004.

20 Joe Mariano, "Organizing Access to Capital: Advocacy and the Democratization of Financial Institutions," in Gregory D. Squires, ed., *Where the Hell Did Billions of Dollars for Reinvestment Come From?*, Temple University Press, 2003, p. 35.

21 Mound, "Stirrings of Revolt: Regressive Levies, the Pocketbook Squeeze, and the 1960s Roots of the 1970s Tax Revolt," p. 107; Ott, "'Leave Something for the Risk-Takers': How the Democrats Rebuilt Structural Racism and Hastened the Great Polarization, 1964–1978," p. 237.

22 Brownlee, "Tax Policy in the United States: Was There a 'Neo-Liberal' Revolution in the 1970s and 1980s?", p. 161; Mound, "Stirrings of Revolt: Regressive Levies, the Pocketbook Squeeze, and the 1960s Roots of the 1970s Tax Revolt," p. 112.

23 Cebul, *Illusions of Progress: Business, Poverty, and Liberalism in the American Century*, p. 217; Mound, "Stirrings of Revolt: Regressive Levies, the Pocketbook Squeeze, and the 1960s Roots of the 1970s Tax Revolt," p. 110.

24 Mound, "Stirrings of Revolt: Regressive Levies, the Pocketbook Squeeze, and the 1960s Roots of the 1970s Tax Revolt," p. 113. From the mid-1950s to the start of the 1970s, the overall tax burden (federal, state, local) on the bottom 90% of the population grew substantially, while for the top 10% of income earners it remained stable and for the very top it came down very significantly (ibid., pp. 113–14).

25 Ibid., p. 107.

26 Collins, *More: The Politics of Economic Growth in Postwar America*, p. 160; W. Carl Biven, *Jimmy Carter's Economy: Policy in an Age of Limits*, University of North Carolina Press, 2003, p. 33.

27 Akard, *The Return of the Market: Corporate Mobilization and the Transformation of U.S. Economic Policy, 1974–1984*, p. 151; Schantz and Schmidt, "The Evolution of Humphrey–Hawkins," p. 369.

28 Akard, *The Return of the Market: Corporate Mobilization and the Transformation of U.S. Economic Policy, 1974–1984*, p. 16.
29 Ibid., p. 167; Patrick Andelic, "'The Old Economic Rules No Longer Apply': The National Planning Idea and the Humphrey–Hawkins Full Employment Act, 1974–1978," *Journal of Policy History*, 31(1), 2019, p. 81.
30 Quoted in Akard, *The Return of the Market: Corporate Mobilization and the Transformation of U.S. Economic Policy, 1974–1984*, p. 154.
31 Andelic, "'The Old Economic Rules No Longer Apply': The National Planning Idea and the Humphrey–Hawkins Full Employment Act, 1974–1978," p. 75; Biven, *Jimmy Carter's Economy: Policy in an Age of Limits*, p. 33.
32 Mathew Forstater, "From Civil Rights to Economic Security: Bayard Rustin and the African-American Struggle for Full Employment, 1945–1978," *International Journal of Political Economy*, 36(3), 2007, p. 65; Benjamin Y. Fong, "The Jobs and Freedom Strategy," *Catalyst*, 7(2), 2023, p. 54.
33 Quoted in Forstater, "From Civil Rights to Economic Security: Bayard Rustin and the African-American Struggle for Full Employment, 1945–1978," pp. 68–9.
34 Fong, "The Jobs and Freedom Strategy," p. 69.
35 Weir, "Full Employment as a Political Issue in the United States," pp. 391–2; Weir, "Innovation and Boundaries in American Employment Policy," p. 259.
36 Paul Frymer, *Black and Blue: African Americans, the Labor Movement, and the Decline of the Democratic Party*, Princeton University Press, 2008, p. 15.
37 Ott, "'Leave Something for the Risk-Takers': How the Democrats Rebuilt Structural Racism and Hastened the Great Polarization, 1964–1978," p. 236.
38 Joshua M. Mound, *Inflated Hopes, Taxing Times: Fiscal Crisis, the Pocketbook Squeeze, and the Roots of the Tax Revolt*, PhD thesis, University of Michigan, 2015, p. 795
39 Stephanie L. Mudge, *Leftism Reinvented: Western Parties from*

Socialism to Neoliberalism, Harvard University Press, 2018, p. 271.

40 Akard, *The Return of the Market: Corporate Mobilization and the Transformation of U.S. Economic Policy, 1974–1984*, pp. 67–8.

41 Ott, "'Leave Something for the Risk-Takers': How the Democrats Rebuilt Structural Racism and Hastened the Great Polarization, 1964–1978," p. 235.

42 In 1950, US pension funds had held 30% of their assets in public debt, 42% in corporate debt, and 16% in stock; by 1972, these numbers were 2%, 18% and 74%, respectively (McCarthy, "Turning Labor into Capital: Pension Funds and the Corporate Control of Finance," p. 459).

43 Ott, "'Leave Something for the Risk-Takers': How the Democrats Rebuilt Structural Racism and Hastened the Great Polarization, 1964–1978," pp. 235–6. To an older generation of fund managers, the idea of investing pension savings in risky ventures was anathema. But fiduciary standards were reshaped by modern portfolio theory, which understood risk as a property not of individual assets but of an investment portfolio as a whole (Natascha van der Zwan, "Financialisation and the Pension System: Lessons from the United States and the Netherlands," *Journal of Modern European History*, 15(4), 2017, p. 566).

44 McCarthy, "Turning Labor into Capital: Pension Funds and the Corporate Control of Finance," p. 469.

45 William Lazonick and Mariana Mazzucato, "The Risk–Reward Nexus in the Innovation–Inequality Relationship: Who Takes the Risks? Who Gets the Rewards?", *Industrial and Corporate Change*, 22(4), 2013, p. 1110.

46 Judith Stein, *Pivotal Decade*, Yale University Press, 2010, p. 177.

47 Collins, *More: The Politics of Economic Growth in Postwar America*, p. 157; Mound, *Inflated Hopes, Taxing Times: Fiscal Crisis, the Pocketbook Squeeze, and the Roots of the Tax Revolt*, p. 812.

48 Biven, *Jimmy Carter's Economy: Policy in an Age of Limits*, p. 34; Phillip J. Cooper, *The War Against Regulation: From Jimmy*

Carter to George W. Bush, University Press of Kansas, 2009, p. 14.

49 Quoted in Biven, *Jimmy Carter's Economy: Policy in an Age of Limits*, p. 68.

50 Bruce J. Schulman, "Slouching Towards the Supply-Side: Jimmy Carter and the New American Political Economy," in Gary M. Fink and Hugh Davis Graham, ed., *The Carter Presidency: Policy Choices in the Post-New Deal Era*, University of Kansas Press, 1998, pp. 54–5.

51 Biven, *Jimmy Carter's Economy: Policy in an Age of Limits*, p. 72.

52 Ibid., p. 89.

53 Schultze quoted in Schulman, "Slouching Towards the Supply-Side: Jimmy Carter and the New American Political Economy," p. 54.

54 Ibid., p. 61.

55 Ibid., p. 62.

56 Ibid., p. 62.

57 Milton Friedman, "The Role of Monetary Policy," *American Economic Review*, 58(1), 1968; Edmund S. Phelps, "Money-Wage Dynamics and Labor-Market Equilibrium," *Journal of Political Economy*, 76(4), 1968; Robert E. Lucas, Jr. and Leonard A. Rapping, "Price Expectations and the Phillips Curve," *American Economic Review*, 59(3), 1969; Robert E. Lucas, Jr., "Expectations and the Neutrality of Money," *Journal of Economic Theory*, 4(2), 1972.

58 Woolley, "Exorcising Inflation-Mindedness: The Transformation of Economic Management in the 1970s."

59 Ginsburg, "Historical Amnesia: The Humphrey–Hawkins Act, Full Employment and Employment as a Right," p. 131.

60 Akard, *The Return of the Market: Corporate Mobilization and the Transformation of U.S. Economic Policy, 1974–1984*, pp. 167–8.

61 Wells, *Economist in an Uncertain World: Arthur F. Burns and the Federal Reserve, 1970–78*, p. 199.

62 Biven, *Jimmy Carter's Economy: Policy in an Age of Limits*, pp. 32–3; Andelic, "'The Old Economic Rules No Longer Apply':

The National Planning Idea and the Humphrey–Hawkins Full Employment Act, 1974–1978," p. 84; Ginsburg, "Historical Amnesia: The Humphrey–Hawkins Act, Full Employment and Employment as a Right," p. 128.

63 Stein, *Pivotal Decade*, p. 149; Biven, *Jimmy Carter's Economy: Policy in an Age of Limits*, p. 33; Collins, *More: The Politics of Economic Growth in Postwar America*, p. 157.

64 Quoted in Akard, *The Return of the Market: Corporate Mobilization and the Transformation of U.S. Economic Policy, 1974–1984*, p. 176.

65 Schantz and Schmidt, "The Evolution of Humphrey–Hawkins," p. 372.

66 Ibid., p. 375.

67 Ibid., p. 374.

68 Schulman, "Slouching Towards the Supply-Side: Jimmy Carter and the New American Political Economy," p. 59.

69 Otis L. Graham, *Losing Time: The Industrial Policy Debate*, Harvard University Press, 1992, p. 29.

70 Collins, *More: The Politics of Economic Growth in Postwar America*, p. 173.

71 Berman shows that progressives found common ground with the Nixon administration in approaching anti-poverty policy in terms of efficiency considerations (Berman, *Thinking like an Economist: How Efficiency Replaced Equality in U.S. Public Policy*, p. 178). When Democrats were back in power with Carter this had become a fait accompli, with all attention focused on technocratic, efficiency-driven "welfare reform" (ibid., p. 197).

72 Ibid., p. 66.

73 Ibid., p. 165; Iwan Morgan, "Jimmy Carter, Bill Clinton, and the New Democratic Economics," *Historical Journal*, 47(4), 2004, p. 1032.

74 Cooper, *The War Against Regulation: From Jimmy Carter to George W. Bush*, p. 15.

75 Katharine C. Lyall, "Public–Private Partnerships in the Carter

Years," *Proceedings of the Academy of Political Science*, 36(2), 1986, p. 5.

76 Biven, *Jimmy Carter's Economy: Policy in an Age of Limits*, p. 138.

77 Quoted in Edward R. Kantowicz, "The Limits of Incrementalism: Carter's Efforts at Tax Reform," *Journal of Policy Analysis and Management*, 4(2), 1985, p. 221.

78 Akard, *The Return of the Market: Corporate Mobilization and the Transformation of U.S. Economic Policy, 1974–1984*, p. 17.

79 Sidney A. Rothstein, "Toward a Discursive Approach to Growth Models: Social Blocs in the Politics of Digital Transformation," *Review of International Political Economy*, 29(4), 2022, p. 1218; Bruce Bartlett, "The Case for Ending the Capital Gains Tax," *Financial Analysts Journal*, 41(3), 1985, pp. 24, 27.

80 Bartlett, "The Case for Ending the Capital Gains Tax," p. 24. In testimony before Congress, Carter's own Budget Director Bert Lance commented: "My personal observation is that as you go through the process of permanent tax reduction, that there is an awfully good argument to be made for the fact that the revenues of the Government actually increase at a given time. I think it has been proven in previous circumstances. I have no problem in following that sort of thing" (quoted in Bruce R. Bartlett, *Reaganomics: Supply Side Economics in Action*, Arlington House, 1981, p. 131).

81 Morgan, "Jimmy Carter, Bill Clinton, and the New Democratic Economics," pp. 1028–9; Mound, *Inflated Hopes, Taxing Times: Fiscal Crisis, the Pocketbook Squeeze, and the Roots of the Tax Revolt*, p. 910; Bartlett, "The Case for Ending the Capital Gains Tax," p. 28.

82 Rothstein, "Toward a Discursive Approach to Growth Models: Social Blocs in the Politics of Digital Transformation," p. 1218; Ott, "'Leave Something for the Risk-Takers': How the Democrats Rebuilt Structural Racism and Hastened the Great Polarization, 1964–1978," p. 241.

83 Mark H. Rose, *Market Rules: Bankers, Presidents, and the Origins of the Great Recession*, 2019, p. 48.

84 Ibid., p. 53.
85 Ibid., p. 55.
86 Ibid., p. 43; Walker, *Unleashing the Financial Sector: Home Loan Deregulation and the Savings and Loan Crisis, 1966–1989*, p. 79.
87 Rose, *Market Rules: Bankers, Presidents, and the Origins of the Great Recession*, p. 55.
88 Ibid., p. 56. As Barton points out, "Democrats did not reluctantly consent to a Republican plan to deregulate the financial industry; rather, the Democratic Party initiated financial deregulation" (Richard Barton, "Upending the New Deal Regulatory Regime: Democratic Party Position Change on Financial Regulation," *Perspectives on Politics*, 2022, p. 1.
89 Quoted in Biven, *Jimmy Carter's Economy: Policy in an Age of Limits*, p. 7.
90 Ibid., pp. 92–3.
91 Akard, *The Return of the Market: Corporate Mobilization and the Transformation of U.S. Economic Policy, 1974–1984*, p. 15.

Chapter 6: Building the Bailout State
1 Quoted in Timiraos, *Trillion Dollar Triage*, p. 34.
2 Arthur F. Burns, *The Anguish of Central Banking*, Per Jacobsson Lecture, 1979, p. 9.
3 Ibid., p. 12.
4 Ibid., p. 21.
5 Panitch and Gindin, *The Making of Global Capitalism: The Political Economy of American Empire*, p. 163.
6 Paul A. Volcker, *The Triumph of Central Banking?*, Per Jacobsson Lecture, 1990, p. 5.
7 Quoted in Wansleben, *The Rise of Central Banks: State Power in Financial Capitalism*, p. 121.
8 Robert E. Weintraub, "Some Neglected Monetary Contributions: Congressman Wright Patman (1893–1976)," *Journal of Money, Credit and Banking*, 9(4), 1977, pp. 526–7; Robert E. Weintraub, "Congressional Supervision of Monetary Policy," *Journal of Monetary Economics*, 4(2), 1978, p. 343.

9 Milton Friedman and Anna Jacobson Schwartz, *A Monetary History of the United States, 1867–1960*, Princeton University Press, 1963.

10 Matusow, *Nixon's Economy: Booms, Bust, Dollars, and Votes*, p. 26.

11 Weintraub, "Some Neglected Monetary Contributions: Congressman Wright Patman (1893–1976)," p. 519.

12 Wells, *Economist in an Uncertain World: Arthur F. Burns and the Federal Reserve, 1970–78*, p. 151.

13 Weintraub, "Some Neglected Monetary Contributions: Congressman Wright Patman (1893–1976)," p. 527.

14 Peter A. Johnson, *The Government of Money: Monetarism in Germany and the United States*, Cornell University Press, 1998, p. 149.

15 Paul A. Volcker, "The Contributions and Limitations of 'Monetary' Analysis," *Federal Reserve Bank of New York Quarterly Review*, 1979, p. 39.

16 Ibid., p. 36.

17 Ibid., p. 36.

18 Paul A. Volcker, "The Role of Monetary Targets in an Age of Inflation," *Journal of Monetary Economics*, 4(2), 1978, pp. 332–3.

19 Iwan Morgan, "Reaganomics and its Legacy," in Cheryl Hudson and Gareth Davies, ed., *Ronal Reagan and the 1980s: Perceptions, Policies, Legacies*, Palgrave, 2008, p. 103.

20 Christoper Leonard, *The Lords of Easy Money: How the Federal Reserve Broke the American Economy*, Simon and Schuster, 2022, p. 58.

21 Morgan, "Reaganomics and its Legacy," p. 104.

22 William Greider, *Secrets of the Temple: How the Federal Reserve Runs the Country*, Simon and Schuster, 1987.

23 Hyman P. Minsky, "Review of 'Secrets of the Temple: How the Federal Reserve Runs the Country'," *Challenge*, 31(3), 1988, p. 59.

24 Knafo, "The Power of Finance in the Age of Market Based Banking," p. 34.

25 George Hanc, "The Banking Crises of the 1980s and Early 1990s: Summary and Implications," *Federal Deposit Insurance Corporation Banking Review*, 11(1), 1998, p. 1.

26 Allen N. Berger, Anil K. Kashyap, Joseph M. Scalise, Mark Gertler and Benjamin M. Friedman, "The Transformation of the U.S. Banking Industry: What a Long, Strange Trip it's Been," *Brookings Papers on Economic Activity*, 2, 1995, p. 67.

27 Volcker, "The Role of Monetary Targets in an Age of Inflation," p. 338.

28 Volcker to the Federal Open Market Committee in 1982, quoted in Panitch and Gindin, *The Making of Global Capitalism: The Political Economy of American Empire*, p. 179.

29 Gary A. Dymski, *The Bank Merger Wave: The Economic Causes and Social Consequences of Financial Consolidation*, Routledge, 1999, p. 41.

30 Rose, *Market Rules: Bankers, Presidents, and the Origins of the Great Recession*, p. 59.

31 William M. Isaac, *Senseless Panic: How Washington Failed America*, Wiley, 2012, pp. 67–8.

32 John F. Bovenzi, *Inside the FDIC: Thirty Years of Bank Failures, Bailouts, and Regulatory Battles*, Wiley, 2015, p. 24.

33 Wistar, *Disorderly Markets: The Federal Reserve, the Banking Lobby, and the Government Securities Market, 1920–1961*, p. 357.

34 Collins, *More: The Politics of Economic Growth in Postwar America*, p. 211.

35 Özgöde, "The Emergence of Systemic Risk: The Federal Reserve, Bailouts, and Monetary Government at the Limits," p. 2057.

36 Ibid., p. 2057; Norbert Gaillard and Rick Michalek, "The Institutionalization of Bailouts, 1970–1984," in Juan Flores Zendejas, Norbert Gaillard and Rick Michalek, ed., *Moral Hazard: A Financial, Legal, and Economic Perspective*, Routledge, 2022, p. 137.

37 George C. Nurisso and Edward Simpson Prescott, "Origins of

Too-Big-To-Fail Policy in the United States," *Financial History Review*, 27(1), 2020, pp. 2–3.

38 Ibid., p. 3.

39 Ibid., p. 3.

40 Ibid., p. 3; Gaillard and Michalek, "The Institutionalization of Bailouts, 1970–1984," pp. 139–40.

41 Nurisso and Prescott, "Origins of Too-Big-To-Fail Policy in the United States," pp. 4–6; Gaillard and Michalek, "The Institutionalization of Bailouts, 1970–1984," pp. 139–40

42 Irvine H. Sprague, *Bailout: An Insider's Account of Bank Failures and Rescues*, Beard Books, 1986, p. 49.

43 Ibid., p. 49.

44 Bovenzi, *Inside the FDIC: Thirty Years of Bank Failures, Bailouts, and Regulatory Battles*, p. 24.

45 Sprague, *Bailout: An Insider's Account of Bank Failures and Rescues*, p. 89.

46 Panitch and Gindin, *The Making of Global Capitalism: The Political Economy of American Empire*, p. 170.

47 Gary A. Dymski, "Genie out of the Bottle: The Evolution of Too-Big-to-Fail Policy and Banking Strategy in the US," *Post-Keynesian Study Group Working Paper*, 2011, p. 13.

48 Ibid., pp. 13–14.

49 Leonard, *The Lords of Easy Money: How the Federal Reserve Broke the American Economy*, p. 66.

50 Sprague, *Bailout: An Insider's Account of Bank Failures and Rescues*, p. 162; Sebastian Mallaby, *The Man Who Knew: The Life and Times of Alan Greenspan*, 2016, p. 300; Isaac, *Senseless Panic: How Washington Failed America*, p. 70.

51 Quoted in Leonard, *The Lords of Easy Money: How the Federal Reserve Broke the American Economy*, p. 67.

52 Dymski, "Genie out of the Bottle: The Evolution of Too-Big-to-Fail Policy and Banking Strategy in the US," p. 9.

53 Wansleben, *The Rise of Central Banks: State Power in Financial Capitalism*, p. 123.

54 Garbade, "The Evolution of Repo Contracting Conventions in the 1980s," p. 33.
55 Ibid., p. 35.
56 Wansleben, *The Rise of Central Banks: State Power in Financial Capitalism*, p. 153.
57 Volcker quoted in ibid., p. 154 (italics in the original).
58 Garbade, "The Evolution of Repo Contracting Conventions in the 1980s," p. 36; Wistar, *Disorderly Markets: The Federal Reserve, the Banking Lobby, and the Government Securities Market, 1920–1961*, pp. 357–8; Leon Wansleben, "Formal Institution Building in Financialized Capitalism: The Case of Repo Markets," *Theory and Society*, 49(2), 2020, p. 198.
59 Wansleben, "Formal Institution Building in Financialized Capitalism: The Case of Repo Markets," p. 200.
60 Bartlett, "The Case for Ending the Capital Gains Tax," p. 26.
61 Edward A. Zelinsky, *The Origins of the Ownership Society: How the Defined Contribution Paradigm Changed America*, Oxford University Press, 2007, p. 52.
62 Ibid., p. 54; van der Zwan, "Financialisation and the Pension System: Lessons from the United States and the Netherlands," p. 568.
63 Bryan Burrough and John Helyar, *Barbarians at the Gate: The Fall of RJR Nabisco*, Harper & Row, 1989.
64 Lazonick and Mazzucato, "The Risk–Reward Nexus in the Innovation–Inequality Relationship: Who Takes the Risks? Who Gets the Rewards?", p. 1111; Knafo, "The Power of Finance in the Age of Market Based Banking," p. 41.
65 Leonard, *The Lords of Easy Money: How the Federal Reserve Broke the American Economy*, pp. 56, 81.
66 Wansleben, *The Rise of Central Banks: State Power in Financial Capitalism*, pp. 124–5.
67 Mark Carlson, "A Brief History of the 1987 Stock Market Crash with a Discussion of the Federal Reserve Response," Finance and Economics Discussion Series, Divisions of Research & Statistics

and Monetary Affairs, Federal Reserve Board, Washington, D.C., 2007.

68 Mallaby, *The Man Who Knew: The Life and Times of Alan Greenspan*, p. 379; Leonard, *The Lords of Easy Money: How the Federal Reserve Broke the American Economy*, p. 83.

69 Degen, *The American Monetary System: A Concise Survey of its Evolution Since 1896*, p. 181; Sarkis Joseph Khoury, *U.S. Banking and its Regulation in the Political Context*, University Press of America, 1997, p. 37.

70 Kitty Calavita, Henry N. Pontell and Robert Tillman, *Big Money Crime: Fraud and Politics in the Savings and Loan Crisis*, University of California Press, 1997, p. 127; Dymski, "Genie out of the Bottle: The Evolution of Too-Big-to-Fail Policy and Banking Strategy in the US," p. 13.

71 Dymski, "Genie out of the Bottle: The Evolution of Too-Big-to-Fail Policy and Banking Strategy in the US," p. 18.

72 Özgöde, "The Emergence of Systemic Risk: The Federal Reserve, Bailouts, and Monetary Government at the Limits," p. 2062.

73 Larry D. Wall, "Too-Big-to-Fail after FDICIA," *Federal Reserve Bank of Atlanta Economic Review*, 78, 1993, p. 14.

74 Quoted in Özgöde, "The Emergence of Systemic Risk: The Federal Reserve, Bailouts, and Monetary Government at the Limits," p. 2062.

75 Wall, "Too-Big-to-Fail after FDICIA," p. 14.

76 Arthur E. Willmarth, "The Transformation of the U.S. Financial Services Industry, 1975–2000: Competition, Consolidation, and Increased Risks," *University of Illinois Law Review*, 215, 2002, p. 300; Özgöde, "The Emergence of Systemic Risk: The Federal Reserve, Bailouts, and Monetary Government at the Limits," p. 2062.

Chapter 7: Asset-Driven Growth

1 Jon F. Hale, "The Making of the New Democrats," *Political Science Quarterly*, 110(2), 1995, pp. 210–11.

2 Ed Burmilla, *Chaotic Neutral: How the Democrats Lost Their*

Soul in the Center, Bold Type Books, 2022, p. 86; Hale, "The Making of the New Democrats," p. 219.

3 Quoted in Robert Pear, "In a Final Draft, Democrats Reject a Part of Their Past," *New York Times*, June 26, 1992.

4 Collins, *More: The Politics of Economic Growth in Postwar America*, pp. 190–1.

5 Richard McGahey, "The Political Economy of Austerity in the United States," *Social Research: An International Quarterly*, 80(3), 2013, p. 730.

6 Isaac William Martin, *The Permanent Tax Revolt: How the Property Tax Transformed American Politics*, Stanford University Press, 2008, pp. 128–9.

7 Ibid., p. 130; Monica Prasad, "The Popular Origins of Neoliberalism in the Reagan Tax Cut of 1981," *Journal of Policy History*, 24(3), 2012, pp. 366–7.

8 Timur Ergen and Inga Rademacher, "The Silicon Valley Imaginary: US Corporate Tax Reform in the 1980s," *Socio-Economic Review*, 21(2), 2021, p. 8.

9 Lancourt, *Benefiting Business: The Fragmented Federal Response to American Deindustrialization*, p. 178.

10 Renée A. Berger, "Private-Sector Initiatives in the Reagan Administration," *Proceedings of the Academy of Political Science*, 36(2), 1986, p. 15.

11 Quoted in Lancourt, *Benefiting Business: The Fragmented Federal Response to American Deindustrialization*, p. 178.

12 Ibid., pp. 178–9; Timothy P.R. Weaver, *Blazing the Neoliberal Trail: Urban Political Development in the United States and the United Kingdom*, University of Pennsylvania Press, 2016, p. 45.

13 Al From, *The New Democrats and the Return to Power*, St. Martin's Press, 2013.

14 Burmilla, *Chaotic Neutral: How the Democrats Lost Their Soul in the Center*, p. 87.

15 Sara Miles, *How to Hack a Party Line: The Democrats and Silicon Valley*, University of California Press, 2001, pp. 54–5;

Michel Feher, "Self-Appreciation; or, the Aspirations of Human Capital," *Public Culture*, 21(1), 2009; Jenny Andersson, *The Library and the Workshop: Social Democracy and Capitalism in the Knowledge Age*, Stanford University Press, 2010, p. 5.

16 Burmilla, *Chaotic Neutral: How the Democrats Lost Their Soul in the Center*, p. 87.

17 Ergen and Rademacher, "The Silicon Valley Imaginary: US Corporate Tax Reform in the 1980s," p. 16.

18 Iwan Morgan, "A New Democrat's New Economics," in Mark White, ed., *The Presidency of Bill Clinton: The Legacy of a New Domestic and Foreign Policy*, I.B. Tauris, 2012, pp. 66–7.

19 Ergen and Rademacher, "The Silicon Valley Imaginary: US Corporate Tax Reform in the 1980s," pp. 11–12.

20 Björn Bremer and Sean McDaniel, "The Ideational Foundations of Social Democratic Austerity in the Context of the Great Recession," *Socio-Economic Review*, 18(2), 2020, p. 445; Flavio Romano, *Clinton and Blair: The Political Economy of the Third Way*, Routledge, 2006.

21 For Democratic state governors, the slow, and above all uneven recovery from the Volcker recession was a major source of concern. They wanted to boost the competitiveness of new industries in ways that were consistent with strong performance on employment and wages, and they were committed to the core ideas of supply-side activism (Lancourt, *Benefiting Business: The Fragmented Federal Response to American Deindustrialization*, p. 179). Massachusetts Governor Michael Dukakis responded to rampant deindustrialization with a program of public–private partnerships dedicated to funneling capital to new high-tech growth industries (David Osborne, *Laboratories of Democracy: A New Breed of Governor Creates Models for National Growth*, Harvard Business School Press, 1988, p. 23). California governor Jerry Brown adopted a similar strategy and supplemented it with extensive public investment in new training programs called "Adjustment Teams" (ibid., pp. 23–4). These models would shape the policies of the Clinton administration.

22 Curtis Atkins, *Forging a New Democratic Party: The Politics of the Third Way from Clinton to Obama*, PhD thesis, York University, 2015, p. 136; Morgan, "Jimmy Carter, Bill Clinton, and the New Democratic Economics", p. 1030.

23 Quoted in Morgan, "Jimmy Carter, Bill Clinton, and the New Democratic Economics," p. 1030.

24 Morgan, "A New Democrat's New Economics," p. 68.

25 Nelson Lichtenstein, "A Fabulous Failure: Clinton's 1990s and the Origins of Our Times," *The American Prospect*, Winter, 2018, p. 40.

26 Morgan, "Jimmy Carter, Bill Clinton, and the New Democratic Economics," p. 1032.

27 Ibid., p. 1031.

28 Lukas Haffert and Philip Mehrtens, "From Austerity to Expansion? Consolidation, Budget Surpluses, and the Decline of Fiscal Capacity," *Politics and Society*, 43(1), 2015, p. 120.

29 David Stein, "The Austerity Imperative: Democratic Deficit Hawks and the Crisis of Keynesianism," in Brent Cebul and Lily Geismer, ed., *Mastery and Drift: Professional-Class Liberals since the 1960s*, University of Chicago Press, 2025.

30 Monte Piliawsky, "The Clinton Administration and African-Americans," *The Black Scholar*, 24(2), 1994, p. 8.

31 Lancourt, *Benefiting Business: The Fragmented Federal Response to American Deindustrialization*, pp. 46, 182.

32 Morgan, "A New Democrat's New Economics," p. 71.

33 Morgan, "Jimmy Carter, Bill Clinton, and the New Democratic Economics," p. 1031.

34 Quoted in Bob Woodward, *The Agenda: Inside the Clinton White House*, Simon and Schuster, 1994, p. 84.

35 Quoted in Morgan, "A New Democrat's New Economics," pp. 69–70.

36 Morgan, "Jimmy Carter, Bill Clinton, and the New Democratic Economics," p. 1033.

37 Ibid., p. 1034.

38 Alan S. Blinder and Janet L. Yellen, *The Fabulous Decade:*

Macroeconomic Lessons from the 1990s, The Century Foundation, 2001, p. 35.

39　Maggie Mahar, *Bull! A History of the Boom and Bust, 1982–2004*, HarperBusiness, 2003, p. 19.

40　Dillon Wamsley, "Crisis Management, New Constitutionalism, and Depoliticisation: Recasting the Politics of Austerity in the US and UK, 2010–16," *New Political Economy*, 28(4), 2023, pp. 6–7.

41　Ibid., p. 7.

42　Ibid., p. 7.

43　Blinder and Yellen, *The Fabulous Decade: Macroeconomic Lessons from the 1990s*, p. 83.

44　Miles, *How to Hack a Party Line: The Democrats and Silicon Valley*, p. 51; Blinder and Yellen, *The Fabulous Decade: Macroeconomic Lessons from the 1990s*, p. 52.

45　Mahar, *Bull! A History of the Boom and Bust, 1982–2004*, pp. 251–3.

46　Leonard, *The Lords of Easy Money: How the Federal Reserve Broke the American Economy*, p. 85.

47　Mahar, *Bull! A History of the Boom and Bust, 1982–2004*, p. 93.

48　Michael McCarthy, *Dismantling Solidarity: Capitalist Politics and American Pensions since the New Deal*, Cornell University Press, 2017, pp. 151, 159; Zelinsky, *The Origins of the Ownership Society: How the Defined Contribution Paradigm Changed America*, pp. 39–45.

49　Mahar, *Bull! A History of the Boom and Bust, 1982–2004*, p. 18.

50　Michael Hudson and Kris Feder, "What's Missing From the Capital Gains Debate? Real Estate and Capital Gains Taxation," *Levy Economics Institute of Bard College*, 1997, p. 14.

51　Richard Barton, *Washington and Wall Street: The Democratic Party, Financial Deregulation, and the Remaking of the American Political Economy*, PhD thesis, Cornell University, 2022, p. 176.

52　Charles W. Calomiris and Stephen Haber, *Fragile by Design: The Political Origins of Banking Crises and Scarce Credit*, Princeton University Press, 2014, p. 239.

53 Quoted in Panitch and Gindin, *The Making of Global Capitalism: The Political Economy of American Empire*, p. 308.

54 Taylor, *Race for Profit: How Banks and the Real Estate Industry Undermined Black Homeownership*, p. 17.

55 Dymski, "Racial Exclusion and the Political Economy of the Subprime Crisis," p. 150.

56 Judd, "Symbolic Politics and Urban Policies: Why African Americans Got So Little from the Democrats," p. 141.

57 Christopher Howard, *The Welfare State Nobody Knows: Debunking Myths About U.S. Social Policy*, Princeton University Press, 2007, pp. 20–1.

58 Timothy J. Sinclair, *The New Masters of Capital: American Bond Rating Agencies and the Politics of Creditworthiness*, Cornell University Press, 2014; Michel Feher, *Rated Agency: Investee Politics in a Speculative Age*, Zone, 2018; Scott Aquanno, *The Crisis of Risk: Subprime Debt and US Financial Power from 1944 to Present*, Edward Elgar, 2021.

59 David J. Erickson, "Community Capitalism: How Housing Advocates, the Private Sector, and Government Forged New Low-Income Housing Policy, 1968–1996," *Journal of Policy History*, 18(2), 2006, p. 168.

60 Ibid., p. 171.

61 Suzanne Mettler, *The Submerged State: How Invisible Government Policies Undermine American Democracy*, University of Chicago Press, 2011; Jacob S. Hacker, "Privatizing Risk without Privatizing the Welfare State: The Hidden Politics of Social Policy Retrenchment in the United States," *American Political Science Review*, 98(2), 2004.

62 Paul Pierson, *Dismantling the Welfare State? Reagan, Thatcher, and the Politics of Retrenchment*, Cambridge University Press, 1994; Geoffrey Garrett, "Global Markets and National Politics: Collision Course or Virtuous Circle?", *International Organization*, 52(4), 1998.

63 Panitch and Gindin, *The Making of Global Capitalism: The Political Economy of American Empire*, p. 270.

64 Adkins, Cooper and Konings, *The Asset Economy: Property Ownership and the New Inequality*.

65 Edward N. Wolff, "Household Wealth Trends in the United States, 1962 to 2016: Has Middle Class Wealth Recovered?", National Bureau of Economic Research, Working Paper 24085, 2017, p. 9.

66 Margaret Weir, "The Collapse of Bill Clinton's Third Way," in Stuart White, ed., *New Labour: The Progressive Future?*, Palgrave Macmillan, 2001, pp. 144–5.

67 Wolff, "Household Wealth Trends in the United States, 1962 to 2016: Has Middle Class Wealth Recovered?", p. 12.

68 Matthias Thiemann, *Taming the Cycles of Finance? Central Banks and the Macro-Prudential Shift in Financial Regulation*, Cambridge University Press, 2024, p. 106.

69 Leonard, *The Lords of Easy Money: How the Federal Reserve Broke the American Economy*, p. 87.

70 Thiemann, *Taming the Cycles of Finance? Central Banks and the Macro-Prudential Shift in Financial Regulation*.

71 Willmarth, "The Transformation of the U.S. Financial Services Industry, 1975–2000: Competition, Consolidation, and Increased Risks," p. 472; Stephen Golub, Ayse Kaya and Michael Reay, "What Were They Thinking? The Federal Reserve in the Run-up to the 2008 Financial Crisis," *Review of International Political Economy*, 22(4), 2015.

72 Olivier Blanchard and Lawrence H. Summers, "Introduction: Rethinking Stabilization Policy: Evolution or Revolution," in Olivier Blanchard and Lawrence H. Summers, ed., *Evolution or Revolution? Rethinking Macroeconomic Policy after the Great Recession*, MIT Press, 2019, p. xvi.

73 Thiemann, *Taming the Cycles of Finance? Central Banks and the Macro-Prudential Shift in Financial Regulation*, p. 112

74 Stefan Eich and Adam Tooze, "The Great Inflation," in Anselm Doering-Manteuffel, Lutz Raphael and Thomas Schlemmer, ed., *Vorgeschichte der Gegenwart. Dimensionen des Strukturbruchs nach dem Boom*, Vandenhoeck & Ruprech, 2015.

75 Perry Mehrling, "Bernanke v. Kindleberger: Which Credit Channel?", Institute for New Economic Thinking, October 13, 2022.

76 Ben S. Bernanke and Mark Gertler, "Should Central Banks Respond to Movements in Asset Prices?", *American Economic Review*, 91(2), 2001.

77 Ben Bernanke, *The Great Moderation*, Remarks by Governor Ben S. Bernanke at the meetings of the Eastern Economic Association, Washington, D.C., February 20, 2004.

78 Ben S. Bernanke, *Courage to Act: A Memoir of a Crisis and its Aftermath*, W. W. Norton & Company, 2015.

79 Timothy Canova, "Legacy of the Clinton Bubble," *Dissent*, 55(3), 2008, p. 46.

80 Barton, *Washington and Wall Street: The Democratic Party, Financial Deregulation, and the Remaking of the American Political Economy*, p. 234.

81 Ibid., p. 234.

82 Willmarth, "The Transformation of the U.S. Financial Services Industry, 1975–2000: Competition, Consolidation, and Increased Risks," pp. 304–5; Panitch and Gindin, *The Making of Global Capitalism: The Political Economy of American Empire*, p. 266.

83 Willmarth, "The Transformation of the U.S. Financial Services Industry, 1975–2000: Competition, Consolidation, and Increased Risks," pp. 305–6.

84 Ibid., p. 305.

85 Ibid., pp. 305–6.

86 Barton, "Upending the New Deal Regulatory Regime: Democratic Party Position Change on Financial Regulation," p. 3.

87 Dymski, "Genie out of the Bottle: The Evolution of Too-Big-to-Fail Policy and Banking Strategy in the US," p. 2

88 Robert L. Hetzel, *The Great Recession*, Cambridge University Press, 2012, p. 153.

89 Willmarth, "The Transformation of the U.S. Financial Services Industry, 1975–2000: Competition, Consolidation, and Increased Risks," p. 306.

90 Wansleben, *The Rise of Central Banks: State Power in Financial Capitalism.*

Chapter 8: Bailouts and Austerity

1 Arthur E. Willmarth, "The Dark Side of Universal Banking: Financial Conglomerates and the Origins of the Subprime Financial Crisis," *Connecticut Law Review*, 41(4), 2009, pp. 1005–6.
2 Ibid.
3 Daniel Béland, "Neo-Liberalism and Social Policy," *Policy Studies Journal*, 28(2), 2007, p. 98.
4 Wolff, "Household Wealth Trends in the United States, 1962 to 2016: Has Middle Class Wealth Recovered?", p. 9.
5 Quoted in Jo Becker, Sheryl Gay Stolberg and Stephen Labaton, "White House Philosophy Stoked Mortgage Bonfire," *New York Times*, November 21, 2008.
6 Panitch and Gindin, *The Making of Global Capitalism: The Political Economy of American Empire*, p. 206.
7 Wolff, "Household Wealth Trends in the United States, 1962 to 2016: Has Middle Class Wealth Recovered?", p. 3.
8 Ibid., p. 4.
9 Panitch and Gindin, *The Making of Global Capitalism: The Political Economy of American Empire*, p. 308.
10 Jeanna Smialek, *Limitless: The Federal Reserve Takes on a New Age of Crisis*, Alfred A. Knopf, 2023, p. 91; Canova, "Legacy of the Clinton Bubble," p. 47.
11 Andra Gillespie, "Race, Real Estate, and Responsiveness: The Obama Administration's Legacy on Housing Policy and Outcomes," in Todd C. Shaw, Robert A. Brown and Joseph P. McCormick II, ed., *After Obama: African American Politics in a Post-Obama Era*, New York University Press, 2021, p. 300.
12 Timothy Shenk, "Taking Off the Neoliberal Lens: The Politics of the Economy, the MIT School of Economics, and the Strange Career of Lawrence Klein," *Modern Intellectual History*, 20(4), 2022, p. 1.

13 Henry M. Paulson, *On the Brink: Inside the Race to Stop the Collapse of the Global Financial System*, Business Plus, 2010, p. 91.
14 Ibid., pp. 91–2.
15 Jeffrey N. Gordon and Christopher Muller, "Avoiding Eight-Alarm Fires in the Political Economy of Systemic Risk Management," *Columbia Law and Economics Research Paper*, 369, 2010, p. 36.
16 Quoted in ibid., p. 29.
17 Paulson, *On the Brink: Inside the Race to Stop the Collapse of the Global Financial System*, p. 3.
18 Ibid., p. 1.
19 Ibid., p. 17.
20 Bernanke, *21st Century Monetary Policy: The Federal Reserve from the Great Inflation to COVID-19*, p. 126.
21 Ibid., p. 127.
22 Ibid., pp. 127–9.
23 Atkins, *Forging a New Democratic Party: The Politics of the Third Way from Clinton to Obama*, p. 2.
24 Reed Hundt, *A Crisis Wasted: Barack Obama's Defining Decisions*, RosettaBooks, 2019, p. 5.
25 Branko Marcetic, *Yesterday's Man: The Case Against Joe Biden*, Verso, 2020, p. 174.
26 Ibid., p. 174.
27 Hundt, *A Crisis Wasted: Barack Obama's Defining Decisions*, p. 90.
28 Ron Suskind, *Confidence Men: Wall Street, Washington, and the Education of a President*, HarperCollins, 2011, p. 9.
29 Eric Rauchway, "Neither a Depression nor a New Deal: Bailout, Stimulus, and the Economy," in Julian E. Zelizer, ed., *The Presidency of Barack Obama: A First Historical Assessment*, Princeton University Press, 2018, p. 40.
30 Tooze, *Crashed: How a Decade of Financial Crises Changed the World*, pp. 280–2; Suzanne Mettler, "Reconstituting the Submerged State: The Challenges of Social Policy Reform in the Obama Era," in Lawrence R. Jacobs and Desmond King, ed.,

Obama at the Crossroads: Politics, Markets, and the Battle for America's Future, Oxford University Press, 2012, p. 86; Leonard, *The Lords of Easy Money: How the Federal Reserve Broke the American Economy*, p. 101

31 Jack Rasmus, *Obama's Economy: Recovery for the Few*, Pluto Press, 2012, p. 151.

32 Panitch and Gindin, *The Making of Global Capitalism: The Political Economy of American Empire*, p. 307.

33 Marcetic, *Yesterday's Man: The Case Against Joe Biden*, pp. 174–5.

34 Ibid.

35 Iwan Morgan, "The Quest for Renewed Economic Prosperity: US Economic Policy in the Twenty-First Century," in John Dumbrell, ed., *Issues in American Politics: Polarized Politics in the Age of Obama*, Routledge, 2013, p. 77.

36 Tooze, *Crashed: How a Decade of Financial Crises Changed the World*, p. 296.

37 Frank Curry, Gary Dymski, Tanita J. Lewis and Hanna K. Szymborska, "Seeing Covid-19 Through a Subprime Crisis Lens: How Structural and Institutional Racism Have Shaped 21st-Century Crises in the U.K. and the U.S.," *Review of Black Political Economy*, 49(1), 2022, p. 84.

38 Bernanke, *21st Century Monetary Policy: The Federal Reserve from the Great Inflation to COVID-19*, p. 130; Neil Barofsky, *Bailout: An Inside Account of How Washington Abandoned Main Street While Rescuing Wall Street*, Free Press, 2012, p. 25.

39 Bernanke, *21st Century Monetary Policy: The Federal Reserve from the Great Inflation to COVID-19*, p. 130.

40 Ibid., p. 130.

41 Barofsky, *Bailout: An Inside Account of How Washington Abandoned Main Street While Rescuing Wall Street*, p. 129.

42 Ibid., p. 130.

43 Ibid., p.130.

44 Ibid., p. 129.

45 Ibid., p. 88.

46 Ibid., p. 94.

47 Ibid., p. 94.

48 Ibid., pp. 26–7.

49 Quoted in ibid., p. 27.

50 Dan Immergluck, *Preventing the Next Mortgage Crisis: The Meltdown, the Federal Response, and the Future of Housing in America*, Rowman & Littlefield, 2015, p. 65.

51 Ibid., p. 77.

52 David Dayen, "The Government Program that Failed Homeowners," *The Guardian*, March 31, 2014.

53 Paul Kiel and Olga Pierce, "Govt's Loan Mod Program Crippled by Lax Oversight and Deference to Banks," *ProPublica*, January 27, 2011.

54 Rasmus, *Obama's Economy: Recovery for the Few*, p. 53; Immergluck, *Preventing the Next Mortgage Crisis: The Meltdown, the Federal Response, and the Future of Housing in America*, p. 73.

55 Wolff, "Household Wealth Trends in the United States, 1962 to 2016: Has Middle Class Wealth Recovered?", p. 3.

56 Arthur Acolin, Jesse Bricker, Paul Calem and Susan Wachter, "Borrowing Constraints and Homeownership," *American Economic Review*, 106(5), 2016, p. 627.

57 Tooze, *Crashed: How a Decade of Financial Crises Changed the World*, p. 281.

58 Curry, Dymski, Lewis and Szymborska, "Seeing Covid-19 Through a Subprime Crisis Lens: How Structural and Institutional Racism Have Shaped 21st-Century Crises in the U.K. and the U.S.," p. 85.

59 Carlos Garriga, Lowell R. Ricketts and Don E. Schlagenhauf, "The Homeownership Experience of Minorities During the Great Recession," *Federal Reserve Bank of St. Louis Review*, 99(1), 2017, p. 150, figure 7.

60 Timothy Smeeding, "Income, Wealth, and Debt and the Great Recession," Russell Sage Foundation and The Stanford Center on Poverty and Inequality, 2012, p. 1.

61 Rasmus, *Obama's Economy: Recovery for the Few*, pp. 86–7.

62 Quoted in Theda Skocpol and Vanessa Williamson, *The Tea*

Party and the Remaking of Republican Conservatism, Oxford University Press, 2016, p. 7.

63 Paul Starr, "Achievement without Credit: The Obama Presidency and Inequality," in Julian E. Zelizer, ed., *The Presidency of Barack Obama: A First Historical Assessment*, Princeton University Press, 2018, p. 51.

64 Geoffrey Kabaservice, *Rule and Ruin: The Downfall of Moderation and the Destruction of the Republican Party, From Eisenhower to the Tea Party*, Oxford University Press, 2012, pp. 387–8.

65 In his 2010 State of the Union address, well before the mid-term elections swung the political balance to a radicalized Republican Party, Obama proclaimed: "Families across the country are tightening their belts and making tough decisions. The federal government should do the same" (quoted in Wamsley, "Crisis Management, New Constitutionalism, and Depoliticisation: Recasting the Politics of Austerity in the US and UK, 2010–16," p. 655).

66 Ibid., pp. 655–6; Morgan, "The Quest for Renewed Economic Prosperity: US Economic Policy in the Twenty-First Century," p. 77.

67 The 2010 compromise package consisted of $802 billion tax cuts and $55 billion unemployment benefits (Rasmus, *Obama's Economy: Recovery for the Few*, p. 94).

68 Joseph Vogl, *The Ascendancy of Finance*, Polity, 2017.

69 Wamsley, "Crisis Management, New Constitutionalism, and Depoliticisation: Recasting the Politics of Austerity in the US and UK, 2010–16," p. 656; Morgan, "The Quest for Renewed Economic Prosperity: US Economic Policy in the Twenty-First Century," p. 77.

70 Rasmus, *Obama's Economy: Recovery for the Few*, p. 63.

Chapter 9: Locked in Place

1 Rasmus, *Obama's Economy: Recovery for the Few*, p. 85.

2 Bernanke, *21st Century Monetary Policy: The Federal Reserve from the Great Inflation to COVID-19*, p. 170.

3 Ibid., p. 138.

4 Aquanno, *The Crisis of Risk: Subprime Debt and US Financial Power from 1944 to Present.*

5 Tooze, *Crashed: How a Decade of Financial Crises Changed the World*, p. 285; Matt Phillips, "Banks Are Bingeing on Bonds, But Not Because They Want To," *New York Times*, August 26, 2021; Wistar, *Disorderly Markets: The Federal Reserve, the Banking Lobby, and the Government Securities Market, 1920–1961*, p. 358.

6 Tooze, *Crashed: How a Decade of Financial Crises Changed the World*, p. 285; Bernanke, *21st Century Monetary Policy: The Federal Reserve from the Great Inflation to COVID-19*, pp. 136–8.

7 Daniela Gabor, "The (Impossible) Repo Trinity: The Political Economy of Repo Markets," *Review of International Political Economy*, 23(6), 2016, p. 969.

8 Steffen Murau, "Shadow Money and the Public Money Supply: The Impact of the 2007–2009 Financial Crisis on the Monetary System," *Review of International Political Economy*, 24(5), 2017; Joscha Wullweber, *Central Bank Capitalism: Monetary Policy in Times of Crisis*, Stanford University Press, 2024.

9 Wistar, *Disorderly Markets: The Federal Reserve, the Banking Lobby, and the Government Securities Market, 1920–1961*, p. 359.

10 Stephen Maher and Scott Aquanno, *The Fall and Rise of American Finance: From J.P. Morgan to Blackrock*, Verso, 2024, p. 155.

11 Daniel McDowell, "The US as 'Sovereign International Last-Resort Lender': The Fed's Currency Swap Programme during the Great Panic of 2007–09," *New Political Economy*, 17(2), 2012; Steffen Murau, Fabian Pape and Tobias Pforr, "International Monetary Hierarchy Through Emergency US-Dollar Liquidity: A Key Currency Approach," *Competition and Change*, 27(3–4), 2023; Panitch and Gindin, *The Making of Global Capitalism: The Political Economy of American Empire*; Tooze, *Crashed: How a Decade of Financial Crises Changed the World*.

12 Hielke Van Doorslaer and Mattias Vermeiren, "Pushing on a

String: Monetary Policy, Growth Models and the Persistence of Low Inflation in Advanced Capitalism," *New Political Economy*, 26(5), 2021.

13 Bernanke, *21st Century Monetary Policy: The Federal Reserve from the Great Inflation to COVID-19*, pp. 141–3; Smialek, *Limitless: The Federal Reserve Takes on a New Age of Crisis*, p. 98; Jonathan Ashworth, *Quantitative Easing: The Great Central Bank Experiment*, Agenda, 2020, p. 48; Leonard, *The Lords of Easy Money: How the Federal Reserve Broke the American Economy*, p. 27.

14 Leonard, *The Lords of Easy Money: How the Federal Reserve Broke the American Economy*, p. 119.

15 J. Nicholas Ziegler and John T. Woolley, "After Dodd–Frank: Ideas and the Post-Enactment Politics of Financial Reform in the United States," *Politics & Society*, 44(2), 2016, pp. 263–4.

16 Thiemann, *Taming the Cycles of Finance? Central Banks and the Macro-Prudential Shift in Financial Regulation*, p. 108.

17 Bernanke, *21st Century Monetary Policy: The Federal Reserve from the Great Inflation to COVID-19*, p. 146; Tooze, *Crashed: How a Decade of Financial Crises Changed the World*, p. 309.

18 Maher and Aquanno, *The Fall and Rise of American Finance: From J.P. Morgan to Blackrock*, p. 152.

19 Tooze, *Crashed: How a Decade of Financial Crises Changed the World*, p. 309.

20 Ibid., p. 310.

21 Thiemann, *Taming the Cycles of Finance? Central Banks and the Macro-Prudential Shift in Financial Regulation*.

22 Daniela Gabor, "Revolution without Revolutionaries: Interrogating the Return of Monetary Financing," *Transformative Responses to the Crisis*, Finanzwende and Heinrich-Böll-Foundation, 2021.

23 Wistar, *Disorderly Markets: The Federal Reserve, the Banking Lobby, and the Government Securities Market, 1920–1961*, p. 359.

24 Oliver Levingston, "Minsky's Moment? The Rise of Depoliticised Keynesianism and Ideational Change at the Federal Reserve

After the Financial Crisis of 2007/08," *Review of International Political Economy*, 28(6), 2021; Will Bateman and Jens van 't Klooster, "The Dysfunctional Taboo: Monetary Financing at the Bank of England, the Federal Reserve, and the European Central Bank," *Review of International Political Economy*, 31(2), 2024.

25 Leonard, *The Lords of Easy Money: How the Federal Reserve Broke the American Economy*, p. 212

26 David Dayen, "A Tale of Two Housing Markets: Mansions for the Rich While Poor Are Priced Out," *The Guardian*, January 21, 2015.

27 See https://fred.stlouisfed.org/series/RELACBW027SBOG

28 Lisa J. Dettling, Joanne W. Hsu and Elizabeth Llanes, "A Wealthless Recovery? Asset Ownership and the Uneven Recovery from the Great Recession," FEDS Notes, Board of Governors of the Federal Reserve System, 2018.

29 Wolff, "Household Wealth Trends in the United States, 1962 to 2016: Has Middle Class Wealth Recovered?", p. 72

30 Acolin, Bricker, Calem and Wachter, "Borrowing Constraints and Homeownership," p. 627.

31 Dettling, Hsu and Llanes, "A Wealthless Recovery? Asset Ownership and the Uneven Recovery from the Great Recession."

32 Smialek, *Limitless: The Federal Reserve Takes on a New Age of Crisis*, p. 99.

33 David Lawder, "U.S. House Passes Fed Audit Bill; Measure Seen Doomed in Senate," *Reuters*, September 18, 2014.

34 Quoted in Shane Ferro, "Janet Yellen Testified to the House of Representatives," *Business Insider*, February 26, 2015.

35 Timiraos, *Trillion Dollar Triage*, p. 53.

36 Tooze, *Crashed: How a Decade of Financial Crises Changed the World*, p. 480.

37 Ashworth, *Quantitative Easing: The Great Central Bank Experiment*, p. 143; Leonard, *The Lords of Easy Money: How the Federal Reserve Broke the American Economy*, pp. 145–6; Wistar, *Disorderly Markets: The Federal Reserve, the Banking Lobby, and the Government Securities Market, 1920–1961*, p. 359.

38 Neil Irwin, "Why Yellen Blinked on Interest Rates," *New York Times*, September 17, 2015.

39 Ferro, "Janet Yellen Testified to the House of Representatives."

40 Pistor, "From Territorial to Monetary Sovereignty."

41 Sirio Aramonte and Fernando Avalos, "The Rise of Private Markets," *BIS Quarterly Review*, December, 2021, p. 76; Brett Christophers, *Our Lives in Their Portfolios: Why Asset Managers Own the World*, Verso, 2023, pp. 70–1.

42 Christophers, *Our Lives in Their Portfolios: Why Asset Managers Own the World*, pp. 98–9.

43 Asset managers like BlackRock pride themselves on not using balance sheet leverage or relying on short-term funding. But as Pozsar (Zoltan Pozsar, "A Macro View of Shadow Banking: Levered Betas and Wholesale Funding in the Context of Secular Stagnation," available at https://ssrn.com/abstract=2558945, 2015, p. 8) points out, this is only true in a technical sense. Their *own* balance sheets are not leveraged, but when one actually looks at how their assets under management are invested, a world of highly leveraged investment becomes visible. Asset managers are fully part of the too-big-to-fail banking complex (Christophers, *Our Lives in Their Portfolios: Why Asset Managers Own the World*, pp. 60–2).

44 Devin Fergus, "Financial Fracking in the Land of the Free, 1980–2008," in Reid Cramer and Trina R. William Shanks, ed., *The Assets Perspective: The Rise of Asset Building and its Impact on Social Policy*, Palgrave, 2014, p. 68.

45 Desiree Fields, "Constructing a New Asset Class: Property-Led Financial Accumulation after the Crisis," *Economic Geography*, 94(2), 2018, p. 126.

46 In 2021, such "dry powder" constituted 34% of the total amount of assets under management by North American asset managers (Aramonte and Avalos, "The Rise of Private Markets," p. 72).

47 Lawrence H. Summers, "Demand Side Secular Stagnation,"

American Economic Review: Papers & Proceedings, 105(5), 2015, p. 60.

48 Lawrence H. Summers, "Secular Stagnation and Monetary Policy," *Federal Reserve Bank of St. Louis Review*, 98(2), 2016, p. 109.

49 Joseph E. Stiglitz, "The Myth of Secular Stagnation," *Project Syndicate*, August 28, 2018.

50 Lawrence H. Summers, "Setting the Record Straight on Secular Stagnation," *Project Syndicate*, September 3, 2018.

51 Lawrence H. Summers, "Jobs for All? Take the Idea Seriously But Not Literally," *Washington Post*, July 2, 2018.

52 Nicholas Eberstadt, *Men Without Work: America's Invisible Crisis*, Templeton Press, 2016, p. 5.

53 https://twitter.com/LHSummers/status/1572433427365826565

54 David Roth Singerman, "Keynesian Eugenics and the Goodness of the World," *Journal of British Studies*, 55(3), 2016; Ute Tellmann, *Life and Money: The Genealogy of the Liberal Economy and the Displacement of Politics*, Columbia University Press, 2017; Melinda Cooper, "Secular Stagnation: Keynesianism and the Demographic Theory of Crisis," *Theory and Event*, 22(2), 2019.

55 Minsky, *John Maynard Keynes*, p. 77.

56 Piketty, *Capital in the Twenty-First Century*.

57 Elga Bartsch, Jean Boivin, Stanley Fischer and Philipp Hildebrand, *Dealing with the Next Downturn: From Unconventional Monetary Policy to Unprecedented Policy Coordination*, BlackRock Investment Institute, 2019, p. 2.

Chapter 10: The Future of Bailouts

1 Alex J. Pollock and Howard B. Adler, *Surprised Again! The Covid Crisis and the New Market Bubble*, Paul Dry Books, 2022, p. 21; Menand, *The Fed Unbound: Central Banking in a Time of Crisis*, p. 46; Tooze, *Shutdown: How Covid Shook the World's Economy*, p. 109.

2 Timiraos, *Trillion Dollar Triage*, p. 126.

3 Tooze, *Shutdown: How Covid Shook the World's Economy*, pp. 121–2; Timiraos, *Trillion Dollar Triage*, p. 137; Menand, *The Fed Unbound: Central Banking in a Time of Crisis*, pp. 40–2; Pollock and Adler, *Surprised Again! The Covid Crisis and the New Market Bubble*, p. 35.
4 Pollock and Adler, *Surprised Again! The Covid Crisis and the New Market Bubble*, pp. 31–2.
5 Ibid., pp. 33–4.
6 See https://fred.stlouisfed.org/series/WALCL
7 Menand, *The Fed Unbound: Central Banking in a Time of Crisis*, pp. 50–60.
8 Timiraos, *Trillion Dollar Triage*, p. 117.
9 Ibid., p. 208.
10 Lev Menand, "The Federal Reserve and the 2020 Economic and Financial Crisis," *Stanford Journal of Law, Business & Finance*, 26(2), 2021, pp. 298–300; Tooze, *Shutdown: How Covid Shook the World's Economy*, pp. 127–9; Bernanke, *21st Century Monetary Policy: The Federal Reserve from the Great Inflation to COVID-19*, pp. 123–4.
11 Bartsch, Boivin, Fischer and Hildebrand, *Dealing with the Next Downturn: From Unconventional Monetary Policy to Unprecedented Policy Coordination*, p. 10.
12 Timiraos, *Trillion Dollar Triage*, p. 209; Smialek, *Limitless: The Federal Reserve Takes on a New Age of Crisis*, p. 189; Dawn Lim and Gregory Zuckerman, "Big Money Managers Take Lead Role in Managing Coronavirus Stimulus," *Wall Street Journal*, May 10, 2020; David Dayen, "Corporate Rescue: How the Fed Bailed Out the Investor Class Without Spending a Cent," *The Intercept*, May 27, 2020.
13 Grace Blakeley, *The Corona Crash: How the Pandemic Will Change Capitalism*, Verso, 2020.
14 Adam Tooze, "What if the Coronavirus Crisis is Just a Trial Run?", *New York Times*, September 1, 2021.
15 Quoted in Scott Pelley, "Federal Reserve Chairman Jerome

Powell on the Coronavirus-Ravaged Economy," *CBS News*, May 18, 2020.

16 Tooze, *Shutdown: How Covid Shook the World's Economy*, pp. 15–16.

17 Dayen, "Corporate Rescue: How the Fed Bailed Out the Investor Class Without Spending a Cent."

18 Thiemann, *Taming the Cycles of Finance? Central Banks and the Macro-Prudential Shift in Financial Regulation*, pp. 191–2; Ryan Banerjee and Boris Hofmann, "The Rise of Zombie Firms: Causes and Consequences," *BIS Quarterly Review*, September, 2018, pp. 70–1; Doorslaer and Vermeiren, "Pushing on a String: Monetary Policy, Growth Models and the Persistence of Low Inflation in Advanced Capitalism," p. 79.

19 Robert J. Shiller, "FOMO Helped Drive Up Housing Prices in the Pandemic. What Can We Expect Next?", *New York Times*, September 28, 2022.

20 Pollock and Adler, *Surprised Again! The Covid Crisis and the New Market Bubble*, p. 114.

21 Ibid., p. 114.

22 Kelton, *The Deficit Myth: Modern Monetary Theory and the Birth of the People's Economy*; Jeanna Smialek, "Is This What Winning Looks Like?", *New York Times*, February 7, 2022.

23 Aaron Timms, "We're Haunted by the Economy of the 1970s," *The New Republic*, October 31, 2022.

24 These columns appeared on July 7, 2021, February 6, 2022, and June 1, 2022, respectively.

25 "Team Transitory Had a Point about Inflation," *Wall Street Journal*, July 19, 2023.

26 Alan S. Blinder, *A Monetary and Fiscal History of the United States, 1961–2021*, Princeton University Press, 2022, p. 62.

27 Jerome Powell, "Transcript: Fed Chief Powell's Postmeeting Press Conference," *Wall Street Journal*, May 4, 2022.

28 Mike Konczal and Niko Lusiani, "Prices, Profits, and Power: An Analysis of 2021 Firm-Level Markups," *Roosevelt Institute*,

2022; Isabella M. Weber and Evan Wasner, "Sellers' Inflation, Profits and Conflict: Why Can Large Firms Hike Prices in an Emergency?", *Review of Keynesian Economics*, 11(2), 2023; Mark Setterfield, "Inflation and Distribution During the Post-COVID Recovery: A Kaleckian Approach," *Journal of Post Keynesian Economics*, 46(4), 2023.

29 Ezra Klein, "The Economic Mistake the Left is Finally Confronting," *New York Times*, September 19, 2021.

30 Max Fraser, "Biden and BlackRock," *New Labor Forum*, 31(2), 2022.

31 Benjamin Braun, "Exit, Control, and Politics: Structural Power and Corporate Governance under Asset Manager Capitalism," *Politics and Society*, 50(4), 2022; Eric Levitz, "Modern Capitalism is Weirder than You Think," *New York Magazine*, March 15, 2022.

32 Adam M. Lowenstein, "For BlackRock, The Climate Crisis is a Win-Win-Win," *The Lever*, April 4, 2022.

33 Geoff Mann, *In the Long Run We Are All Dead: Keynesianism, Political Economy, and Revolution*, Verso, 2017; Zachary Carter, *The Price of Peace: Money, Democracy, and the Life of John Maynard Keynes*, Random House, 2020.

34 Of course, Marxist authors are more likely to emphasize that this is a symptom of deeper contradictions and that the objective is not just to get rid of rentiers but of capitalism as a whole. But those are just political afterthoughts to frame an otherwise near-identical analysis that revolves around the difference between productive and unproductive investment and the idea that a sphere of speculative finance has become unmoored from the productive economy.

35 Bezemer and Hudson, "Finance is not the Economy: Reviving the Conceptual Distinction," p. 746.

36 In 2007, on the eve of the financial crisis, the bottom half of income earners owed a total of 15% of household debt; the top 10% owed 31%, and the 40% in between owed 51% (J.W. Mason, "Income Distribution, Household Debt, and Aggregate Demand:

A Critical Assessment," *Levy Economics Institute Working Paper*, 93, 2018, p. 31).

37 Adkins, Cooper and Konings, *The Asset Economy: Property Ownership and the New Inequality.*

38 Stefano Sgambati, "Who Owes? Class Struggle, Inequality and the Political Economy of Leverage in the Twenty-First Century," *Finance and Society*, 8(1), 2022, p. 9.

39 Colin Crouch, "Privatised Keynesianism: An Unacknowledged Policy Regime," *British Journal of Politics and International Relations*, 11(3), 2009; Greta R. Krippner, *Capitalizing on Crisis: The Political Origins of the Rise of Finance*, Harvard University Press, 2011; Andreas Wiedemann, *Indebted Societies: Credit and Welfare in Rich Democracies*, Cambridge University Press, 2021; Judge, *Democracy in Default: Finance and the Rise of Neoliberalism in America.*

40 Etienne Lepers, "Fiscal Policy as Credit Policy: Reassessing the Fiscal Spending vs. Private Debt Trade-Off," CITYPERC Working Paper, 2021-04, 2021.

41 Ibid., p. 5.

42 E.g., Benjamin Lemoine, "The Politics of Public Debt Structures: How Uneven Claims on the State Colonize the Future," *Near Futures Online*, 1, 2016; Wolfgang Streeck, *Buying Time: The Delayed Crisis of Democratic Capitalism*, Verso, 2014; Sandy Brian Hager, *Public Debt, Inequality, and Power: The Making of a Modern Debt State*, University of California Press, 2016; Jerome E. Roos, *Why Not Default? The Political Economy of Sovereign Debt*, Princeton University Press, 2019.

43 My thanks to Stefano Sgambati for suggesting this term.

44 Ben Spies-Butcher and Gareth Bryant, "The History and Future of the Tax State: Possibilities for a New Fiscal Politics Beyond Neoliberalism," *Critical Perspectives on Accounting*, 98(January), 2014.

45 Minsky, *John Maynard Keynes*, p. 158.

46 Costas Lapavitsas, *Profiting Without Producing: How Finance Exploits Us All*, Verso, 2014; Brett Christophers, *Rentier*

Capitalism: Who Owns the Economy, and Who Pays for It?, Verso, 2020; Mariana Mazzucato, *The Value of Everything: Making and Taking in the Global Economy*, PublicAffairs, 2020; Guy Standing, *The Corruption of Capitalism: Why Rentiers Thrive and Work Does Not Pay*, BiteBack, 2021.

47 Adair Turner, *Between Debt and the Devil: Money, Credit, and Fixing Global Finance*, Princeton University Press, 2016; Rana Foroohar, *Makers and Takers: How Wall Street Destroyed Main Street*, Currency, 2017; Martin Wolf, *The Crisis of Democratic Capitalism*, Penguin, 2023.

48 McKenzie Wark, *Capital is Dead: Is This Something Worse?*, Verso, 2019; Jodi Dean, "Neofeudalism: The End of Capitalism?", *Los Angeles Review of Books*, May 12, 2020; Yanis Varoufakis, *Technofeudalism: What Killed Capitalism*, Melville House, 2024.

49 Minsky, *Stabilizing an Unstable Economy*, p. 328.

Postscript

1 Konings, *The Development of American Finance*.

2 Martijn Konings, *Capital and Time: For a Ne w Critique of Neoliberal Reason*, Stanford University Press, 2018.